11.50

RICHARD III
AND THE PRINCES IN THE TOWER

raison   fortune   vertu

Fortune, attended by Reason and Virtue, turns her wheel full circle as a new king rises, the current ruler topples and the old is crushed. This was a familiar and commonplace image in the fifteenth century. Contemporaries well knew that Fortune was fickle, as events after Edward IV's death amply demonstrated

RICHARD III

AND THE PRINCES IN THE TOWER

A. J. POLLARD

ALAN SUTTON

First published in the United Kingdom in 1991 by
Alan Sutton Publishing Limited
Phoenix Mill, Far Thrupp, Stroud, Gloucestershire, GL5 2BU.

British Library Cataloguing in Publication Data

Pollard, A. J. (Anthony James) *1941–*
    Richard III and the princes in the Tower.
    1. Monarchs. Richard III. King of England *1452–1485*
    I. Title
    942.046092

    ISBN (case) 0–86299–660–0
    ISBN (paperback) 0–86299–990–1

Typeset in 12/13 Garamond
Typesetting and origination by
Alan Sutton Publishing Limited.
Printed in Great Britain by
Eagle Colourbooks, Glasgow.

For
Bumble, Jenna and H301

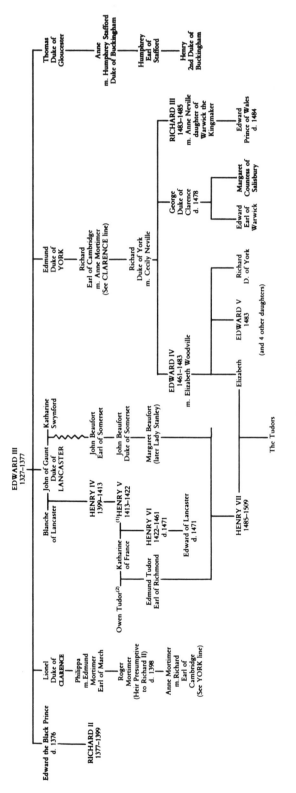

Genealogical table

Contents

List of Illustrations

Picture Essays

Maps

Picture Credits

Photographs and illustrations were supplied by, or are reproduced by courtesy of and the kind permission of the following: the author (96, picture essay 15); Bantam Books (145); The Bodleian Library, Oxford (8, 13, 15, 65, 123, 135); Bridgeman Art Library (picture essay 4, 34, 35, 51); British Library (1, 2, 4, 7, 9, 10, 14, 16, 22, 24, 25, 26, 28, 33, 34, 36, 38, 40, 44, 50, 51, 52, 53, 62,

Acknowledgements

This book would not have been written had not Alan Sutton twisted my arm. The concept owes much to him; the execution to Peter Clifford and Jaqueline Mitchell who not only saw it through the press but also played a major role in its formation. But the concept could not have been realized without the tireless and frequently inspired picture research of Margaret Condon. In the attempt to match illustration with text, there has in reality been joint authorship. I would also like to record my thanks to Carole Rawcliffe, Pauline Bennett and Marie Dixon for helping with astrology and saints; to Geoffrey Wheeler for making both his substantial collection of photographs and his archive of cuttings and photocopies available to me; and to Carolyn Hammond for helping to hunt down some of the more bizarre manifestations of Ricardian enthusiasm. To both Geoffrey and Carolyn I apologise for the absence of frying pans. I would also like to express my gratitude to my family for putting up with long periods of seclusion in the study while I pursued this boring obsession; and to Dr Barnes Mair-Goyder for answering successive mayday appeals. Finally I would like to acknowledge the part played by several generations of final year students at Teesside Polytechnic with whom the ideas in this book were worked out. To them and other friends it is dedicated.

Hurworth-on-Tees
September 1990

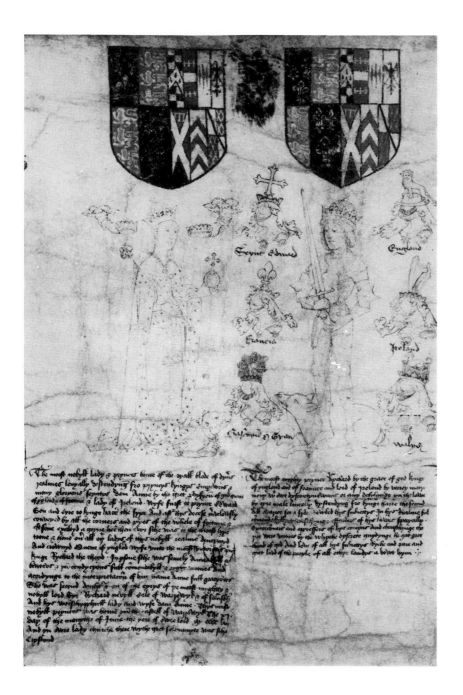

Richard III and Queen Anne in full glory as king and queen of England, taken from the version of the Rous Roll completed between 1483 and 1485. It contains a eulogy of the king and a description of the queen as 'semely, amiable and beuteus . . . and accordynge to the interpretation of hire name, Anne, full gracyous'

Chapter 1

Early Stories of Richard III

Richard III has divided opinion for five hundred years. To many he has always been a villain, a bloody tyrant and detestable child murderer deservedly overthrown. To others he was and remains a hero, a noble prince and enlightened statesman tragically slain. So strong is his appeal in the twentieth century that a flourishing society exists, dedicated to the task of clearing his name. Uniquely among the kings of medieval England he has the power to generate passionate commitment and blind devotion. In the eyes of some followers there are only anti-Ricardians and pro-Ricardians; pro-Ricardians fighting anti-Ricardians to vindicate Richard's reputation. There are those for whom Richard's innocence of the charges laid against him, especially that he murdered the Princes in the Tower, is an article of faith. In the study of history, in which it is assumed that historians approach their subject with an open and objective mind, this is, to say the least, unusual.

The subject of Richard III and the Princes in the Tower thus transcends conventional history. In the late twentieth century the discipline of history has come to mean the methodical search for and assessment of evidence of the past and the dispassionate recording and interpretation of that evidence. It is, as near as it can be, scientific in approach. But it was not always so. As the very word 'history' (*storia* in Italian) suggests, it was once, and some would argue essentially still is, a form of story-telling. What distinguished

A teacher imparts moral and political lessons to his pupils. From a woodcut published by Wynkyn de Worde at approximately the same time as Thomas More was writing his history of Richard III with a similar purpose

history from, say, epic or tragedy is that its stories were true stories from the past: poetic licence was excluded. In reality, while the power of the historian's stories derived from the fact that they were believed to be true, it never was and never has been possible for the historian to tell the facts as they were. As Sir Philip Sidney acidly commented in the sixteenth century, he was 'loaden with old mouse-eaten records, authorising himself (for the most part) upon other histories, whose greatest authorities are built upon the notable foundation of hearsay'.[1] Furthermore in telling the story built upon the foundation of hearsay the historian embellished and adorned it to impart moral and political lessons. Thus dialogue would be invented or unspecified reliable sources would be called upon. This is exactly what Sir Thomas More did to brilliant effect in his influential *History of King Richard III*.

An appreciation of the literary nature of history is of particular importance in the matter of Richard III precisely because there are two contradictory stories in circulation. The conventional historical assumption would be that one is true, the other is false; the historian's function being to deploy all his or her sophisticated professional skills to determine which. But, not only does the very nature of the events at the time and the inadequacy of the surviving evidence make it impossible to resolve many of the contradictions, it is also apparent that after five hundred years the stories have generated lives of their own that transcend any mere factual truth that lies hidden and lost to the searching historian: they have themselves become inseparable from the past of which they tell.

The earliest, best known and dominant story is that of the cruel tyrant who murdered his innocent nephews in the Tower. It is enshrined in William Shakespeare's *King Richard III*, written and first performed in the 1590s. The play has left its indelible mark on perceptions of Richard III. Shakespeare neither invented the story nor wrote Tudor propaganda; all he did was to dramatize the widely believed and conventional account of his day. One hundred years after the events, he recreated on the stage what he believed in good faith to have happened. His main sources, such as Holinshed's Chronicles, carried the standard and accepted account of the life and times of Richard III and the terrible murders of the Princes in the Tower. The origins of Shakespeare's portrait of Richard III may lie in Henry VII's propaganda, but by the late sixteenth century propaganda had been transformed into historical fact.

Henry VII, even before he was king, presented himself as a saviour rescuing England from evil tyranny. His messages to supporters in England described Richard III as 'that homicide and unnatural tyrant which now unjustly bears dominion over you'.[2] Soon after he took the throne Henry condemned Richard as 'the enemy of nature' and, in his first Parliament, as a man guilty of the crime of the 'shedding of infants' blood'.[3] Government-inspired publications lost no time at all in presenting the late king as an evil tyrant and the new monarch as a healer of old wounds and a restorer of justice.

Propaganda is not necessarily ill-founded. Would historians today wish to dismiss as a complete tissue of lies the propaganda put out by the Allies against Hitler during and immediately after the Second World War? Governments often need to exploit all the media at their disposal to explain their policies. Independent and

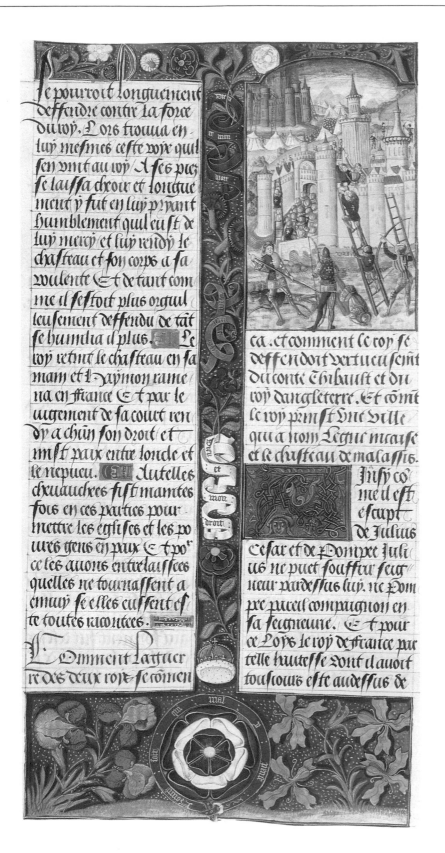

An unusual reversed Tudor Rose set in a garter forms part of the decorative border of a chronicle acquired by Henry VII. From the beginning of his reign he deployed the union rose to symbolize the creation of harmony and peace out of the civil war illustrated by a siege in progress at the top of the page

impartial contemporary evidence is always needed to distinguish between that which is information and that which is disinformation. Unfortunately, this is almost totally lacking for Richard III. All the accounts of his reign written after Henry VII became king in 1485 are compromised. The works of Sir Thomas More and Polydore Vergil, both composed some thirty years after the event, are histories, not sources, heavily influenced by the official interpretation and the memories of the victors. In the case of Vergil the reminiscences of men like Fox, Bray and Urswick who happily recalled the experience of exile and conspiracy before 1485 are invaluable, but the viewpoint is inevitably partisan.

London chroniclers, such as Robert Fabyan, author of the *Great Chronicle* , were men who had lived through and witnessed some of the most dramatic events in 1483, but they wrote about them much later and were influenced by orthodox interpretation. It is now almost impossible to determine how much of what they wrote was their own independent opinion and an accurate recollection of the events they described two decades later. Similarly one cannot rely on John Rous, writing in his *History of the Kings of England* between 1487 and 1491, as supplying direct, impartial evidence. His hostility to Richard III in this account, although absent from an earlier comment on the king written before 1485, is transparent. Moreover, an old chantry priest living in seclusion near Warwick, while he would have known about Richard's religious benefactions and have been at hand when the royal progress passed by in August 1483, would have been too far from the centre of events to pick up more than gossip on most of the main political issues.

A self-portrait by John Rous, the Warwickshire chantry priest whose history of the reign of Richard III is unreliable as much because he was out of touch with events as because he was highly partisan

Lastly, for all its apparent objectivity and immediacy, the memoir known as *The Second Contination of the Crowland Chronicle* is not necessarily trustworthy. It was written in the spring of 1486 by a senior civil servant who had been, unlike Rous, at the very centre of events since 1459. However, this was still seven months after Henry VII's victory; time enough for him to have been influenced by the new king's propaganda. Thus he greets Henry as, 'an angel sent from Heaven through whom God had deigned to visit his people and to free them from the evils which had hitherto afflicted them beyond measure'.[4] His awareness that a red rose had avenged the white reveals that he was already familiar with the symbolism deployed by the the new king in his propaganda. His story, too, is coloured by his knowledge of what happened on and after 22 August 1485 and the current perception of the immediate past. He may independently, of his own conviction, have shared that view; but how can we be sure?

There is but one narrative account of events in 1483 and a handful of passing comments which predate Richard III's death.

The memorial brass of Christopher Urswick and a portrait of Sir Reginald Bray as donor in the Magnificat window at Great Malvern. Urswick and Bray were two of Henry VII's closest aides, who provided Polydore Vergil with valuable first-hand accounts of recent history

The monks of Crowland kneel before three kings in the illuminated initial letter of the confirmation of their charters issued in 1393. The second continuation of their chronicle was written not by one of their number, but by an anonymous visitor in April 1486

Dominic Mancini was an Italian friar who happened to be in London during the spring and early summer of 1483 and thus a witness to the events which saw Richard become king. He wrote the story of what he had seen before the end of November of that year. Not discovered until 1934, Mancini's account remarkably confirmed the character sketch and interpretation offered by early-Tudor writers. Mancini too, in 1483, suspected that the princes had been murdered, although he honestly admitted that he did not know for sure. In Mancini there appears superficially to lie independent support for the official account. However, a close reading of his text reveals that the author, who probably did not speak English, relied for his information on gossip being picked up by the Italian community in London and the heart-rending story told to him by John Argentine, physician to Edward V and the last of his household to remain in attendance on him. Argentine's story, as incorporated in the text, is therefore the story of those loyal to Edward V whom Richard III removed from power. In so far as Mancini tells a story deeply hostile to Richard III, it is the story of the losers in 1483 who became the victors in 1485. It is the story from the same side. Indeed Argentine prospered after 1485; he was known by both More and Vergil and may well have been one of the oral sources for their histories. Far from being independent of the 'Tudor myth', it is closely linked with it.

All that is left for the historian from before 1485 with which to

The memorial brass of John Argentine, physician to Edward V, who was Mancini's principal source of information for the events of the summer of 1483

attempt to test the official account are scraps of praise from miscellaneous sources. Thomas Langton, bishop of St David's wrote in August 1483 to his friend the prior of Christ Church, Canterbury telling him what a fine king Richard promised to make:

> he contents the people where he goes best that ever did prince; for many a poor man that hath suffered wrong many days have been relieved and helped by him and his commands in his progress. And in many great cities and towns were great sums of money given him which he hath refused. On my trouth I liked never the condition of any prince so well as his; God hath sent him to us for the weal of us all.[5]

Here is the very reverse of Henry VII's propaganda. Richard is the saviour sent from heaven. But this too is to be treated with caution. The author was party to Richard's triumphal progress undertaken shortly after his coronation and shared the euphoria of the event. He had also been promised promotion to the see of Salisbury by his king. He was not exactly impartial himself. Sadly, no one took it upon himself, either before or immediately after 1485, to write a full narrative account of Richard's reign from the king's side for us to balance against the other hostile histories.

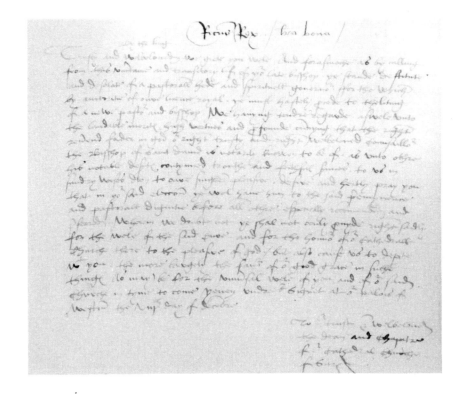

Dated 8 October 1483 and noted at the head as a model letter, this is the office copy of Richard III's recommendation of Thomas Langton to the Dean and Chapter of Salisbury Cathedral as their next bishop. Richard's patronage of Langton helps explain his favourable opinion of the king

There is, therefore, no reliable, well-informed, independent and impartial source upon which the historian can call for the events of 1483–5. Although there are grounds for doubt, it is not possible to verify the version propagated by Henry VII. It has been argued that both Mancini and Crowland were close enough to events for their interpretations to be relied upon. In truth neither is to be perceived as offering objective evidence; they are highly subjective, indeed self-consciously literary, tales. Mancini's patron, Angelo Cato, was so fascinated by what had happened in England in the summer of 1483 that he could not hear it told too often:

A portrait medallion of Angelo Cato, archbishop of Vienne, who was Mancini's patron and the commissioner of his history of Richard III's seizure of the throne

> You have often besought me, Angelo Cato, most reverend father in God, to put in writing by what machinations Richard the Third who is now reigning in England, attained the high degree of kingship, a story which I had repeatedly gone over in your presence.[6]

And so Mancini did. He told a good story. It is the tale of how Richard III, who all but the most discerning believed to be a man of honour and probity, successfully plotted to seize the throne from his nephew. 'Actuated by ambition and an insane lust for power', Richard cunningly exploited hostility to the queen and most of her family first of all to make himself protector and then king. He used his high standing and popularity as a screen. He was a master of deceit and duplicity. Only occasionally, as when his brother Clarence was killed, could he not dissimulate as well. So complete was his duplicity that only a few realized what he was up to. Only when it was too late was it generally realized what his aim was. But then he was cursed with a fate worthy of his crimes.[7] It is a highly moral tale on the theme of devilish deceit, but one in which the author cannot disguise his grudging admiration for the sheer cunning of its central character.

Duplicity is a central characteristic of Richard III in all the early tellings of this tale. 'He contrived a desolate deceit; here's his deceit between his eyes', exulted Dafydd Llwyd, the bard celebrating Henry VII's victory in 1486.[8] Two or three years later John Rous strikingly commented:

> And like a scorpion he combined a smooth front with a stinging tale. He received his lord king Edward V blandly with embraces and kisses, and within three months or a little more he killed him together with his brother.[9]

He was both a Judas and a poisonous arachnid. Polydore Vergil, more prosaically said the same: 'truly he had a sharp wit, provident

Judas betrays Christ with a kiss in the garden of Gethsemane, an image exploited by Rous and More when they wrote of Richard III's disloyalty to Edward V. This is taken from a fifteenth-century book of hours

and subtle, apt both to counterfeit and dissemble'.[10] But Thomas More returned to the Judas theme. 'He was close and secret, a deep dissembler, lowly of countenance, arrogant of heart, outwardly companionable where he inwardly hated, not letting to kiss whom he thought to kill.'[11] The figure made famous by Shakespeare was clearly established from a very early date.

Another of Shakespeare's themes was introduced into the story after 1485; the idea that after committing his terrible crimes in 1483, Richard was wracked by a guilty conscience and finally punished by God for his sins. In 1486 the Crowland Chronicler told

Devils attack murderers and tyrants with spears and halberds as they lie in Hell. An image such as this, from a contemporary treatise on Antichrist, was probably in the mind of the Crowland Continuator when he wrote that Richard dreamt of being tormented by demons

of the report that on the night before Bosworth he had seen 'in a terrible dream, a multitude of demons apparently surrounding him';[12] a tale upon which More elaborated with relish:

> For I have heard by credible report of such as were secret with his chamberers that, after this abominable deed was done [the murder of the princes], he never had quiet of mind. . . . He took ill rest at nights, lay long waking and musing. . . . troubled with fearful dreams, suddenly sometimes start up, leap out of his bed and run about his chamber; so was his restless heart continually tossed and tumbled with the tedious impression and stormy rememberance of his abominable deed.[13]

And Vergil completed the moral. Despite his efforts subsequently by good deeds to merit God's pardon, 'the miserable man had suddenly such an end [at Bosworth] as wont is to happen to them that have right and law, both of God and of man, in like estimation as will, impiety and wickedness.'[14] The sinner, in the end, meets his just deserts, destroyed in part from within by his own conscience.

The message is clear; cheats do not prosper, crime does not pay. A third strand was quickly added to this configuration. Richard III was said to be physically deformed; the physical deformity symbolizing his moral depravity. Rous was the first to comment on his uneven shoulders; although he had to add subsequently which shoulder was higher than the other.[15] Two or three years later, a drunken schoolmaster in York was reported to have declared that the late king was a crookback.[16] By the second decade of the sixteenth century this physique was well established. More wrote, 'He was little of stature, ill-featured of limbs, crook-backed, his left shoulder much higher than his right.' For good measure he added, 'It is for truth reported that the Duchess his mother had so much ado in her travail that she could not be delivered of him uncut; and that he came into the world feet forward. . . . and (as the fame runneth) also not untoothed.'[17] He thus added to Rous's tale of an unusual birth, full of ominous portent.

However, there is no contemporary description of Richard III to confirm any physical deformity. Mancini, who saw him, says nothing of his appearance, which would seem to suggest that it was unexceptional. A German visitor in 1484, Nicholas von Poppelau wrote later in his journal that the king was three fingers taller than him, much leaner and more delicate. He noted no deformity.[18] The earliest surviving copy of a contemporary portrait of the king (c. 1512–20) gives no indication of a hunchback; only later were

(Right) The frontispiece to the book of Leviticus *in a biblical history owned by Edward IV shows animals being sacrificed in the temple while the hunchback is excluded as unfit to enter the Holy of Holies. The depiction of Richard III as a hunchback, unfit to be king, almost certainly derives from this literary source*

portraits doctored to give the 'correct' resemblance. The inspiration
for Richard III's physical deformity is almost certainly biblical.
Leviticus, 21: 16–23 sets down that a hunchback is one of the
blemishes which exclude a man from the Holy of Holies. By
extension, a crooked body contained a crooked mind. Thus was the

idea of deformity elaborated and enlarged to stand as an emblem for the inner wickedness of the man.[19]

The moral and literary dimensions to the early story of Richard III were brought together to powerful effect in Sir Thomas More's *History of the Reign of Richard III*, written during the second decade

The two-faced Antichrist, whose devilish features are hidden behind a smooth front, sows discord in the world. Thomas More portrayed Richard as just such a figure

of the sixteenth century. This is not a history in the modern sense. Although it contains a few memories of remarks heard in his childhood and some oral testimony gleaned from contemporaries, it is a complex work of literature. Yet it is not to be dismissed as mere Tudor propaganda. On one level it was conceived as an exercise in humanist historical writing; the deliberate attempt of a modern to imitate the ancients. The structure is borrowed from Tacitus and the style inspired by Suetonius. It also carries a warning against the tyranny into which More feared kingship, not only then, but also in the future, could so readily degenerate. At a deeper level still the story was used to demonstrate how God would allow the Devil to manifest himself from time to time as Antichrist, in this instance in the person of Richard III, to be a source of tribulation and suffering for his people. All is written in a satirical tone, classically inspired again, so as to make more effective comment through black humour; true word is spoken in jest. The idea of satire has even been taken to the extent of suggesting that the work itself is one big leg-pull, a joke at the expense of over-serious historians. This last suggestion may well be too extreme, but it reinforces the fundamental point that More's *History* is not to be read as a literal statement of facts.

All the strands of the early literary tradition ultimately came together in the most famous of all the versions of the story: Shakespeare's *King Richard III*. As is now evident, Shakespeare did not invent the demonic character who dominates his play: he merely retold the tale familiar to him and his audience. While the play stands on its own, it is also the conclusion of an eight-part cycle in which a chain of events set off by the deposition of Richard II in 1399 is finally brought to an end with the triumph of Henry VII on Bosworth Field. This scheme, covering almost a century of English history, owes much to Polydore Vergil's perception of the unfolding of divine providence. It gives the whole history a mythical quality in which Richard III is the final, dire, consequence of the crime of deposing the Lord's annointed. Thus the future Richard III is first introduced in the third part of *Henry VI* and his character established in two long soliloquies. The leitmotif is again duplicity:

> Why I can smile, and murther whiles I smile,
> And cry, Content, to that which grieves my heart,
> And wet my cheeks with artificial tears,
> And frame my face to all occasions.
> I'll drown more sailors than the mermaid shall,
> I'll slay more gazers than the basilisk,
> I'll play the orator as well as Nestor,
> Deceive more slily than Ulysses could,

And like a Sinon, take another Troy.
I can add colours to the chameleon,
Change shapes with Proteus, for advantages,
And set the murtherous Machiavel to school.[20]

He is a figure, moreover, without moral or social restraint, totally
devoid of conscience:

I have no Brother, I am like no Brother:
And this word [Love] which greybeards call divine,
Be resident in men like one another,
And not in me: I am myself alone.[21]

Richard is dangerous because he recognizes none of the bonds and
obligations which men normally take for granted, and which others
whom he destroys assume he possesses. Because of this he sweeps all
before him. Only after he has gained the crown, the fixed objective of
all his scheming and treachery, does he lose his power. He loses it as a
result of developing a conscience. Once emasculated by an insidious
sense of guilt, he is destroyed from within and his world falls apart.

Shakespeare drew upon the tradition of the morality play:
Richard III, as in More, is the Antichrist, the Devil. It is vital for

*The basilisk, the fabulous king
of serpents, which was reputed to
kill by looking into his victim's
eyes, was one of the many types of
murderers to whom Shakespeare's
Richard III likened himself. In
this miniature the beast has just
killed a man who has fallen
dead in the foreground*

the successful working of the play that we, the audience, develop a rapport with the character. We collude with him, laugh at his jokes and share his triumph when he pulls the wool over the eyes of yet another dupe, or seduces the widow of the man he has just killed. For a brief while we enjoy the fantasy of being like the character on the stage – free of all constraint. He is the archetypal man we love to hate: the model for J.R. Ewing in the long-running soap opera *Dallas*.

It is curious then that many should claim that they have felt compelled to clear Richard III's name after seeing Shakespeare's play. Perhaps there is an unwillingness to accept that evil can be attractive; and a compulsion, therefore, to make what is attractive good. To this extent they too might be unwittingly ensnared by Shakespeare's art. For art it is. History, in the sense of what really happened at the end of the fifteenth century, has little to do with the action of the play. Shakespeare reduced fourteen years (1471–85) to the passing of no more than four months. He also extended Margaret of Anjou's life so that she could play a vital choral role. None of this matters any more than the historical accuracy of the portrayal of the king in what is poetic drama, not scientific history.

Indeed much of the force of Shakespeare's tale, as also of the earlier chronicles and accounts upon which he drew, derives from it being grafted on to a common archetype recurring in western European literature: the story of the wicked guardian who murders his or her wards. This becomes evident if one compares the play with another contemporary variation and popular version of the same archetype, the story of the children in the wood. The earliest surviving English version of this tale also dates from the late sixteenth century. It is almost certainly a much older story: echoes of it are to be found in Chaucer's *The Clerk's Tale* in which a nobleman pretends to murder his children in order to test the love and constancy of his low-born wife. The late sixteenth-century *Babes in the Wood* tells how a Norfolk gentleman and his wife, both on their deathbeds, leave their two young children in the charge of his brother. The brother, however, greedy for the children's inheritance, hires two ruffians to take the children into a wood and kill them. Although the murderers themselves fall out, the children are abandoned to die, lost and alone. The wicked uncle duly enters the inheritance of the children who have disappeared. However, his world begins to fall apart:

> And now the heavy wrath of God,
> Upon their Uncle fell,
> Yea, fearfull fiends did haunt his house,
> His conscience felt an Hell.

Scenes from a late eighteenth-century chapbook, telling the story of the two children in the wood, which illustrate (above) the death of their father, and (below) their being abandoned in the woods by the murderers. The story, first printed in the late sixteenth century, is reflected in Shakespeare's Richard III

Seven years later, when one of the murderers confesses, the truth is revealed and he dies in disgrace.[22]

The commonly recurring nature of this story is instantly recognizable. It is to be found in *Hansel and Gretel* and in *Snow White*, both popularized by Grimm in the nineteenth century. In both these versions the children are victims of a wicked stepmother and they survive their ordeal in the woods; as of course they do in the modern pantomime version of *The Babes in the Wood* itself. It is remarkable, too, how similar the sixteenth-century ballad is to the story of Richard III as transmitted after 1485. The father, like Edward IV, entrusts his children to his younger brother; the brother, a wicked uncle, contrives to have them murdered secretly; the babes have no proper Christian burial; the wicked uncle does not prosper; and some time later the murderer confesses to the crime.

The headpiece, from what appears to be a seventeenth-century woodcut, to the story of the children in the wood shows the murderers falling out, just as the murderers of Clarence fall out in Richard III. *In the background the children lie dead and someone hangs for the crime*

What is even more remarkable, however, is the occasional textual closeness between the printed ballad and Shakespeare's text. The children's death is told in the ballad in the following way:

> Thus wandered these poor innocents,
> Till death did end their grief,
> In one another's arms they died,
> As wanting due relief.[23]

In the play, Tyrell tells what his henchmen had reported to him:

> Dighton and Forrest, whom I did suborn
> To do this piece of ruthless butchery,
> Albeit they were fleshed villains, bloody dogs,
> Melting with tenderness and mild compassion,
> Wept like to children in their death's sad story.
> 'O thus', quoth Dighton, 'lay the gentle babes'.
> 'Thus, thus', quoth Forrest, 'girdling one another
> Within their alabaster innocent arms'.[24]

In the ballad the two murderers fall out. One is moved to pity by the pretty speech, the appeal for mercy made by the children.[25] Shakespeare employs the same dramatic device in the murder of Clarence, where the two murderers fall out in a similar way. Indeed Gloucester has warned them:

> For Clarence is well-spoken, and perhaps
> May move your hearts to pity, if you mark him.[26]

These textual similarities are too close for coincidence.

It so happens that the dates of registration of both works with the Stationers' Company is known. The ballad was registered in 1595; Shakespeare's play, written *c.* 1592–4, was registered in 1597. But the ballad, like an earlier version of a play about Richard III was almost certainly in circulation long before it was registered. It is highly likely that Shakespeare knew and drew upon the ballad. In the nineteenth century, Sharon Turner and Caroline Halsted, who first drew attention to these similarities, supposed that the ballad itself was composed as a disguised recital of the story of Richard III and the Princes.[27] Most recently Desmond Seward repeated, 'Richard III would be commemorated as the Wicked Uncle in the ballad of the Babes in the Wood, which may have an origin earlier than the sixteenth century, but was undoubtedly inspired by the fate of the little king and his brother'.[28] This has it the wrong way round. The story of Richard III and his nephews, as it was repeated and elaborated after his death, fitted easily into the model of one of Europe's oldest folk tales concerning children who fall into the hands of an ogre. In detail it developed an uncanny resemblance to another version then current in England. Both were variants on the same archetypal story. History and literature are as one in these, the first stories of Richard III.

There is, therefore, an inescapable literary dimension to the history of Richard III and the Princes in the Tower. No telling of the story can avoid reference to the original archetype. Moreover, in the light of the overwhelming literary character of the early history of Richard III and the Princes, it is unlikely that what in the twentieth century is called the historical truth will ever be revealed by modern research. A twentieth-century historian is trained to gather, sift and evaluate the evidence out of which the pattern of the past will be revealed. However assiduously or 'scientifically' the historian of the late fifteenth century researches, conclusive, object-ive and incontrovertible evidence on the fate of the Princes in the Tower is unlikely to emerge. It is even less remotely possible that evidence will surface which will resolve the ambiguities and enigma within the character and personality of Richard III himself. So much remains hidden and so little direct and impartial information exists that no account can hope to establish 'the facts' independently of the received story.

The primary source material for the subject, as distinct from early histories, is essentially of two kinds: that of contemporaries who wrote down what they knew of what was going on around them, with varying degrees of ignorance and partiality; and that of the routine paper work of administrators. Much in contemporary chronicles which is taken for fact is really no more than rumour,

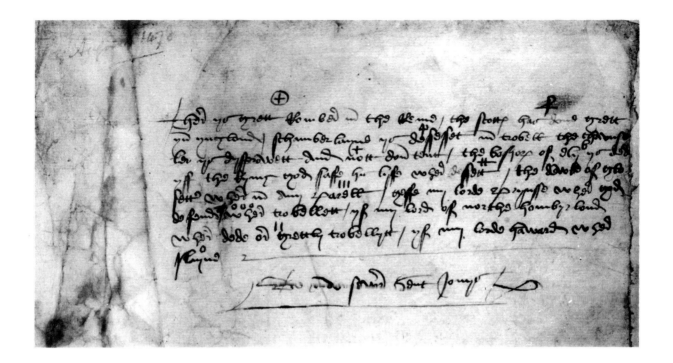

gossip or propaganda – a notable foundation of hearsay. Very few really knew what was going on. This is most dramatically apparent during the two weeks of 13–26 June 1483 when Richard III became king. George Cely, a prominent merchant of the Staple based in London, found himself so confused shortly after 13 June that he jotted down a note of the rumours flying around. He divided them into two categories: those that he had heard as 'facts' and those that were just 'fears'. Five facts included a Scottish invasion, the death of the bishop of Ely and the death of Lord Hastings. Only the last was true. Among the fears were that the king had been put to death, that the life of his brother, Richard of York was in danger, that the earl of Northumberland's life was threatened, and that the duke of Gloucester was in peril.[29] The last may reflect the information put about by the duke himself that he had unearthed a plot against him. Cely no doubt found out more of the truth on all these counts, but he seems not to have recorded it. Historians five hundred years later are far less able than he to discover what was true, what was deliberate disinformation and what was entirely make-believe.

To some extent it is possible to check, clarify and amplify the contemporary accounts of events by reference to the administrative record. This has been done recently to good effect in the case of Richard III by use of the document known as Harley 433, a record of letters sent out under the king's signet between 1483 and 1485. However, rarely do documents such as these reveal anything of

George Cely scribbled a hurried note in June 1483, recording the rumours then flying around. Modern historians are hardly more certain than he was about what happened that month

policy or motivation. The historian has to rely extensively on deduction and the balance of probability. He or she (in this case he) may be convinced that he has arrived at sound conclusions based on a knowledge of the sources and a perceptive use of them; but his readers may not be. Thus, he cannot insist that he possesses a monopoly of the truth or that he alone knows the definitive answers. His perception too is coloured by the common literary heritage and his reaction to it.

This work will return at its end to a discussion of the writings on the subject of Richard III and the Princes since the sixteenth century. In the retelling of the story itself, which now follows, it seeks to unravel some of the knots, especially in relationship to the perennial mystery of the fate of the princes and the enigma of Richard III's character, and to explain why things happened rather more than present an unadorned narrative. In the modern mode of historical writing it attempts to be both objective and dispassionate. It tries to follow the precept that the historian is not a judge, least of all a hanging judge. Given the nature of the topic, it is hard to put this into practice. However, it is hoped that at least a sense of informed understanding of Richard III's life will emerge.

Chapter 2

Childhood and
Youth, 1452–71

Richard III was born at Fotheringhay in Northamptonshire on 2 October 1452. He was the eleventh and last surviving child of Richard, duke of York and Cecily Neville. He was probably christened Richard after his godfather; who that was we do not know, but it might have been his mother's eldest brother, Richard Neville, earl of Salisbury, or even Neville's son Richard, earl of Warwick.

This portrait in glass preserved in Penrith parish church in Cumbria used to be identified as Cecily, duchess of York. It is now believed to be of her mother, and Richard III's grandmother, Joan Beaufort, countess of Westmorland

Nearly forty years later John Rous wrote that Richard's mother's pregnancy lasted two years and that he was born 'with teeth and hair to his shoulders'.[1] Even later Thomas More threw in for good measure that he was a breach birth delivered by caesarian section.[2] Because of the symbolic significance of an unnatural and difficult birth, it is usually assumed that these details were entirely fabricated. However, it may just be possible that Rous had heard that the birth was unusual. His patron, Anne Beauchamp, countess of Warwick (Richard's future mother-in-law) was, he wrote, 'glad to be at and with women that travailed of child, full comfortable and plenteous then of all things that should be helping to them'.[3] If not present herself, Anne may well have heard about the confinement from the duchess of York. And while a two-year pregnancy is impossible, it is not unknown for women to mistake the date of conception; and children are occasionally born with gums that look like teeth and a body covered with hair-like down. There may have been something about Richard's birth which later gave rise to the exaggerated reports.

Richard III's Birth Sign

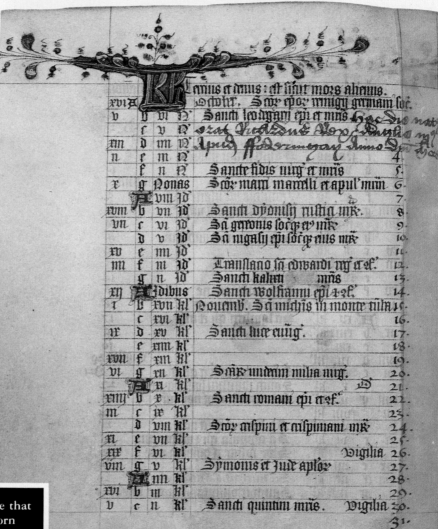

John Rous wrote that Richard was born under the sign of Scorpio and like a scorpion combined a smooth front with a stinging tail. His birthday was 2 October, the day illustrated here in his own book of hours.

Dc acre chauls de sera eschuffee
et douleur en aura Aux mais
et aux piedz se douldra . Douleur
de ventre soufftra Contre elle z
contre ses enfans seront faictes
sourfaictures . de hault cherra . au
cun de ses membres aura desloye
Au col aucunessops mal aura . la
neau de ses espousailles perdra
de quoy grand domauge aura Le
vendredy ne doit lauer sa teste
ne robe neuue teslu . De sa part
occident est bien fortunee en
toutes choses . Dymenche luy est
bon / lundy mardy mercredy no .
          ℂPour lôme
ℂSensuit la .iij. face de libra et
la premiere de scorpio pour lôme
qui sera ne de puis le xij iour docto
bre uisques au xv dicesuy moys .

ℂ ladauit ou asadachil est
appelle sa fin de libra et
la teste de lescorpion a

Strictly speaking,
however, Scorpio
does not begin until
5 October. In this
annotated, astrological
calendar of c. 1480 it is
stated that Scorpio
began to replace Libra
(the scales) on that date
as is shown in the
right-hand miniature.

Octobre a xxxi Jo.
La lune xxix.

			Saint remy.
.v.	b	M'	Saint ligier.
.xiii.	c	N'	Saint victor.
.ii.	d	M'	S' francois.
	e	M'	Sainte xpine.
.x.	f	N'	Sainte foy.
	g	N'	Saint marc
xviii		Id'	S' denettre.
.vii.	b	Id'	Saint denis.
	c	Id'	Saint geron.
xv.	d	Id'	S' madaine.
.iii.	e	Id'	Saint cyrien
	f	Id'	Saint uenant.
iii.	g	Id'	Saint caliste
.i.		Id'	Saint oran

Nevertheless, in many books of hours, as in this entry for October, it was the practice to link the whole of a month with a particular zodiacal sign. Rous's perception of the zodiac is likely to have been shaped by this loose association with Scorpio.

In medieval medical science each sign of the zodiac was related to a particular part of the body. Scorpio was the sign for the genitals. In the Tres Riches Heures of the Duc de Berry the representation of the human body was androgynous and the scorpion could be either male or female.

But in the Guild Book of the Barber Surgeons of York Scorpio was unequivocally associated with the penis.

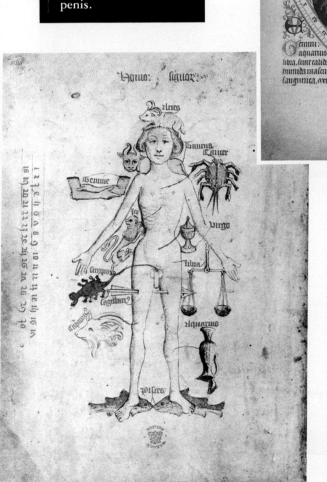

According to contemporary medical wisdom the astrological conjunction afforded Richard protection against injury in the groin. It is not known in which part of his body he received his fatal wound on 22 August 1485.

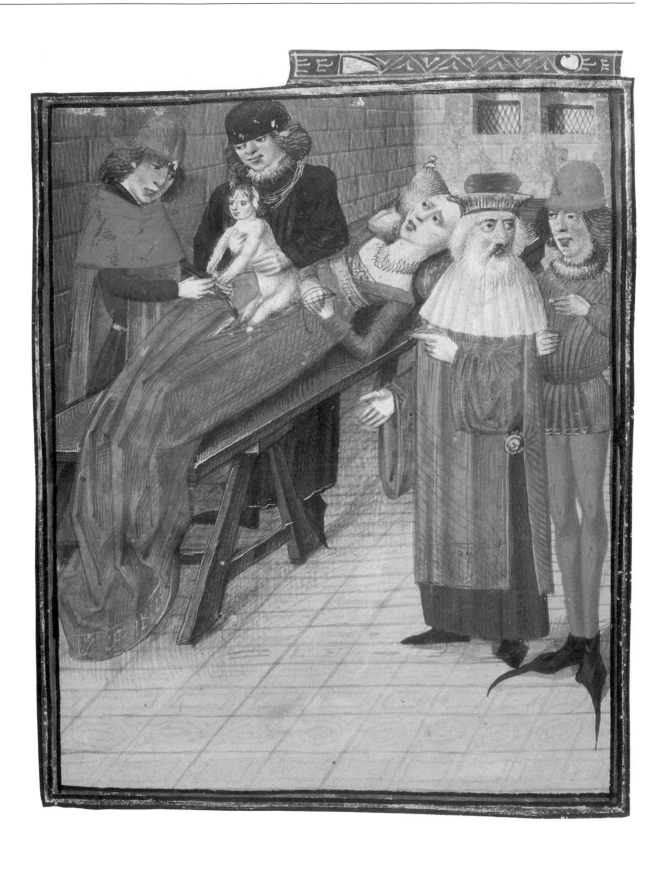

There is no evidence whatsoever that as the child grew a deformity became apparent. One may speculate, as did Kendall, that over-vigorous chivalric exercise led to one shoulder being larger; one might even surmise that as an adult he stooped. But no one in his lifetime thought a physical deformity was worth reporting. Only after his death, and again first through Rous, was the suggestion of deformity made. He was said in his lifetime to look like his father, and was in two or three sources described as little. Nicolas von Poppelau described him in 1484 as taller and thinner than himself, with delicate arms and legs; but how tall was von Poppelau?[4] There is, therefore, some justification for supposing that he grew to be a slight man, perhaps even a slight man with a stoop. It has sometimes been suggested that he was a sickly child, but this derives only from a report that he was still alive, which in its original context clearly meant no more than that he was the only one of his mother's last three children to have survived infancy.[5]

Richard of York is commemorated in glass in the hall of Trinity College, Cambridge. At the time of his youngest child's birth he was the king's mightiest subject

At the time of Richard's birth his father was heir presumptive to the English throne: that is to say York was next in line of succession should Henry VI die childless. He was the greatest magnate of the realm; not only of close royal blood, but also the king's wealthiest subject. However, in October 1452 Richard of York was excluded from power and favour. He himself believed that his birth and wealth entitled him to a place at court and council, yet this was denied him by a king fearful that York might make use of an inherited claim to the throne itself and who was himself easily led by a group of the duke's rivals. Having unsuccessfully tried several times to force himself on the king between September 1450 and March 1452, the bitter and resentful duke was languishing in the political wilderness when his youngest child was born. Only Henry VI's unexpected mental collapse in August 1453 rescued York and gave him a fortuitous opportunity to establish himself in power. Recalled to the royal council, after six months intensive political jockeying he was made Protector of the Realm in March 1454. Thereafter he was never again willing to lose power and the house of York was set on a course that would lead to the accession of Richard's eldest brother, Edward, to the throne seven years later.

Richard of Gloucester was born into an England on the verge of a civil war in which his father and eldest brother were to be principal protagonists. His England was a small, rural kingdom on the western periphery of Christendom. In population (some two and a quarter million), wealth and grandeur it could not match Italy, France or even the Netherlands. By continental standards its only real town was London. Its role in the European economy was as a supplier of raw materials, especially wool, to continental manufacturers. This trade brought to its ports merchants from the Baltic

In this contemporary illustration (left) of a birth by Caesarian section, a large baby, like Richard III supposedly blessed with a full head of hair, is drawn out of his mother's womb. An elaborate tale was constructed about Richard's birth giving portent of evils to follow

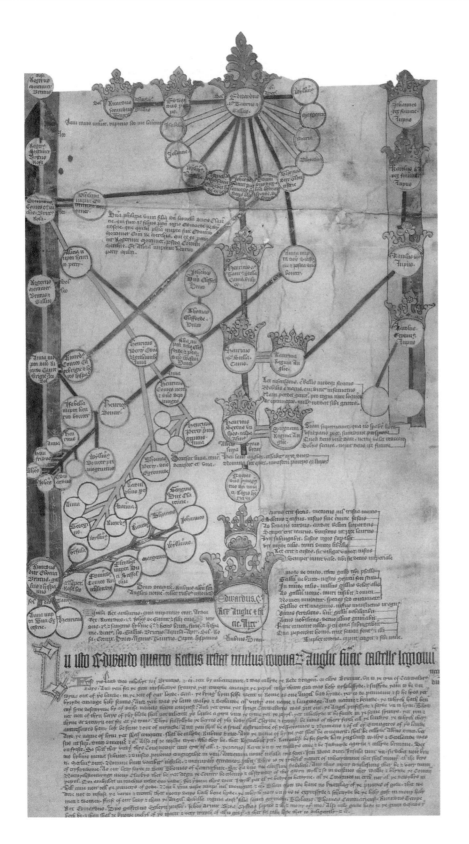

Genealogies were frequently drawn in the fifteenth century for propaganda purposes. This genealogy of the house of York, emphasizing the legitimacy of its claim to the throne, was executed during Edward IV's reign. It names all the children of Richard of York, including the youngest, Richard

and Mediterranean. Yet, because of the success and fame of two of its recent warrior kings, Edward III and Henry V, it was a military power not to be taken lightly by its neighbours. Moreover, in comparison with its larger, more populous and richer continental neighbours – France, Spain or Germany – it was a remarkably integrated and unified state. Its kings, unlike the kings of France, did not have to contend with semi-independent rulers within the bounds of the realm. Over the centuries successive kings of England had been able to develop a sophisticated central bureaucracy housed in the royal palace of Westminster. Royal authority was exercised throughout the realm through the offices of Chancery and Exchequer and through the central law courts. Small it might have been, but England enjoyed the advantages of homogeneity and centralization.

On the other hand, kings of England found their authority curtailed and limited in ways not experienced by their continental cousins. While claiming and displaying in the mystique and trappings of royalty an absolute power under God, ritually imparted by the ceremony of coronation, by custom the king could neither make law nor tax his subjects without their prior consent. By the mid-fifteenth century, parliament, a body representative of the whole community of the realm, had emerged as the institution through which these customary limitations were exercised. Fifteenth-century parliaments were not like twentieth-century parliaments: they were called and dismissed at the will of the monarch; they made no claim to share in his government. Because the monarchy was poorly endowed and found it difficult to make ends meet on its revenues from feudal rights and land, especially to

Sheep being let out of a barn and into the fields made an appropriate illustration for the month of April in this late fifteenth-century book of hours. They also supplied their wool for England's principal export and a rapidly growing textile industry

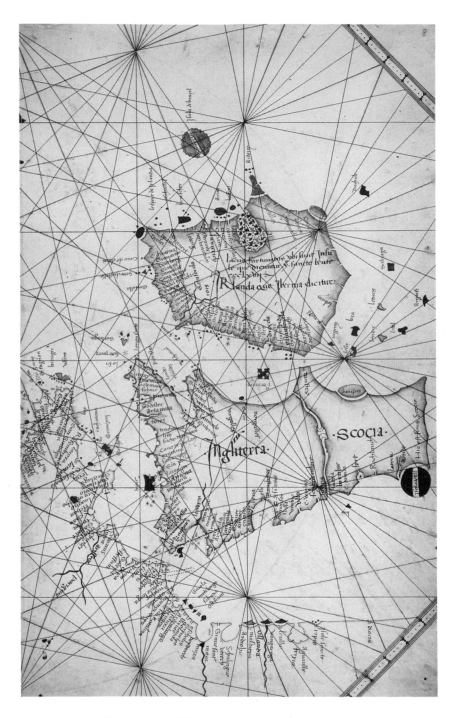

This contemporary map of the British Isles (oriented to the west), compiled in 1473 for Italian merchants, suggests that Britain, a distant land, was but imperfectly known to the cartographer

cover extraordinary costs like the defence of the realm, it needed to call upon its subjects, through parliament, to supply subsidies, or taxes; and parliament had already discovered that it could paralyse an unpopular regime by its refusal to do so.

Parliament itself was a body composed of two houses. The Lords

The king in parliament, with his lords spiritual and lay behind him. The illustration is taken from the initial letter introducing Richard III's statutes transcribed in the Corporation of London's Cartae Antiquae

were some fifty families of the greater nobility who sat by hereditary right with the bishops and the abbots of leading religious houses. The Commons were the representatives of the lesser nobility (the gentry) and the towns sitting as knights of the shires and burgesses drawn from and elected by the realm at large. Parliament was only an occasional gathering; it was only in session for a total of 112 weeks over the 32 years of Richard III's lifetime. When parliament was not in session, which was most of the time, the king still needed to be sure of the support and cooperation of his subjects, especially his greater subjects, through whom, in practice, he ruled the localities. This rule was both formal and informal: it was formal in that lords and gentry served as stewards, constables, sheriffs, justices of the peace and other local government officers; and it was informal in that they, great lords in particular, were courtiers, companions-in-arms and, in some instances, kinsmen. But a poorly endowed monarchy had no paid civil service in the shires and boroughs and no standing police force at hand throughout the realm; the king relied on voluntary service and a sense of obligation, duty and allegiance. Compared with today's omnipotent state, the central government of fifteenth-century England was puny.

The king's principal subjects thus enjoyed considerable political power and autonomy. Among them were a dozen or so magnates, dukes and earls, several with royal blood coursing through their veins, all very rich with huge estates in their possession. Prestige might have been derived from lineage, titles and lavish lifestyles, but power rested on wealth and the men at their command. Around themselves the magnates created affinities, or retinues, of servants employed to manage their estates, settle their legal affairs, attend them on prestigious occasions, even hold public office on their behalf, and, if it came to it, fight their battles for them. Some servants were formally retained by indenture, contracted to serve for life in peace and war in return for an annual fee: others, far more numerous, rendered many services on an informal basis in return for favours granted as part of good lordship. This arrangement, characterized by the legal instrument of the indenture of retainer, is known as 'bastard feudalism', but it was merely a form of the patronage which lay at the heart of English political society until modern times.

Political life in the provinces moved around these affinities and not the king himself. A lord was expected to satisfy the aspirations of his followers. If he did so he attracted more to his service and himself became a more influential figure, and enhanced his own 'worship'. To fail to do so was to risk losing influence and worship, especially if rivals benefited. It was, therefore, essential for lords seeking political influence and power (and not all individuals were necessarily that ambitious) to enjoy royal favour, through which offices, pensions and promotion for their followers could be found. If royal favour was denied a lord, his own local standing was diminished. The desirability of royal favour became even more pressing when local lords competed for dominance.

In fifteenth-century England particular families dominated particular districts, even whole regions, especially where they held substantial estates. Thus, the Courtenay earls of Devon and the Beauchamp earls of Warwick dominated the west country and the west midlands until the middle of the century. The Percy earls of Northumberland dominated Northumberland; the Nevilles of Middleham controlled northern Yorkshire; and the de la Pole dukes

Richard's retainers sported a badge, the white boar, to declare their attachment to him. The retainers of kings and great lords often wore livery collars. The illuminator of this text of Nicholas Upton's treatise on chivalry showed the king of France bestowing one such collar on one of his knights

of Suffolk, the de Vere earls of Oxford and the Mowbray dukes of Norfolk competed for pre-eminence in East Anglia when Richard III was born. His own father, Richard of York, was dominant in the central Welsh Marches and the border counties and a force to be reckoned with in the east midlands and Cambridgeshire. A political map of magnate domination could be drawn, but it would be a constantly changing map as local power was shifting and unstable. The Courtenays were challenged in the west country by the Bonvilles after 1440; after the failure of the Beauchamps in the male line in 1449, Richard Neville, earl of Warwick and Humphrey Stafford, duke of Buckingham competed for the succession to their hegemony; and in Yorkshire after 1450 the Percys sought to break

Many tomb effigies have survived in which the deceased proudly wears a livery collar, proclaiming that he was a member of the king's household. This is Sir Thomas Wykeham, Knight of the Body, who died in 1470 and was buried at Broughton in Oxfordshire

the tightening control of the Nevilles. In a society in which young men were educated in the warrior code of chivalry, violence was never far from the surface. Rivalry could easily lead to the use of physical force; as happened in Yorkshire in 1453 and 1454 when the Percys took up arms against the Nevilles.

Keeping the peace, maintaining the law and controlling the magnates was no easy matter for a fifteenth-century king. Yet it was vital for the well-being of his kingdom that he was able to assert his authority. One strategy was to develop and deploy his own retinue, the royal household, occupying strategic local offices in the provinces and supported by his own estates. Both Richard II and the early Lancastrian kings had adopted this practice. Knights and Esquires of the Body, the king's own retainers drawn from the local gentry, had one foot in the country and one at court. They could exercise his authority in their own localities and represent local interests at court. By this means a royal presence could be maintained in several parts of the kingdom, most notably in Cheshire and the districts dominated by the duchy of Lancaster. But royal resources were too limited for this expedient to be adopted everywhere. In some regions, such as the far north and the Welsh marches where the king's own landed estate was negligible, he had to rely on local lords. Without their support he could not govern; and if they withdrew their loyalty he himself was threatened. The political system was a delicate mechanism. The king needed to exercise tact and firmness to maintain its balance.

In an hereditary, personal monarchy there was no guaranteeing that the king would possess the necessary abilities to rule

Sir John Donne was portrayed by Memlinc as a Knight of the Body of Edward IV being presented to the Virgin Mary and the infant Christ

effectively. At the best of times exceptional qualities were required; but neither was the mid-fifteenth century the best of times, nor was Henry VI the most able of kings. During the first half of the century economic recession and financial crisis put pressure on Crown and subject alike. Regular royal revenues possibly fell by as much as two-thirds between 1377 and 1461. Nobles faced growing economic and financial difficulties, especially after 1440. Demands made on royal patronage increased at the same time as the Crown's capacity to satisfy them diminished. Matters were exacerbated by the aftermath of defeat in war – the long, costly and futile effort to maintain Henry V's conquests in France, which led ultimately in 1453 to the loss of all the French territories except Calais. Nearly forty years of war so injudiciously initiated by Henry V bankrupted the house of Lancaster. The times demanded a man of character: instead Henry VI was one of the most spineless men ever to have sat on the throne. Vacillating, feckless and profligate; revulsed by war and the code of chivalry; and fundamentally uninterested in government, he was the creature of a series of factions who shamelessly exploited royal authority for their own ends. Private quarrels and feuds proliferated as his subjects took the law into their own hands. To confound confusion, in 1453 his mental health collapsed, and although he regained his sanity at the end of 1454, for the rest of his life he was an invalid and little more than a

This worried and feeble-looking Henry VI is a contemporary sketch on the King's Bench plea roll for the early part of 1460, after the rout of the Yorkists at Ludford and their proscription for treason. The mottoes read, in translation, 'God Save the King', 'Judge Rightly' and 'God Give Us Peace'. The dragon firing a gun from its mouth (presumably at the rebel Yorkists) might well represent a basilisk; basilisk was also the name given to a large brass cannon

puppet. Saintly he may have been in his private life, but as a king he was a disaster.

As the credibility of the Lancastrian regime collapsed in the 1450s Richard III's father put himself forward as the leader of an alternative government in the king's name. While there is reason to suppose that York was motivated as much by pride, ambition, bitter resentment at exclusion from office and a desire for revenge on Edmund Beaufort, duke of Somerset who had ousted him from command in Normandy in 1447, he was also able to present himself to the political nation as a reformer. He articulated disenchantment with the failure of English arms abroad and the sense of chivalric dishonour felt keenly in conservative quarters; he offered a more vigorous enforcement of the law; and he championed financial retrenchment by the means of resumption of royal grants. He would, in short, restore good governance. However, he failed to secure office and establish himself in power, even by force. After two protectorates, in 1454–5 and 1455–6, the second having been secured by arms at the first battle of St Albans in 1455, he became even more politically isolated. His major support came from the Neville of Middleham family, father and son, earl of Salisbury and earl of Warwick, who rallied to his cause during the first protectorate. They did so then in order to retain royal favour in their own disputes with the earl of Northumberland and duke of Somerset. After the killings of Somerset and Northumberland at St Albans they had little choice but to stick with York. They did indeed provide substantial support, especially in the north where Richard Neville the elder had amassed great power, but the majority of the peerage and the political nation at large was not convinced of the rightness of York's cause. He himself seems to have lacked political finesse: possessing great advantages in his birth and wealth, he nevertheless was always out-manouevred by his rivals.

Richard of York's eventual revival of the Mortimer claim to the throne had, therefore, something of an air of desperation about it.

A petition presented to Richard of York during his first protectorate. His signature is prominent among those of other councillors who have collectively granted the request

The claim to the throne through the Mortimer descent, which Richard of York revived in 1460, is emphasized in the genealogy which shows Edward IV, in full armour, as the legitimate king, while the usurper Henry IV lops the branch from which Richard II falls

The claim, inherited through his uncle the last earl of March, had lain dormant since the beginning of the century. York may have long harboured this ambition, but it is more likely that it was seized upon as a last resort after the disastrous failure of yet another attempt to force himself into office in 1459. Attainted for treason after the Rout of Ludford and facing complete ruin as he and his supporters were proscribed by the victorious Queen Margaret and her allies, he and the Nevilles decided that they could only be secure if they took the momentous step of deposing Henry VI. The opportunity arose after the capture of the unfortunate king by the earl of Warwick at the battle of Northampton in July 1460. Returning from exile in Ireland in October 1460, York immediately

laid claim to the throne. Although at first he had to accept a compromise, obviously unworkable, whereby he was officially adopted as Henry's heir, his right was accepted reluctantly by parliament. However, in the all-out civil war between supporters of the houses of York and Lancaster that followed, he himself was killed (Wakefield, 30 December 1460). Nevertheless, his eldest son and heir, Edward, a dashing eighteen year old of altogether greater ability than his father, snatched victory from the proverbial jaws of defeat. Having occupied the throne early in March 1461, he decisively defeated the combined forces of the house of Lancaster at Towton at the end of the month. The eight-year-old Richard was now the youngest brother of a king – Edward IV.

Richard III passed his childhood through turbulent and unsettled times. Very little is known of it, not even where he lived. His

An imaginary, and imaginative, contemporary illustration of the battle of Northampton in July 1460 at which the Yorkists seized power and started down the road which led to Edward IV's usurpation of the throne the following March

Richard of York's castle at Sandal from an official survey made in 1562–4. Although the duke rode out to his death from its gate at the end of 1460, he was not a frequent visitor except when affairs of state took him north. His youngest son Richard may have spent some of his childhood there

father's principal country residences were at Fotheringhay, Ludlow and Sandal, and he kept a town house, Baynards Castle, in London. These are the places at which Richard, with his mother, probably spent most of his time as a child. According to one report they were at Ludlow in October 1459 when his father was routed outside the town at Ludford.[6] In the winter of 1461, after his father's death he and his elder brother, George, were sent for safekeeping to the Netherlands. The boys did not return until late May, the crisis over, in time to participate in Edward IV's coronation on 28 June. As the king's brother, Richard was now accorded the highest respect and deference. Two days before the ceremony he was created a Knight of the Bath and he was present throughout the days of feasting and celebration that followed. On 1 November he was created duke of Gloucester and on 4 February 1462, still only aged nine, was admitted to the Order of the Garter.

The care and upbringing of the king's youngest brother was a matter of importance. For the first four years of Edward IV's reign most of the cost of his maintenance was borne by the office of the Wardrobe, indicating that he was in the overall charge of the royal household. He may have resided on occasion at Greenwich; and he might also have stayed for some of the time with Archbishop Bourgchier of Canterbury. It was not until 1465, when he was twelve, that he was considered old enough to be boarded out, as was customary with noble youths, to complete his education in the household of a great aristocrat. The household he joined was that of his cousin, possibly his godfather, Richard Neville, earl of Warwick.

Warwick was the most mighty of mighty subjects in Edward IV's England. In 1465 he was at the zenith of his fame and power. He

The bear, the badge of Warwick the Kingmaker, here illustrated from Fenn's Book of Badges, a scrapbook compiled from a herald's manuscript of 1467–70

had inherited from his father the lion's share of the estates of the earldom of Westmorland, concentrated in the two great lordships of Middleham and Sheriff Hutton in northern Yorkshire. From his mother who was still alive he was due to inherit the estates of the earldom of Salisbury concentrated in Wessex. In the name of his countess, the heiress of Beauchamp, he also held the huge earldom of Warwick with lands in the Midlands and the West Country as well as the lordship of Barnard Castle in County Durham. In particular Warwick was the lord of the north, succeeding to and emulating his father. Although the Nevilles owed their political rise to their Lancastrian connection (Warwick's grandmother was Joan Beaufort, daughter of John of Gaunt), their support had been decisive in helping Edward IV take the throne. Moreover, his brother John, Lord Montagu had with him worked tirelessly in the first three years of the reign to secure the far north against Lancastrian counter attacks. It was reported to Louis XI in 1464, not entirely in jest, that there were but two kings of England: 'M. de Warwick and another whose name escapes me'.[7] Not for nothing did he become known as Warwick the Kingmaker.

By 1465 the Nevilles of Middleham were in total control of northern England. Although the junior line of the family, they had eclipsed the impoverished senior line which retained the title of earl of Westmorland, but held only a truncated estate concentrated in County Durham. Moreover, they had also triumphed over the Percys who were stripped of land and titles after Towton. Warwick, Montagu and the young George, duke of Clarence shared possession of the forfeited ·Percy estates. Montagu, who held those in Northumberland and the office of warden of the east march, was raised to the earldom of Northumberland in 1464. Warwick himself was warden of the west march and occupied the Percy lands in Cumberland. He and his brother dominated the county palatine of Durham, where Bishop Booth had been browbeaten into subservience. For fifteen months in 1462–4 the temporalities of the bishopric (its government) had been taken into royal hands, and the administration dominated by the Nevilles. While Booth had been restored in April 1464, John Neville, earl of Northumberland remained his steward. To tie it all up, in March 1465 Warwick's youngest brother, George was promoted to be archbishop of York. Not only the spiritual authority within the whole of the northern province, but also the secular authority in Hexham, Beverley and Ripon was annexed to the Neville empire. As one contemporary later commented, 'he and his brothers had the rule of the land and had gathered great riches'.[8]

The twelve-year-old Richard of Gloucester entered this world in 1465. He was in the care of the earl of Warwick before the end of

Sheriff Hutton, now in ruins, was one of the principal residences of the Nevilles in northern England. Richard III almost certainly stayed here from time to time when he was under the tutelage of the earl of Warwick

the year, by which time Warwick had been granted £1,000 towards the cost of his maintenance. He was a member of the household by 22 September when he was present, in the company of the earl's ten-year-old daughter Anne, at the great feast in York celebrating the enthronement of Archbishop George Neville.[9] It is reasonable to assume that he spent a good part of the next three and a half years in the north, staying at Warwick's principal castles of Barnard Castle, Middleham, Penrith and Sheriff Hutton. He need not necessarily have spent his whole youth there; Warwick had other residences. Indeed Richard is known to have been at Warwick itself before March 1466. Apart from a record that he was received with his guardian by the city of York in 1468, his precise movements are undocumented.[10] How well he came to know the earl is equally hard to discern. Warwick withdrew, disgruntled, from public affairs during the winter of 1467–8; the adolescent might have become closer to him then. He might have known others in Warwick's circle better: his fellow ward, Francis, Lord Lovell and prominent retainers of the earl such as Sir John Conyers, Sir James Strangways and Thomas Metcalfe. No doubt he also became more familiar with the landscape and society of northern England. Of his formal education nothing is known. It was presumably conventional. Had it followed the course outlined by the Northumbrian John Hardyng in his contemporary chronicle it would have concentrated on the physical arts of the chase and chivalry:

> At fourteen they shall to field I sure
> At hunt the deer; and catch an hardiness. . . .
> At sixteen year to war and to wage,
> To joust and ride, and castles to assail.[11]

A stag is raised by a harbourer, hounds and huntsmen give chase, in this scene from Gaston Phoebus', Livre de Chace. As a youth Richard III would have learnt how to hunt in the extensive Pennine forests, then the preserve of red deer

Whether at school under Warwick or elsewhere, Richard certainly did 'catch an hardiness' and learn 'to war and to wage'. Ironically, however, he was first to demonstrate the success of his upbringing in arms against his guardian.

Edward IV recalled his youngest brother to court early in 1469. For the first time he was granted a substantial landed estate appropriate for the support of a royal duke, drawn from the forfeited estates of the Beaufort and Hungerford families, still unreconciled Lancastrians in exile. It is possible that he was considered to have come of age on his sixteenth birthday in October 1468: in the fifteenth century sixteen was considered old enough to play an active role in public affairs. In any case by February 1469 Edward IV had good cause to remove Richard from Warwick's custody. Although king and earl had patched up their differences in 1468, relationships between the two had continued to deteriorate. By the spring of 1469 Warwick was plotting rebellion. There were several causes for the rift between Edward IV and the Kingmaker. Once the first flush of victory had passed, it had been difficult for the two to co-exist: Edward IV needed to assert his full, independent authority; Warwick wished to consolidate his pre-eminence. The king's secret marriage to Elizabeth Woodville in 1464, by its manner an insult and in its effect an injury, did little to improve relations. The immediate cause of disagreement was the direction of foreign policy, in which Warwick, somewhat idiosyncratically, favoured a French alliance. He found himself no longer indispensable and was elbowed out of favour by new men, in particular the Earl Rivers (the queen's father) and the earls of Pembroke and Devon. Like the duke of York before him, Warwick at length resorted to the expedient of forcing himself upon the king. He stirred up popular rebellion in Yorkshire, forged an alliance with the king's disaffected brother George, duke of Clarence, and, his men having defeated and killed the king's supporters at Edgecote in July 1469, took Edward IV himself prisoner. But it proved even less feasible for Warwick to rule in the name of a captive but vigorous Edward IV than it had been for York to rule in the name of a captive but sick Henry VI. Disturbances in the far north created by the rival branch of the Neville family forced Warwick to release the king in September. Although Edward, once he had returned to Westminster, publicly declared that he was once again reconciled with Warwick, privately he prepared to reduce Warwick's power.

Young and inexperienced though he was, Richard of Gloucester, as the king's brother, now had an important part to play in Edward IV's plans. Shortly after his seventeenth birthday, on 17 October 1469, he was created constable of England in succession to the late Earl Rivers, and was subsequently appointed to several offices in the duchy of Lancaster. To enhance his estate as a royal duke he was also granted the lordship of Sudeley in Gloucestershire. His specific charge was to represent the king's authority in Wales where the earl of Pembroke had, until the summer of 1469, been all powerful and whose offices Warwick had taken into his own hands after Pembroke's death at Edgecote. Between 7 November 1469 and 7 February 1470 Richard was granted the chief offices of the principality, men experienced in Welsh affairs were nominated to his council, and he established his own household in Wales. His immediate task, for which he was granted a commission of array at the end of October 1469, was to recover Carmarthen and Cardigan from allies of Warwick. While at first Richard's promotion might have been welcome to the earl (after all he had until recently been his ward and was in no way associated with the old regime), his appointments in Wales, where Warwick for long had harboured his own ambitions, were a direct snub and a resounding declaration that Gloucester was the king's man. As the lines were being drawn for a renewal of civil war it became apparent that the young duke was to take side against the earl.

It is not known whether Gloucester stayed to establish himself in Wales during the winter of 1469–70 or returned to court. He did, however, occupy his offices in the duchy of Lancaster and, as a result, come into dispute with Thomas, Lord Stanley (Warwick's brother-in-law) from whom they had been taken. In March 1470 Edward IV had additionally to deal with the 'variance late fallen' between 'his right entirely beloved brother' and Stanley.[12] In largely obscure circumstances the duke allied himself with Sir James Harrington against Stanley's son Edward in a dispute over possession of Hornby castle in Lonsdale. He was at Hornby on 26 March 1470, when the castle was being threatened by Stanley's men; and it was possibly at this time that a skirmish took place, which was later recalled in a sixteenth-century poem celebrating the Stanleys, between his and Stanley's men on the banks of the Ribble near Preston.[13]

By March 1470, however, any private quarrel with Lord Stanley had been overtaken by renewal of conflict between Warwick and the king. This time, once more in alliance with Clarence, Warwick planned to depose Edward IV and replace him with his brother. Edward, however, was not to be caught unawares a second time. The plot was largely as before: a popular rising, this time in Lincolnshire, was to lure the king into a trap. Once caught, Warwick was to declare his hand. But Edward moved decisively against the rebels, who broke and fled on the appropriately named Losecoat field. The king quickly discovered the nature of Warwick and Clarence's intentions from his prisoners and moved against them. The earl and duke, having attempted to link up with Stanley in Lancashire, turned and fled south, finally taking a boat to France from Dartmouth. Gloucester stood firmly by Edward throughout the crisis. Although caught up in a private feud in Lancashire while the king faced Warwick's allies in Lincolnshire, he effectively prevented Stanley from throwing his weight behind the rebellion. As soon as news reached Edward that Warwick and Clarence had fled, Richard was ordered to march south to raise men in Gloucestershire and Herefordshire against them.

A portrait medal of Margaret of Anjou, struck c. 1463. Described by a contemporary as 'a strong laboured woman', she fought uncompromisingly for her son's right to the throne of England until his death in battle in 1471

During the summer of 1470 Edward IV did his utmost to consolidate his position. Besides his brother Richard, he turned to Henry Percy whom he restored to the earldom of Northumberland, and Laurence Booth to whom he restored the lordship of Barnard Castle. His intention was to undermine Warwick's immense residual power in the north; but time was not on his side. Warwick, in France, entered into an agreement with Louis XI and Margaret of Anjou to restore Henry VI with French help. As part of the deal he married his younger daughter Anne to Henry's son and heir, Edward, Prince of Wales. He then sent messengers to England with orders for his northern followers to rise once more in rebellion. By the beginning of August Lord FitzHugh was in arms in northern Yorkshire and Cumbria. Edward, who well knew how serious a threat such northern risings were, once more called out his retainers and immediately set off to crush it. The rebels dispersed on his approach, many happily sueing for pardons, but Edward understood that the rising was Warwick's work, and so on 26 August took the step over which until then he had hesitated – the removal of the earl from the wardenship of the west march. In his place he appointed his brother Richard. It may well be that it was at this time, while Edward was in Yorkshire, that he first decided to use Richard as his agent in the region as an alternative to Warwick. But it was too late. In the middle of September, while Edward was still seeking to secure his authority in the north, Warwick and Clarence landed in Devon. They immediately declared for Henry VI and numbers of noblemen, including Lord Stanley, came in to support them with substantial retinues. Edward, Gloucester and others marched to meet the ever-increasing threat, but before they had reached Nottingham, Edward heard news that Warwick's brother, Lord Montagu, who he believed was bringing reinforcements from the north, had also declared against him. Trapped between two hostile armies Edward and his principal companions immediately fled through Lincolnshire to King's Lynn, where, on 2 October (Richard's eighteenth birthday) they took ship for the Low Countries. As Gloucester fled into exile for the second time in his life, his short career as a royal duke appeared to be at end.

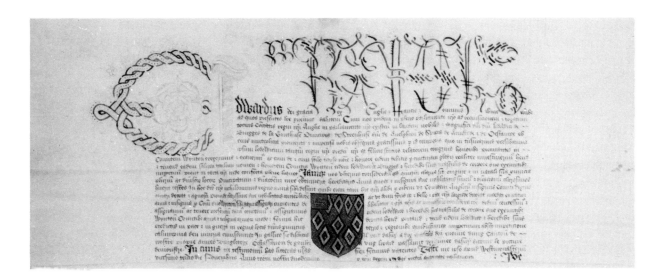

The winter of 1470–71 was the low point of Gloucester's life. Exile was endured in the hospitality of Louis of Bruges, Lord of Gruythuyse, the governor of Holland for Charles, duke of Burgundy. However, a chance to turn the tables on Warwick and his new allies arose when, in accordance with the terms extracted by Louis XI for his support, the new Lancastrian government declared war on Burgundy in February 1471. The duke's response was to sponsor a Yorkist descent on England. A fleet was fitted out and on 11 March a small expedition of barely a thousand men set sail from Flushing. It was a desperate venture, the gamble of men who had little to lose but all to gain. An attempted landing in East Anglia failed, but the band successfully disembarked on Ravenspur at the mouth of the Humber. At first, Edward, taking a leaf out of Henry IV's book, claimed only to be seeking restoration of his right as duke of York. This gained valuable time in hostile country. More critically Henry Percy, earl of Northumberland showed his gratitude for his restoration a year earlier (and his resentment at having been removed from the wardenship of the east march by the new regime) by allowing Edward and his men to proceed unmolested. However, the Yorkists received little support in an area where memories of the

Louis of Bruges, Lord of Gruythuyse was created earl of Winchester by Edward IV in 1471 in gratitude for his hospitality while in exile. The grant of arms to the new earl was lovingly executed, including a white rose in the initial letter

Thomas Stephenson of Boston was one of several merchants who lent money to Edward IV in exile. The four chevron cancellation marks demonstrate that Edward kept his promise to repay the £100 lent to him at Bruges in February 1471

slaughter of Towton were still vivid, not even at Wakefield which was part of Edward's duchy. Not until they had safely left Yorkshire behind them did they begin to attract support. Nothing daunted they pressed on to confront Warwick who was recruiting men in the midlands. The tide turned when, on 2 April, Clarence threw in his lot with his brother. Attempts were made to induce Warwick, safely behind the walls of Coventry, to come out to fight, but he refused and so Edward marched up to London to seize control of the administration. Warwick followed behind. Eventually the two armies came to blows outside Barnet on Easter Sunday, 14 April.

The battle of Barnet was Richard of Gloucester's first taste of war. In it he won his spurs. The battle was confused; because Edward had moved up at night, the two lines were not directly opposite each other; each right wing extending beyond the enemy's left. Moreover, battle was joined at dawn in thick fog. In the confusion the Lancastrian right routed the Yorkist left and on the other flank the Yorkists gained the upper hand. In the centre a fierce hand-to-hand

The owner of this book of hours used its calendar to record the battles of Barnet and Tewkesbury and the deaths of the Earl of Warwick and Prince of Wales

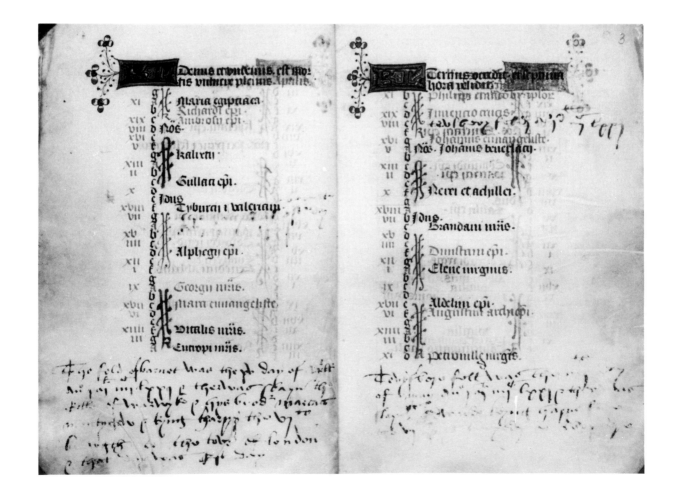

mêlée developed. When troops of the Lancastrian right regrouped and returned to the fray they came up on their own men, and in the fog they were mistaken for the enemy. Cries of treason were set up and the Lancastrian line broke. Warwick was killed in flight and his brother died on the field. Richard of Gloucester was in the thick of the fighting. Several members of his retinue were killed at his side and he clearly acquitted himself with honour.

On the same day as Barnet was fought, Queen Margaret of Anjou landed at Weymouth with a long-promised army of Lancastrian reinforcements. Too late to assist Warwick, she still might be able to defeat Edward. She first went to Exeter to recruit troops loyal to the Courtenay family, and then advanced through Somerset to Bath. Edward IV himself hastily raised new men. On 24 April, he set out from Windsor for Cirencester to intercept the queen's army. Discovering that she intended to cross the Severn, he gave chase. After a forced march, he caught up with the Lancastrian army south of Tewkesbury as it prepared to ford the river. On the following day, 4 May, he sent Gloucester into a frontal attack in command of the first division. He was met by the duke of Somerset. After bitter hand-to-hand fighting Gloucester's men gained the upper hand and Somerset fell back. Edward IV then led his division against troops led by Edward, Prince of Wales, which were routed. The whole Lancastrian army broke and fled. The prince was killed and other leaders took refuge in Tewkesbury Abbey. They were probably seized by force from sanctuary and on 6 May a dozen or so, of whom the most prominent was Edmund Beaufort, duke of Somerset, were brought to trial in a court of chivalry convened under Richard of Gloucester as constable, found guilty of treason and executed.

Within two months Edward had defeated all his enemies and re-occupied the throne which he lost six months earlier. Edward IV's recovery of the throne was one of the most remarkable changes of fortune in English history. The battles of Barnet and Tewkesbury removed all but a handful of the enemies of the house of York and brought to a decisive end the first round of the Wars of the Roses between Lancaster and York. Richard of Gloucester had shared his brother's exile and had been at his side throughout the campaign. He had emerged as a soldier of renown. He also shared in the responsibility for summary executions after the battles. His role as constable presiding over the court of chivalry was not exceptional, nor was the summary justice exercised unusual. Polydore Vergil and later Tudor writers, however, told an elaborate story of how the Prince of Wales was cruelly murdered by Clarence, Gloucester and Hastings after he had been taken alive and berated by Edward IV. There is no contemporary evidence to support this story. The earliest accounts of the battle state that he was killed 'in the field'

perhaps 'fleeing towards the town'.[14] Warkworth suggested that he 'cried for succour to his brother-in-law the duke of Clarence',[15] but none even hinted at cold-blooded murder at the hands of the duke of Gloucester.

If Richard can be excused complicity in the supposed murder of the Prince of Wales, he cannot be exonerated from his part in the death of Henry VI. Henry VI had been a prisoner in the Tower since 1465. He had been allowed to live because of the very fact that his son and heir was alive and at large in France. Before 1471 the killing of Henry VI would have been politically counterproductive; it would not only have created bad publicity for Edward IV, but would also have opened the way for a more plausible and effective Lancastrian claimant. After Edward, the Prince of Wales was dead, himself childless, Henry VI was doomed. The official account of

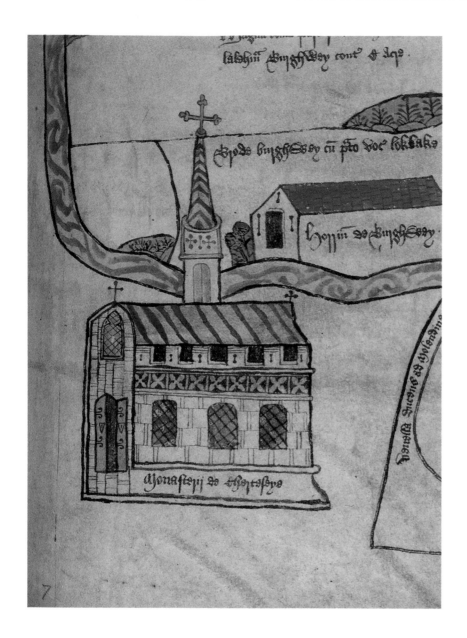

*A mid-fifteenth-century
manuscript illustration of
Chertsey Abbey where Henry VI
was buried after his murder.
Soon afterwards a cult developed
around the memory of the saintly
king and Chertsey began to
attract pilgrims*

Edward IV's recovery of the throne disingenuously declared that
Henry died of 'pure displeasure and melancholy' on hearing of the
fate of his cause at Tewkesbury.[16] A less partial and more plausible
account was given by John Warkworth of Peterhouse, Cambridge,
who wrote in his chronicle in 1480 that the king was put to death on
the night of the Yorkists' triumphant return to London (21–22 May),
'between eleven and twelve of the clock, being then at the Tower
the Duke of Gloucester and many others'.[17] Five years later the
Crowland Chronicler wrote that the body was discovered in the
Tower, but added:

may God have mercy upon and give time for repentance to him, whoever it might be, who dared to lay sacrilegious hands on the Lord's annointed! And so let the doer merit the title of tyrant and the victim that of glorious martyr.[18]

This might seem also to implicate the duke of Gloucester. Only later, well after his death, did 'men constantly say' that Richard had himself killed Henry with his own hands and, according to More, without the knowledge of the king.[19] It is highly unlikely that Henry would have been killed on any authority but the king's. At worst Richard, if involved, was but Edward's agent; there is no reason at all to suppose that he personally stabbed Henry to death with his own dagger crying 'Down, down to hell, and say I sent thee thither'.[20] There is nothing in the events of 1471 to mark out the eighteen-year-old Richard as a cold-blooded and heartless murderer. It had become common for defeated enemies to be killed after battle. Richard Neville, earl of Salisbury had been one of the first victims in 1460, and his sons were not renowned for the quality of mercy shown to their rivals. As a deposed king, Henry VI, like Richard II before him, could not have expected to live long.

Richard of Gloucester's adolescence came to an end in the spring of 1471. The turmoil of the years 1469–71 formed an extended rite of passage from boyhood to manhood. It no doubt shaped the man he was to become. In which ways it is hard to tell: while aspects of his personality became apparent in the calmer years to follow, the likely effect of these turbulent years should not be overlooked. His experiences then perhaps influenced his reactions to crisis and uncertainty again in 1483. He might have noted the advantages of acting promptly and decisively; he might have appreciated the need to win and keep the initiative; and he might have observed that it was often expedient not to take too much notice of the niceties of the law. Richard had reached maturity in a hard school in an uncertain world and he was likely to have taken its lessons to heart.

Representations of
Richard III are to
be found in several
manuscripts executed
during his lifetime.
Most make no attempt
at a likeness.

Portraits of Richard III

An illustration of Anthony, earl Rivers presenting a book to Edward IV shows Duke Richard of Gloucester, identified by a coronet, as the king's right-hand man.

In the Salisbury Roll he and his duchess were represented heraldically.

In the Rous Roll Richard was presented as an idealized monarch.

The early Tudor portraits, the first of which was completed approximately thirty years after his death, were probably based on a lost contemporary likeness. That held by the Society of Antiquaries (above) is the only version not to suggest a hunchback.

Modern examination has revealed that in the copy of approximately the same date (*c.* 1520) held by Her Majesty the Queen (left below, and above), the right shoulder has been crudely overpainted so as to suggest a deformity.

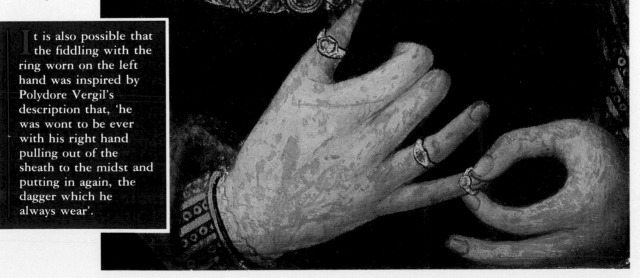

It is also possible that the fiddling with the ring worn on the left hand was inspired by Polydore Vergil's description that, 'he was wont to be ever with his right hand pulling out of the sheath to the midst and putting in again, the dagger which he always wear'.

Chapter 3

Richard in the North, 1471–83

At the age of eighteen Richard of Gloucester succeeded Warwick the Kingmaker as the lord of the north. Richard owed his initial promotion to his brother the king, but he subsequently achieved an unassailable power in the region by his own effort and enterprise. Edward IV clearly owed him a huge debt of gratitude for his unswerving loyalty throughout the crises of 1469–71. Asking Gloucester to take over Warwick's mantle in the north had much to commend it. It is possible that in June 1471 Edward IV was only executing what he had already decided to do in August 1470; it was then that Gloucester had been made warden of the west march. In the summer of 1471 other royal offices previously held by Warwick as well as the lion's share of his northern estates quickly followed into Gloucester's hands. In particular Gloucester succeeded to the office of chief steward of the duchy of Lancaster in the north, which placed him at the head of the most substantial royal interest there. It is conceivable that Edward first intended Richard to exercise royal authority in the region on this basis: in the early 1470s Pontefract, the headquarters of the duchy in Yorkshire, was the duke's most frequent residence. But additionally, Richard was granted the Neville of Middleham estates in Yorkshire and Cumberland, based on Middleham, Sheriff Hutton and Penrith: Richard set out to make these the bases of his own power in the region, independent of the king.

(Right) A mid-sixteenth-century elevation of Pontefract castle, showing the town and parish church beyond. Pontefract was Richard of Gloucester's headquarters in the north and possibly his principal residence at the beginning of the 1470s

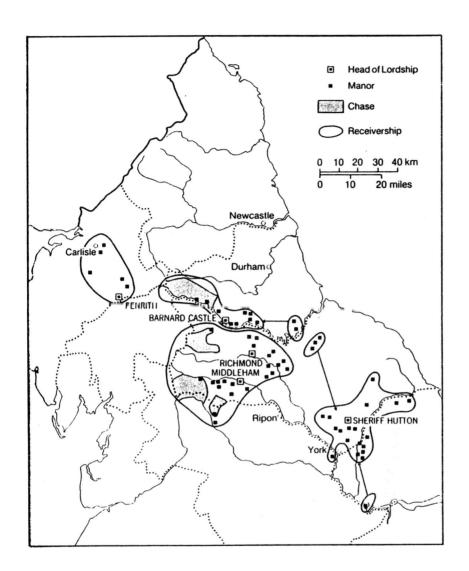

Richard of Gloucester's principal estates in the north

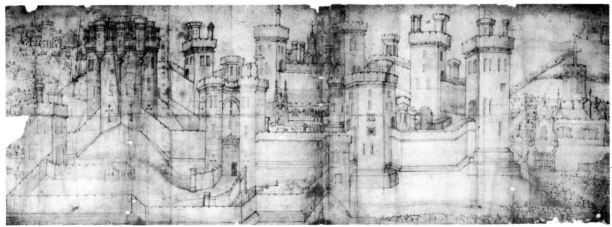

Although the city of York was five days' hard riding from Westminster, the region of which it was capital was by no means remote, backward or barbarous. The vale of York itself, the north-east coastal plain and the valleys west of the Pennines were rich grain producing districts, settled and farmed in the same time-honoured way as midland and southern England. Pastoral farming, both sheep and cattle rearing, was more extensive on the wide sweeps of northern moorland, but it was not economically dominant. As a result the region supported a numerous and substantial peerage and gentry, who were an integral part, socially, culturally and politically of the English nobility as a whole. They were not, as is sometimes still thought, a group of Squire Westons, cut off from their more sophisticated southern cousins. In some respects northern society was culturally more lively than the south. Cheshire and Lancashire were the seedbeds of a thriving tradition of alliterative poetry; Yorkshire produced some of the leading proponents of the new cult of Christian mysticism, especially in the cloisters of Mount Grace Priory; and Durham Cathedral was one of the principal centres of English musical composition, admired throughout Europe.

Yet there were features that set England north of the Trent apart from the rest of the realm. Proximity to England's only land frontier with a hostile neighbour – Scotland – shaped regional consciousness. Near the border itself, in the upper reaches of Tynedale and Coquetdale, a uniquely disordered society of cattle thieves had emerged in the wake of almost two centuries of war, already being celebrated in ballad and verse. But elsewhere, even as far south as Derbyshire and Nottinghamshire, fear of Scottish invasion, created a willingness to serve on the border in time of emergency and ensured that a more conservative and defensive style of building was retained than was becoming fashionable further south. For the same reason chivalry may have enjoyed a more immediate appeal and possessed a more direct relevance for northern lords and gentry than for many living in the south-east.

The north too was religiously distinct and tended to be doctrinally more conservative. It formed its own ecclesiastical province; although York was significantly less well endowed than Canterbury. It enjoyed its own special saints, especially St Cuthbert whose shrine at Durham was a national as well as regional attraction. While in central and south-eastern counties the foundation and support of chantries and prayers for the dead was slackening, in Yorkshire and Lancashire belief in purgatory and the need to lessen its pains remained unabated until the Reformation. The religious houses retained a strong appeal to lay patrons well into the sixteenth century. And whereas educational provision in London and among

Mount Grace Priory near Osmotherley in North Yorkshire was one of the leading Carthusian houses in England, renowned for the quality of its spiritual life and for its contributions to mystical literature

advanced intellectual circles in the south was beginning to reflect the new humanism, in northern centres, while educational opportunities were equally valued, they were firmly rooted in the traditional mould.

Economically the north was not backward, but in the second half of the fifteenth century it was suffering the effects of recession and decline. Agrarian crisis at the end of the fourth decade of the century had hit the north-eastern lowlands particularly severely. Population declined, land was taken out of cultivation and rents fell. Limited recovery after 1460 stabilized the agricultural

When he was king, Richard III gave a licence to Margaret Clifford to donate property to the nuns of Esholt in Yorkshire. The illustrated initial letter of his grant, capped with a crown, shows nuns praying before an image of the Virgin and child. In northern England monastic houses were still held in high esteem

economy, but losses incurred earlier in the century were not completely made good. At the same time, contraction of the domestic market, a shortage of circulating coin and competition from Hanseatic merchants led to severe commercial and industrial depression in the second half of the century, adversely affecting most of the old towns, but particularly the city of York. The situation was exacerbated by the buoyancy of the economy in south-eastern England after 1470 and the loss of trade to London and other southern centres. The region suffered relative as well as absolute decline.

Thus, while it was not cut off from the rest of the kingdom, the north was a distinctive region, differing in important respects from the southern counties and enjoying its own common identity. Awareness of this distinction was summed up in the use of the contemporary phrase 'the north parts'. It was a region already known to Richard of Gloucester when he returned there in the summer of 1471; it was the part of England with which he was to become inseparably identified over the following twelve years.

The seal of the Hanseatic town of Lübeck. Domination of North Sea trade by the Hanseatic League in the second half of the fifteenth century contributed towards the decline of northern commerce

Edward IV's grant of the northern Neville lordships to Richard of Gloucester in the summer of 1471 was but the beginning of a complicated and ultimately incomplete process by which the duke was established as a great landowner in the region. In 1471, at the time of the initial grant, it was assumed that Warwick would be attainted for treason and his lands forfeited. In the event this did not happen. The main reason was that neither Gloucester nor his brother Clarence, with whom he shared possession of the Warwick inheritance, wanted it to happen. Neither brother was willing to accept property merely as a gift of the king, which would have been the case had the lands been forfeit. Richard in particular, as the youngest brother, as yet unmarried, had no right to a part of his father's inheritance. Despite his royal blood, he had to depend on the generosity of his brother to create for him a landed estate worthy of his status. But Richard did have a relatively strong hand with which to play. Edward not only owed him a debt of gratitude for past loyal services, but he also needed him as one of the principal supports of his new regime. Richard could insist on more than a grant of forfeited lands only for as long as the king pleased. However, in his determination to extract not only the most land but also the best terms from the king he ran into the vested interests of others and against awkward legal impediments.

One way to strengthen his hand was to marry Warwick's younger daughter, Anne, the sixteen-year-old widow of the Lancastrian Prince of Wales killed at Tewkesbury. The marriage took place in the spring of 1472. Although the young couple had known each other in childhood, there is no evidence that theirs was a love-match. One might be drawn by the romantic notion that it was, particularly since Richard does indeed seem to have rescued the unfortunate girl from virtual arrest in Clarence's household. Sadly there were mundane and material reasons for the match on both sides. Anne and her sister Isabel, already duchess of Clarence, were the joint heiresses of the earl and countess of Warwick. Held under house arrest by her sister and her husband, Anne was thus prevented from claiming her share in the Warwick inheritance; she was rescued so that she could. It was the sweep of her potential acres not the comeliness of her person that attracted the landless Gloucester. Marriage to Anne Neville also gave credence locally to the young duke's presentation of himself as the social and political heir of Warwick in the north.

In law the marriage was of little immediate advantage. The Neville estates in the north were entailed in the male line; that is to say neither Anne nor her sister Isabel would benefit, Warwick's male heir being George, a boy of six, the only son of his brother John. Anne and Isabel still stood to inherit a substantial estate from

Anne, countess of Warwick, the daughter and heiress of Richard Beauchamp, earl of Warwick, was Rous's patron. Her treatment at the hands of her sons-in-law, especially Richard of Gloucester, angered Rous whose animosity later coloured his short history of Richard's reign

their mother Anne, but she was alive and well, if sheltering in sanctuary at Beaulieu Abbey in Hampshire. Only after her death could the sisters and their husbands hope to succeed to the Beauchamp and Despenser lands which made up half of the Warwick inheritance. It is clear, however, that Richard, like George, wanted immediate possession of a substantial estate created out of that inheritance. George knew this too, which was why when he declared that Richard 'may well have my Lady his sister in law', he sought to insist that he and his duchess 'shall part no livelihood'.[1]

Between 1472 and 1475 an undignified and bitter squabble over the spoils of the Warwick inheritance, to which neither party was entitled, dragged on between the dukes and their duchesses. In the autumn of 1474 they nearly came to blows: only the king's intervention and enforced compromise settled things. This highly political compromise, worked out in stages, rode roughshod over the rights of both George Neville and the dowager countess Anne. In the process any idea of attainting Warwick and his brother was

Anne Neville and her two husbands, one a prince of Wales and the other a king, both of whom look towards her in this gentle portrait in the Beauchamp Pageant. Anne was a sixteen-year-old widow when she married Richard of Gloucester

Isabel Neville and her husband George, duke of Clarence. Isabel and George tried to prevent her sister Anne from taking a share of their mother's inheritance and for a while held Anne under virtual arrest

abandoned. The outcome was that George Neville was disinherited and nearly all his estates, which Gloucester had occupied since the summer of 1471, were granted to him, his duchess and the heirs of their body by authority of an act of parliament. Similarly, also by act of parliament, the dowager countess was stripped of her inheritance, although she had committed no offence, and her lands were divided between her daughters as if she were dead. As her chaplain John Rous put it, she 'had in her days great tribulation for her lord's sake'.[2] The Gloucesters' share was the lordship of Barnard Castle in County Durham. In 1473 she left sanctuary at Beaulieu to be escorted north by servants of her younger son-in-law. There she spent the next decade or so hidden from the world, either in voluntary retreat, or, as Rous alleged, imprisoned by Gloucester. She outlived both her daughters and their husbands and was to receive partial recompense from Henry VII.

The Warwick inheritance was thus partitioned between the avaricious brothers of the king and their wives. Gloucester took the northern half. He did not enter these estates as the husband of the legal heiress of the late earl of Warwick. The marriage at best secured an ultimate right to Barnard Castle as well as a sentimental continuity of kinship between Warwick and the duke. Edward IV knew what he was doing; he had no choice but to satisfy his brothers on whom he depended. But the final settlement completed in 1475 left Gloucester tied to his brother's favour by one unusual knot. While the entail on the Neville lands was broken in Richard's favour, the act of parliament clearly laid down that the title should

lie with him and his duchess jointly in descent to their male heirs
only as long as there were also heirs male of the body of John
Neville, late Marquess Montagu living. Should George Neville, his
son, die without a male heir himself, Gloucester's title would revert
to a life interest. This extraordinary clause seems to have been
designed to protect the interests of residual Neville legatees,
particularly Richard, Lord Latimer, also a minor, and to make it
clear that the act was limited to punishing John Neville for his
treason. From Gloucester's point of view it was clearly less than
ideal. It hardly provided a secure basis upon which to establish his
own line. One can only conclude that he never considered it more
than a stop-gap arrangement to be amended to his advantage at a
future date.

It is important to appreciate the flawed nature of Richard's title
to his northern estates, upon which all his future power depended,
for it left his position in the world uncertain and impermanent. An
opportunity for Richard to have persuaded Edward IV to amend the
settlement of 1475 in his favour would seem to have arisen in 1478
after the trial and execution of Clarence for treason. But, while
Richard made small territorial gains in return for his tacit support,
no alteration to the title to the Neville estates was secured; only a
further degradation of George Neville who lost his title of duke of
Bedford. Thereafter, as if he sensed that amendment in the near

*The eagle badge and motto ('As
it Plese God') of Thomas
Bourgchier, the elderly
Archbishop of Canterbury, from
Fenn's scrapbook. His possession
of the wardship of the young
Richard Neville, Lord Latimer,
helped frustrate Gloucester's
attempts to tighten his shaky hold
on his northern estates*

future was unlikely, Richard stepped up efforts to protect himself from the potential consequences of the settlement. Ralph, Lord Neville, the heir to the earl of Westmorland, formally agreed to quit the claim of the senior branch of the Nevilles. An unsuccessful attempt was made to secure the custody of Richard Neville, Lord Latimer; but although the support of one or two of his kinswomen and the custody of his Yorkshire estates were won, the wardship remained firmly in the hands of Thomas Bourgchier, archbishop of Canterbury. Richard did, however, succeed by 1480 in gaining the custody of George Neville himself, upon whose life and reproductive capacity his own line depended. Yet he seems to have been unable to induce George to marry let alone produce a legitimate child. When Edward IV died in April 1483 the matter was still unresolved. Throughout Edward IV's reign therefore there was an underlying uncertainty to Richard's position in the north. In the spring of 1483, when George died, it was to become an issue of immediate and pressing concern; but for the rest of Edward's reign it was only a small cloud on the horizon, which would hopefully disappear. In the immediate future, Richard had other interests and ambitions to pursue.

Richard of Gloucester acquired other lands than a share of the Warwick inheritance. In 1474 and later in 1478 he increased his holding of forfeited Hungerford lands. In 1471 he was granted the confiscated estates of John de Vere, earl of Oxford. He also browbeat the earl's elderly mother into surrendering her own estates to him in January 1473. At a hearing twenty years later, witness after witness gave evidence as to the manner in which Gloucester's servants bullied the old countess into signing an agreement to hand over her own inheritance to the duke 'by coercion and compulsion'. According to Henry Preston she gave in when he threatened that he would 'send her to Middleham there to be kept', and she, 'considering her great age, the great journey and the great cold which then was of frost and snow, thought that she could not endure to be conveyed thither without great jeopardy of her life.'[3] A defenceless widow, whose son was a disgraced traitor, she was like the countess of Warwick, vulnerable to the duke's strong-arm tactics. Edward IV, who was reported to be unhappy about his brother's behaviour, nevertheless acquiesced. The parallel with the treatment of the countess of Warwick at the same time is, to say the least, thought-provoking. Gloucester was not particularly scrupulous about the legality of the steps he took to create for himself a landed estate to match his birth and station. He was determined to establish himself as a magnate independent of the king by whatever means.

Richard of Gloucester held estates throughout England. The

The gateway to Hornby Castle in Richmondshire, now standing in the Burrell Collection in Glasgow, was completed in the early sixteenth century by the first Lord Conyers. His predecessor and grandfather, Sir John, was the leading figure in local society in the second half of the fifteenth century

de Vere property made him significant in East Anglia, but the north was from the first his principal interest. It was here, from the summer of 1471, that he concentrated on creating his own personal following. Several men from the earl of Warwick's affinity were quickly offered indentures of retainer, most with enhanced fees. Of particular importance to Richard in persuading Warwick's men to enter his service (and in enabling those men quickly to secure the protection of the king's brother) was Sir John Conyers of Hornby in Richmondshire. Conyers was the head of one of the wealthiest gentry families in the north east, whose grandson and heir was to be promoted to the peerage in the early sixteenth century. Sir John, a man in his fifties, had served the Nevilles in all their causes since 1450 and had succeeded his father as steward of Middleham in the early 1460s. He had ridden successive political storms since 1459 and was at hand to welcome the young duke in 1471. Conyers delivered the northern Neville affinity to Gloucester; Richard's lordship offered instant protection from prosecution for the treasonable support many of them had given to Warwick over the previous two years.

The old Neville affinity, built around the Conyers, Harrington, Huddleston, Strangways and Metcalfe families became the core of Richard's following. The Conyers family itself (Sir John was one of twenty-four siblings and half-siblings and himself fathered twelve children) provided many retainers who were themselves substantial landed gentlemen in Durham and North Yorkshire. To this nucleus were added men from further south in Yorkshire retained on the basis of the stewardship of the duchy of Lancaster; men in County Durham recruited through the lordship of Barnard Castle; and Cumbrians retained through the wardenship of the west march. The lesser peerage too, Lords FitzHugh, Greystoke and Scrope of Bolton quickly saw the wisdom of entering the service of such a favoured royal prince. In 1476 he secured the custody of the young Lord Scrope of Masham, who later became his committed supporter. Other young men, of lower social status, from outside the existing establishment and several, like him, younger sons, entered his service at this time and became his most confidential servants. Prominent among these were Robert Brackenbury and Richard Ratcliffe.

Gloucester's dramatic intrusion into northern society was not universally welcomed. Three powerful men in particular resented and resisted his advancement: Henry Percy, earl of Northumberland; Laurence Booth, bishop of Durham; and Thomas, Lord Stanley. All three found their own hopes of benefiting from Warwick's fall frustrated by Richard. Northumberland had anticipated that he would be the principal beneficiary. He had been

William Burgh (below) of Brough Hall near Catterick, Sir John Conyers' brother-in-law, was retained by Richard of Gloucester. His brass is to be seen in the parish church of St Anne. Sir Richard Conyers, Sir John's brother, the receiver (estate manager) of Middleham, set himself up as lord of the nearby South Cowton. Here he built himself a fine new fortified manor house (left) and established a chantry in the parish church where he was buried (below left)

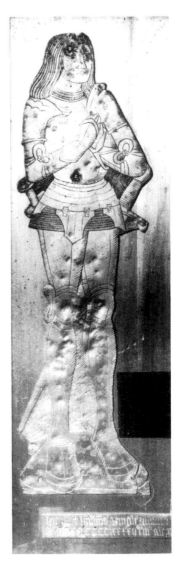

Knaresborough Castle, the centre of the duchy of Lancaster lordship, pictured here in the mid-sixteenth century, was the focal point of conflict between Gloucester and the earl of Northumberland in the early 1470s

restored by Edward IV in 1470 as a counterweight to the overbearing earl and in 1471 he had returned the favour by his benevolent neutrality. In the early 1470s, as Gloucester effortlessly stepped into Warwick's shoes, the old rivalry and conflict between Percy and Neville interests threatened to revive. Tension focused on the honour of Knaresborough in which Northumberland was the principal landholder and steward of the duchy of Lancaster. Gloucester as chief steward, and reviving long-standing Neville ambitions, challenged the earl's dominance. By 1473 it was necessary for the king to intervene to stifle the growing conflict, and in 1474 he secured a settlement whereby Gloucester agreed not to compete for retainers in return for the earl entering the duke's service. In effect, Northumberland conceded defeat. Laurence Booth, too, had been no friend of Warwick, with whom he had had a long-standing quarrel over possession of Barnard Castle. He too had benefited in 1470 by the recovery of that lordship from the heirs of Beauchamp, but he was required to surrender it to Gloucester before the autumn of 1474. Until his promotion to York in 1476 he excluded the duke from his palatinate. Lord Stanley's quarrel with Gloucester was already well established as a result of the duke's intervention in 1470 on the side of the Harringtons in the dispute over Hornby in Lonsdale. It was again not until 1474 that a compromise over this was reached. Thus, Gloucester's arrival in the north as the political heir of Warwick initially threatened the continuation of strife, not the end of disorder.

The headstrong and ambitious Richard was an unsettling force in the early 1470s. It needed all Edward IV's personal authority to restrain him. This is revealed clearly in instructions given to his ambassador to Scotland in 1475. At the time, a few months after the treaty of Edinburgh, the king was completing his final preparations for an invasion of France. Part of the diplomatic groundwork for this was the truce with Scotland so as to secure his rear. Yet Gloucester, warden of the west march, was dragging his feet. In 1473 it had been reported in Scotland that he wanted to launch an invasion. Now, by his reluctance to implement the terms of the treaty and by his own insubordinate acts of piracy, he was threatening to undermine all Edward IV's efforts in the north. As a result the ambassador, Alexander Lee, was instructed by the king in February 1475 to order the duke to hold march days as required and to 'advertise' him that he, 'according the king's pleasure for his honour and surety, proved in this case as it apperuaineth': in other words, he should do as he was told.[4] Richard was almost as much of a handful as his brother George.

Richard III's admiralty seal. As admiral of England before 1483, he once incurred his brother's displeasure by an act of piracy against a Scottish ship at a time when Edward IV was striving to maintain the peace

The invasion of France itself offered the opportunity and occasion to reunite the bickering magnates. All the outstanding issues between Gloucester and his northern rivals were settled, for the most part in Gloucester's favour, in the year before they set sail together for Calais with dreams of emulating Agincourt. Although the expedition hardly lived up to this, ending as it did in Louis XI buying off the leaders at the treaty of Picquigny and the troops becoming roaring drunk in Amiens, a new spirit of harmony seems subsequently to have been created between the northern lords. After 1475 Gloucester's supremacy was accepted and the duke, now established as the leading magnate of the north, seems to have become a less abrasive and more accommodating figure. He no longer needed to prove himself. It was during the next eight years, when Richard was sure of his personal predominance, that he established his reputation as the benevolent lord of the north.

It is significant that from 1475 Richard began not only to spend more time in the north, but also, at some expense, to concentrate his landed estate in the region. He sold, released or exchanged estates granted to him in Wales and the west country so as to add Scarborough, Cottingham, Skipton and Helmsley, the latter forfeited properties of the Clifford and Scrope families, to his Yorkshire holdings. To secure some of these acquisitions he had to pay substantial sums. As a result, but clearly by his own choice, he became more exclusively a northern lord and his interests elsewhere, although never totally neglected, became more peripheral. While he spent the winters of 1476–7 and 1477–8 in London, he stayed for the rest of those years on his northern estates. Middleham, Barnard Castle and Sheriff Hutton now became his principal residences, the centres of a lavish display of largesse suggested by heavy expenditure

Richard made Middleham Castle his principal residence in the north in the late 1470s. His son and heir was born there; he established an annual fair for the town; and he transformed its parish church into a lavishly endowed college

on jewels, clothing and feasting which gave rise to his reputation as 'a great and magnificent housekeeper'.[5]

Richard also concentrated his religious patronage in the north. While he was a major founder of Queens' College, Cambridge (establishing four fellowships whose holders were to pray for the good estate of the founder and his family and for the souls of servants slain at Barnet and Tewkesbury) and a patron of Allhallows Barking by the Tower, his principal benefactions and foundations were northern. From 1474 he was, with his duchess, a member of the fraternity of Durham priory; by 1476 he was considered to be

the priory's very special lord, and he was an almost annual visitor to the cathedral, probably on the occasion of one of St Cuthbert's two feasts. He took up the responsibilities of the lord of Middleham as patron of Coverham Abbey generously. In 1478 he received permission to found and endow two ambitious collegiate chapels, one at Middleham with six priests which was established in 1480, the other at Barnard Castle with twelve priests which did not materialize. An altogether more ambitious and grandiose scheme for a chantry served by no fewer than 100 priests in York Minster was launched after he became king. This, probably his intended mausoleum, more than anything else demonstrates the extent to which he identified himself with his adopted region.

As Duke Richard focused his personal interest on the north, so he also extended and consolidated his political influence. In 1476, William Dudley, dean of the Chapel Royal, succeeded Laurence Booth as bishop of Durham. Dudley became Richard's creature, allowing him to tap the resources of the palatinate to reward his

The choir of Durham Cathedral. As members of the fraternity of St Cuthbert, the duke and duchess of Gloucester were entitled to participate in the celebration of mass in the choir, a privilege they seem to have exercised from time to time if their donations to the saint's shrine are a guide

servants, and appointing the duke and his men to important political and administrative posts. By 1480 at the latest the bishop was routinely consulting the duke over palatine affairs while his subjects were as a matter of course appealing to Gloucester to intervene in legal matters on their behalf. Where the bishop led, if Dudley can ever be said to have led, the Nevilles of Raby followed. Ralph, Lord Neville, heir to the elderly and simple earl of Westmorland, who at the beginning of the decade had allied himself with Bishop Booth, now put himself in Gloucester's service and his uncle's castle of Raby at his disposal. Similarly in York, the mayor and corporation were eager to please: by 1482 it was customary for them to shower lavish gifts on him whenever he visited the city and on 16 March twenty-five of them agreed to attend on him at the Austin Friary there to give 'a laudable thank for his good and benevolent lordship that he at all times have had unto this city'.[6] Even the residentiary canons of the Minster, not withstanding the reluctance of successive archbishops to become too closely associated with the duke, assiduously cultivated Richard's patronage, even approaching him on at least one occasion for assistance in ecclesiastical matters. By 1480 there was barely a lord or gentleman, corporation or religious body in Cumbria, Northumberland, Durham and Yorkshire who did not hope to benefit, directly or indirectly, from his good lordship. In short, by the end of the decade Richard of Gloucester had created a hegemony more complete and more comprehensive than even that enjoyed by his predecessor, the earl of Warwick. Within an exceedingly brief period he had risen from the distrusted interloper to the acknowledged lord of the north.

The seal of William Dudley as dean of Wolverhampton, before he became bishop of Durham in 1476. A personal servant of Edward IV, he proved to be one of the more spineless prince bishops of the palatinate, happy to let its administration be dominated by the king's brother

The use to which Richard put his power was largely beneficial to the north. By the healing of old wounds between Neville and Neville, and Neville and Percy he removed the principal cause of the civil strife and disorder which had plagued the region since 1453. Conflict now gave way to cooperation. Richard deliberately set out to pacify quarrels between lesser men that might threaten to disturb the peace, and actively promoted the cause of impartial justice. His councillors were fully employed as arbitrators in disputes such as that between Richard Clervaux of Croft and Roland Place of Halnaby, neighbours in the parish of Croft in North Yorkshire, which both parties put to him for resolution at Middleham in March 1478. The award, declared a month later, settled such diverse issues as seating arrangements in the parish church, property boundaries and the trespass of hounds on each other's land when hunting. In its preamble the duke expressed his desire to see 'good concord, rest and friendly unity' between them for the peace and weal of the country in which they lived.[7]

Duke Richard's concern to maintain the peace and weal of the country extended beyond the landed gentry. In 1480 a humble husbandman, John Randson of Burntoft in County Durham, appealed to him against Sir Robert Claxton of Horden, one of the leading gentry of the palatinate, who, Randson claimed, was preventing him from working his land. It was, in fact, a dispute over possession of the property. Gloucester did not hesitate to intervene on Randson's behalf, warning Claxton 'so to demean you that we have no cause to provide his lawful remedy in this behalf';[8] and this notwithstanding the fact that Claxton was the father of one of his retainers and the father-in-law of another. Most lords would have maintained the cause of the kinsman of their own retainers, especially in a case such as this. Richard took the side of the lesser man.

But Gloucester went out of his way to uphold the law even against his own men. A petition by Katherine Williamson of Riccall in Yorkshire received in the February–April session of parliament in 1473 told how Gloucester had unwittingly taken into his service Thomas Farnell, the father of her husband's murderers, but how on discovering that he had aided and abetted his criminal sons, notwithstanding that he wore his livery, Gloucester had commanded 'the said Thomas should be brought unto the gaol of York, there to abide, unto the time that he . . . were lawfully acquitted or attainted'.[9] Richard himself may have sponsored her petition, which called for Farnell and his sons to be brought for trial before the King's Bench. He acted similarly in 1482 when he handed over Thomas Redhead, a servant of the treasurer of his household, to the mayor of York, 'to correct and punish him for his said offence and upon that to commit him to prison'.[10] One may suspect that the duke had an eye to the good that such acts might do for his reputation, especially in the case of Katherine Williamson, which coincided with his own harassment of another widow, the countess of Oxford. Nevertheless, whatever his own personal motive, it was on cases like those of Randson, Williamson and Redhead that his reputation as a man of justice was built. The work that his ducal council undertook on his instruction in settling disputes and responding to the petitions of the weak and oppressed, gave rise to the establishment of a court of poor requests and the council of the north when he was king. It is hard not to conclude that, where his own immediate self interest was not concerned, Richard had a desire to ensure the administration of impartial justice.

Richard was responsive too to the economic plight of the region. Evidence of his efforts here focus on the city of York, suffering a deep depression and extended decline. But York's plight was symptomatic of the north as a whole during the 1470s. The mayor and corporation placed the blame for their difficulties on two things: unfair competition from London and the obstruction of Yorkshire waterways by fishgarths. The duke acted vigorously on the city's behalf on both issues, lobbying the king to discriminate against London in York's favour (in which he failed), and backing the city's campaign to clear fishgarths (in which he succeeded). In 1482 he took up the city's case for a reduction in its fee farm, the annual payment to the Crown for the right to be self-governing; once king he granted it. He was indeed a benevolent lord to York; although, since the city's misfortunes were caused by other

The Guildhall, York, before it was damaged by enemy action during the Second World War. The citizens, or at least a dominant party of their number, became enthusiastic supporters of the duke of Gloucester, who did his best to further their interests with the king

James III of Scotland, here portrayed with his heir, the future James IV, was the proud repossessor of Berwick for his kingdom. It was wrested from him by Richard of Gloucester in 1482

economic forces beyond government control, his efforts made very little difference. Nevertheless he did all that was in his power, and was seen to do all that he could, to help the city.

Above all Richard was responsive to regional opinion in the matter of war against Scotland. The lords and gentry of the northern counties were perpetually anxious about the security of the border; and some were itching for the opportunity of war. In the 1470s they were still smarting from the ignominy of losses suffered between 1448 and 1464 when the Scots had gained the upper hand. In particular the cession of Berwick by Margaret of Anjou in 1461 rankled not only because of pride but also because it left the east coast route into England exposed. Richard himself was temperamentally at one with the more aggressive elements in northern society. As we have seen he was a reluctant executant of the treaty of Edinburgh in 1474. For five years the truce survived and Gloucester kept the peace, but in 1479 the truce crumbled and in 1480 open war between the two kingdoms was renewed. It is not really known why the perpetual peace in the isle of Britain promised by the treaty was so short-lived, but one important factor in its failure was that the principal magnates on either side of the border, Gloucester and his Scottish counterpart, the duke of Albany, did not want it to succeed. When war came Duke Richard, twice the king's appointed lieutenant-general, in 1480 and 1482 led the English successfully in the field. From the point of view of the wider diplomatic interest of the realm, the war was ill-advised since it diverted men and materials northwards and thus allowed Louis XI of France to humiliate Edward IV in the Low Countries, but from the point of view of northern England the war was a triumphant success. Not only did Richard contain all Scottish raids within a few miles of the border, but he also led a series of devastating and profitable raids of his own deep into Scotland, culminating in 1482 in an unopposed march on Edinburgh. Above all in the same year his troops recaptured Berwick. By the end of that campaigning season, after three years of warfare, the tables had been turned on the Scots. Once more the initiative lay firmly in English hands.

Victory in war against the Scots sealed Richard of Gloucester's reputation in the north and assured his continuing political domination. His achievement was recognized and rewarded in February 1483 by the creation for him of a county palatine comprising Cumberland and a large stretch of south-west Scotland which it was his declared intention to conquer. The wardenship of the west march was to become his hereditary possession; he was set on a new phase in his career in which, it seems, he hoped to establish himself as the hereditary ruler of a new marcher principality lying between the two kingdoms. At the age of thirty

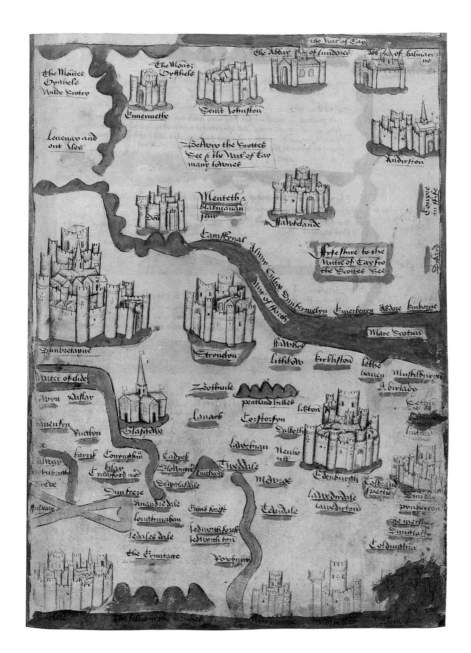

John Hardyng, who died in the early 1460s, was a Northumbrian squire who spent his life fighting the Scots. He wrote a rhyming history of England, a revised version of which was dedicated to Edward IV, in which he urged a conquest of Scotland. It was left to Richard of Gloucester in the early 1480s to wage the kind of war Hardyng appreciated: this map was designed to help the invader

Richard was the greatest subject in the realm, admired and respected in the south as well as in the north. Constable, Admiral and Great Chamberlain, the brother of the king, he was not just a distant northern lord. He participated in all the great occasions of state after 1475: the solemn reburial of his father at Fotheringhay in August 1476; the marriage of his nephew Richard of York at Westminster in January 1478; and the treaty of Fotheringhay with Alexander of Albany in June 1482. He was a witness to all royal charters until 1483, which may not mean that he was actually present, but does mean that he was *persona grata* at court. He had, at the least tacitly, supported Edward IV during the trial of their brother George in 1478; he offered no opposition and he helped pack the parliament which condemned Clarence.

Richard had benefited from his fall to the extent of a small addition to his estates, an office and a title for his son. Early historians were divided as to whether he was privately upset by what happened or secretly rejoiced. Mancini heard five years later that 'Richard duke of Gloucester was so overcome with grief for his brother, that he could not dissimulate so well, but that he was overheard to say that he would one day avenge his brother's death'.[11] More, on the other hand, a considerable time later, considered that he dissimulated all too effectively, for he commented that:

> Some wise men also ween that his drift covertly conveyed, lacked not in helping forth his brother of Clarence to his death, which he resisted openly, howbeit somewhat (as men deemed) more faintly than he that were heartily minded to his wealth.[12]

Where the truth lay is now impossible to discern. Richard may have sought to distance himself as much as possible from what went on, doing no more than his duty to his king. Nevertheless the event left him even higher in favour.

Mancini also reported that after Clarence's death Richard came very rarely to court and kept himself within his own lands so as to 'avoid the jealousy of the queen'.[13] What little is known of his itinerary confirms that he went down to Middleham in March 1478 and only occasionally visited London or Westminster thereafter. The city of York in the autumn of 1485 commented in its petition to Henry VII to confirm the reduction in its fee farm that the duke of Gloucester had in his day been 'continually among' his northern subjects.[14] Yet there is little contemporary evidence to suggest a rift between Richard and the queen. On the surface his relationship in these years with Edward IV, his queen and her sons was amicable; beneath the surface we cannot see. Nor is there evidence of hostility between Richard and the queen's brother Anthony, Earl Rivers before the king's death. Indeed at the end of March 1483, just a week or two before Edward died, Rivers and Roger Townshend, serjeant-at-law, agreed to put their dispute over property in Norfolk to Gloucester's arbitration.[15] After Edward's death Richard and Queen Elizabeth became deadly rivals, but Mancini and all subsequent writers who suggested that Gloucester always resented the power and influence enjoyed at court by upstart Woodvilles in the last years of Edward's reign read back from later events, and later propaganda, into the past. They also chose to overlook the overwhelming evidence of Richard's high favour with the king until the very last months of the reign. No one who has a county palatinate created for him can complain that he lacks royal favour. And even if, as has been argued, the queen was by this time exercising considerable influence, it follows that it cannot have been used against her brother-in-law on this occasion.

The precise relationship between Edward and Richard is hard to determine. On the one hand, Edward had promoted his brother, rewarded him and placed great trust in him. Initially it was Edward's choice to put him at the head of the royal household and Neville affinity in the north. It was part of a pattern whereby Edward entrusted control of the more distant provinces of the realm to a handful of relatives and close companions: Rivers in Wales; Clarence, then the queen's son Thomas, marquess of Dorset in the West Country; Hastings in the north and west midlands; Gloucester in the north. In the north it had proved a wise and successful decision. Gloucester secured a potentially rebellious region for him. In 1476 he used his authority to quell disturbances there which followed the return of troops from France.[16] When in the following year a violent quarrel blew up between two of the king's own household men in Yorkshire (Sir John Pilkington and John Saville), Gloucester headed a judicial enquiry to calm things down.[17] He served his brother well.

But perhaps Richard took more for himself than Edward intended; as we have seen Gloucester had a mind of his own. He pursued ambitions of his own in the face of his brother's disapproval. It was possibly so as to retain ultimate control over these ambitions that Edward imposed an unusual but restricting limitation on the title to his brother's northern estates which left him still dependent on his favour. Yet, Gloucester was nevertheless able to create for himself a power in the region greater than Edward could have anticipated. It is noticeable that he recruited to his service several men who, before 1471, had been the king's foremost knights of the body in Yorkshire: Sir Ralph Ashton, Sir Edmund Hastings, Sir John Pilkington and John Saville. By the end of Edward's reign these men (or their heirs) were more closely attached to Richard than to the king. And after the fall of Clarence in 1478 Edward was in no position to risk offending his younger brother. While Gloucester still relied on his brother's favour, Edward was no doubt conscious of the need to keep Richard happy. This is the most satisfactory explanation for Edward's continued prosecution of the war against Scotland even when it undermined his wider diplomatic interests. Richard wanted war, and Edward was not prepared to run the risk of driving him into opposition by refusing him. He had learnt to his cost earlier in his reign the consequences of excluding a

Edward IV died, it was said, as a result of a chill caught while out boating on the Thames. If so, his messing about on the river, like these courtiers illustrated in one of his own books, changed the course of history

powerful northern lord from office; it was not a mistake he was prepared to repeat.

At the beginning of 1483 Richard of Gloucester was riding the crest of a wave; high in the king's favour, backed by a powerful retinue, respected and admired by his countrymen, he dominated the north of England. But all may not have been quite as it seemed. Although there is no direct and irrefutable evidence it is possible that he had grossly overstretched his finances. More certainly he was still stuck with an unsatisfactory title to the Neville estates in the north and had yet to make a reality of his palatine ambitions in the west march. He still depended as much on Edward IV as Edward IV depended on him. But on 9 April, after a short illness, Edward IV died. Edward's unexpected and untimely death put Richard's whole future and everything he had achieved since 1471 at risk. Whatever happened he could not now afford to lose royal favour under the new king, his twelve-year-old nephew, Edward V.

Pigs and Boars

Richard III's badge of the white boar may well have been adopted as a pun on *Eboracum*, latin for York into which house he was born.

The boar is to be found carved in stone in Barnard Castle . . .

. . . painted on glass at St Martin-cum-Gregory in York . . .

. . . in wax on his seal . . . .

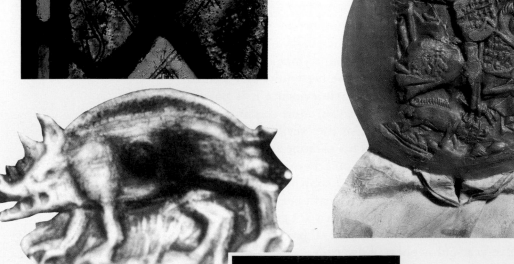

. . . and in the form of a hat badge dug up from the moat at Middleham.

narré:

sabia

On the one hand, the boar was a wild and dangerous animal – 'a proud beast and fierce and perilous' – as the author of the standard treatise on hunting, *The Master of Game*, put it. Erasmus later noted in his *Institution of the Christian Prince* that such a wild beast was a suitable metaphor for a tyrant. And indeed in the shamelessly propagandist *Twelve Triumphs of Henry VII*, probably written by Bernard Andre in 1497, the third feat of Hercules with which Henry is credited was the slaying on the field of battle of the wild boar of Arcadia, who had had for his device 'The Great Hog, which is a very foul animal.' It would seem too that Polydore Vergil in his account of Bosworth drew upon a familiar literary source to describe the boar at bay. Vergil wrote:

> while the battle continued thus hot on both sides, king Richard understood where earl Henry was afar off with small force of soldiers about him, wherefore, all inflamed with ire, he struck his horse with the spurs, and ran against him . . . king Richard alone was killed fighting manfully in the thickest press of his enemies.

The Master of Game describes how, 'when the boar is heated, or wrathful, or hurt, then he runneth upon all things that he sees before him. And for no stroke or wound that men do him will he complain or cry.' To his enemies, Richard's badge of the boar was a most appropriate symbol. Scenes of the boar hunt in the Devonshire Tapestries, completed in the mid-fifteenth century, illustrate what they had in mind.

On the other hand, the wild pig was the symbol of the hermit saint, Anthony of Egypt, because a boar had protected him from all danger for twenty-four years in the wilderness. According to the legend, the boar not only himself refused to threaten St Anthony at the behest of demons, but he also drove off all the other beasts that did. He thus symbolized St Anthony's own ascetic virtue and rejection of the pleasures of the flesh. St Anthony was one of Richard III's special saints: it is conceivable that he perceived his badge of the white boar as a symbol of his own virtue and struggle against sexual temptation. Richard would almost certainly have been familiar with the recently executed panel painting of the legend of St Anthony on the back of the choir stalls at Carlisle cathedral. This scene depicts the pig driving away the other beasts.

Richard would also have known the fraternity of St Anthony in York, on the roof of whose hall the symbol of St Anthony's pig bearing a cross was depicted on bosses in the nineteenth century.

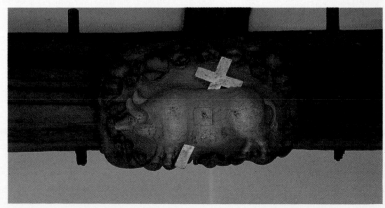

Chapter 4

Usurpation and Rebellion, 1483

The events of 9 April to 6 July 1483, between the death of Edward IV and the coronation of Richard III, lie at the heart of our story. Would the well-informed political commentator surveying the scene after Edward's death have predicted that within three months his brother would have made himself king? It is to be doubted. One or two claimed to be wise after the event. Sir Thomas More knew someone who clearly remembered that on the very night that Edward IV died one Potter declared 'By my troth, then will my master, the duke of Gloucester be king'.[1] But the surprise by which almost everyone was taken when Richard of all people deposed his nephew Edward V suggests that few had access to such privileged inside information. What happened in these months was unexpected and to many inexplicable. For these reasons alone the accession of Richard III will never cease to intrigue and divide opinion.

The events can be quickly summarized. Richard, residing at one of his northern castles, heard the news of Edward IV's death on or about 15 April. He may have been forewarned, for Edward had been ill for three weeks and a false rumour of his death had already spread. Richard's first reported public act was to go to York Minster and there pledge his loyalty to his new king, Edward V. At the same time he entered into correspondence with at least two noblemen who were to be his allies in the immediate future: Henry

Stafford, duke of Buckingham and William, Lord Hastings. Buckingham was a magnate who had been almost totally excluded from power by Edward IV. He was of the royal blood, and held extensive lands in the midlands and Wales. He almost certainly resented the way in which Edward IV had promoted Lords Stanley and Hastings in regions where he had a vested interest. He also had a long-standing claim to a share of the old Bohun inheritance held by the crown. His exclusion from the Yorkist elite is difficult to understand unless it were on grounds of a suspicion of his own royal ambitions, or of a judgement that he was personally unreliable and unfitted for high office. There is no evidence of association between Buckingham and Richard before 1483. It is perhaps of significance, however, that Richard was so quickly in contact with one who had been so clearly out of favour in recent years. Hastings was the very opposite: he had been Edward IV's right-hand man for most of his reign and as chamberlain of his household the key figure in leading and coordinating the knights and esquires of the body through whom Edward IV had exercised his personal authority. He had shared exile with Edward and Richard in 1470 and their triumphal return in 1471. Like Richard, he was an insider. But he was involved in a notorious quarrel with the queen's family, especially her son Thomas Grey, marquess of Dorset, and was no doubt anxious about his future at court under the new regime. These three, Richard and Buckingham in the country and Hastings in London, quickly forged an alliance.

From London Hastings reported to the dukes the deliberations of the royal council making arrangements for the government of the realm during the minority. The council was divided. Some, one assumes Hastings prominent in their number, wanted to make Gloucester, as the king's paternal uncle, an interim protector of the realm; others, including the queen and Dorset, wanted to proceed to an immediate coronation. A compromise agreement was apparently reached for an early coronation on 4 May, as soon as the king and his uncles had reached London, and for Gloucester to become chief councillor. Gloucester and Buckingham joined forces, both accompanied only by modestly sized retinues, at Northampton on 29 April. There they entertained Earl Rivers and his principal officers who, with the king, had reached Stony Stratford on their road up from Ludlow. Rivers assumed that on the morrow they would join together to accompany the king in state to London and his coronation five days later in Westminster Abbey. Anthony Woodville, Earl Rivers was the queen's brother. Like Richard and Hastings he had shared exile with Edward IV in 1470–1. Like Richard he enjoyed a reputation as a cultured, pious and chivalric man; but he was also a hard-headed politician who had used his

The seal of William, Lord Hastings attached to an indenture for his garrison at Calais. In the spring of 1483 he threatened to call upon these troops if he did not get his way in the establishment of the minority government for Edward V

The signatures and mottoes of Edward V, Richard of Gloucester and Henry Stafford, duke of Buckingham on a document dating from the protectorate. In the light of later events Richard's motto, meaning 'loyalty binds me', carefully written in a clear hand beneath his king's signature, is full of tragic irony

position as governor of the Prince of Wales and head of his household to enhance his own power and influence. He was not the sort of man to take risks if he sensed any danger. On the night of 29 April he clearly believed that he, Gloucester and Buckingham were as one over the immediate arrangements for the government. At dawn on 30 April, however, he was seized in his bed by the dukes' retainers and immediately taken the ten miles back to Stony Stratford where the dukes confronted the young king, dismissed his personal attendants and arrested Sir Richard Grey (the queen's younger son by her first marriage) and Sir Thomas Vaughan, the treasurer of the king's household. According to what reads like an eyewitness account given to Mancini, Gloucester, 'who exhibited a mournful countenance',[2] told the king that Rivers and his family were morally unsuited to be royal ministers, that they had conspired to kill him and that they had sought to deny him the protectorate promised by Edward IV. Despite a spirited defence of Rivers, the king saw that he had no choice but to surrender himself to the care of his paternal uncle. While Richard and Buckingham, now with Edward V firmly under their control, resumed their journey to London, Rivers, Grey and Vaughan were sent north to imprisonment at Middleham and Sheriff Hutton. News of this palace coup quickly reached London where the queen, having initially tried to raise the city on her behalf, fled to sanctuary in Westminster with her younger son, Richard of York, her daughters and Dorset. London was held for the dukes by Lord Hastings who welcomed them to the city a few days later.

On 10 May, at a formal meeting of council, Richard was installed as protector, the coronation was put back to 24 June (later altered to

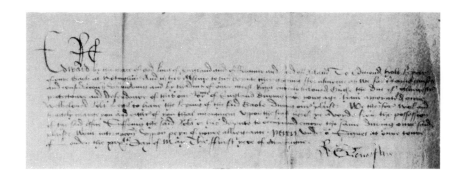

This letter, dated 19 May 1483 in the name of the king, but over the signature of the duke of Gloucester, which orders the keeper of Nottingham gaol to resign and surrender his office to Robert Leigh, shows that Richard was tightening his grip on the government of the kingdom

Sunday 22 June) and all the lords in London as well as the mayor and aldermen were required to swear an oath of fealty to the young king. This, and Gloucester's declaration of intent, reassured the city. Once Gloucester was established as protector, royal government carried on much as before. Rivers, Dorset and their closest associates were stripped of offices and grants; Buckingham was lavishly rewarded and established with almost vice-regal power in Wales. The triumvirate seemed to have achieved its objective of excluding the queen's family. While the council refused to support Gloucester's demand that Rivers should be tried for treason, preparations were nevertheless set in train for the coronation and the meeting of parliament that would follow immediately, and discussion was initiated on the form of government to be put into operation once the king was crowned and, as was expected, the protectorate came to an end.

The apparent calm was shattered when on Friday 13 June, during a council meeting at the Tower, the protector suddenly accused Hastings, Lord Stanley, Archbishop Rotherham of York and Bishop Morton of Ely of treason. Hastings was seized, taken outside and beheaded without even the pretence of a trial. The other three were thrown into prison. It is now known that on 10 June Richard had sent letters north to the city of York, Lord Neville and, no doubt, many others including the earl of Northumberland, calling on them to raise troops to rescue him from the danger he and his men faced in London from the plots and sorcery of the queen and her adherents, who threatened 'the final destruction' of all who followed him.[3] On 13 June he justified his actions on the grounds of the same Woodville plot against him. Events moved rapidly. On Monday 16 June Richard surrounded the Westminster precinct with a large force, threatening to enter and seize the young duke of York. The archbishop of Canterbury, fearing more the desecration of sanctuary than the safety of the ten-year-old prince, persuaded Queen Elizabeth to hand him over. Writs were now issued cancelling the parliament called to meet after the coronation, and

(Opposite) Richard of Gloucester's seige of the sanctuary of Westminster in June 1483, where the king's younger brother, the Duke of York, had taken refuge with his mother, must have resembled this scene of troops surrounding a church in the centre of a town

Archbishop Thomas Rotherham of York, dismissed from office as chancellor after Edward IV's death, was one of those whom Richard arrested immediately before he made his bid for the throne. Here Rotherham's closeness to Edward IV and his family is emphasized in the frontispiece to the Luton Guild Book

the coronation itself was postponed once more until November. By now all routine government business had come to a halt.

On Sunday 22 June, the day Edward V was to have been crowned, Ralph Shaw preached a sermon at St Paul's Cross in which Richard's claim to the throne as the only legitimate heir of York was first advanced. Two days later another claim was put forward by the

A later copy of an entry in the Garter Book compiled by Sir Thomas Writh, Garter King of Arms in the early sixteenth century, shows Earl Rivers's coat of arms. The biographical note celebrates his jousting fame and laments that this 'couragious knight and gentill' was 'pituously put to dethe at Pumfret'

duke of Buckingham before a gathering of the mayor and aldermen of London in the Guildhall. On 25 June, the day on which parliament was to have met, a group of lords, knights and gentlemen attended Richard at Baynard's Castle, his mother's London house, and petitioned him in the name of the three estates to take the throne. They did so again on the following day, 26 June, when he formally took possession and sat in the king's chair in the court of King's Bench in the Great Hall at Westminster. While these events were happening in London a substantial army was being gathered in the north. The York contingent did not set out until 21 June; and troops were still mustering at Pontefract on 25 June when, on Richard's orders, Rivers, Grey and Vaughan were executed, like Hastings, without trial. The northern army, numbering some 4,000 men, finally arrived in London on 2 or 3 July in time to police the coronation which was held on 6 July.

That is what happened: why it happened is much harder to tell. The earliest story, followed by Shakespeare, was that Richard had long intended to take the throne for himself and had only been awaiting the opportunity. This can be safely discounted. There is no evidence to suggest that Richard entertained such ambitions before Edward IV died; on the contrary the whole purpose and direction of his career until 9 April was to establish himself as a great northern magnate. Only two months earlier he had been granted a marcher palatine in the north-west. Ambition for the throne was only awakened after Edward IV's death. The decision might have been taken immediately, or only hesitatingly and reluctantly just before he became king. Much depends on the interpretation placed on his actions, and the actions of others, during these months.

First to be explained is the seizure by force of the person of the king at Stony Stratford on 30 April. This *coup d'état* can be seen either as the first calculated step towards seizing the throne itself or as merely a means of making sure of the office of protector. It is impossible to be certain which. We know that while Richard, Buckingham and Edward V were converging on London, the council in Westminster was debating the structure of the new government. The precise divisions of opinion were reported second-hand by Mancini and cryptically by the Crowland Chronicler who appears to have been present. Two inter-related issues were paramount: what constitutional precedent should be adopted and who should be the head of the minority government in the king's name? A rumour circulated in London that Edward IV had nominated Richard of Gloucester as protector shortly before his death. Crowland refers to a codicil to the king's will, but gives no details.[4] No actual documentation of Edward's supposed last wishes seems otherwise to have existed. According to Mancini, Richard claimed that he had been nominated protector, but this may have been put out to support his claim to such an office.[5] Even if Edward had nominated his brother to this office, as the precedent of Henry V showed, the council was not bound to follow the wishes of a dead king. It was free to make its own decision. In fact, it seems that this option was discussed and rejected. The decision was made, according to Crowland, that Edward V 'should succeed his father in all his glory'.[6] This probably means that he should be crowned at once, so obviating the need for a protectorate. In other words the precedent of Richard II, who was ten when he succeeded to the throne, rather than Henry VI who was nine months, was to be followed. This was logical, since Edward V, like Richard II before him, was old enough for immediate coronation. Moreover, in the precedent of Henry VI the protectorate had officially ended when the king was eventually crowned, aged seven, in 1429. The conciliar decision, therefore, to fix the coronation for 4 May and to dispense with a formal protectorate was, as far as this can be said, constitutionally correct.

The burning political question was who should preside over the council which would govern the realm until the king was old enough to rule himself – at the earliest November 1486 when he would be sixteen. It is apparent from both contemporary accounts that the queen and Dorset themselves made a bid for power, perhaps to exclude Gloucester altogether. Dorset was reported to Mancini as boasting that his party was so important, 'that even without the king's uncle we can make and enforce decisions'.[7] It is also apparent that Hastings was deeply opposed to a Woodville dominated council. He and others feared that Earl Rivers would, in the company of the king, arrive in London with such force, that he would impose a Woodville regime. The most bitter dispute seems to have focused not on the constitutional arrangements but on the size of retinues brought up to Westminster for the coronation. Hastings even threatened to withdraw to Calais, of which he was captain and where he had troops, if the queen did not advise her son to bring only a modest retinue.[8] On this he had his way. Although he and his allies themselves wished to exclude the Woodvilles, a compromise seems to have been reached in which it was agreed that Gloucester should become chief councillor.

While one can trace the lines of dispute in the royal council at Westminster, it is impossible to tell what Gloucester was thinking. He apparently wrote reassuring letters to the council; he probably advanced his claim to be made protector. 'According to the common report, the chamberlain, Hastings reported all these deliberations by letter and messenger to the duke of Gloucester.'[9] If Mancini is to be believed, Hastings is likely to have told him that although it had been agreed that he was to be chief councillor, the Woodvilles did not whole-heartedly support him and were still to be included in the government. It seems that Richard was set on becoming protector and would accept no compromise. Thus on 30 April he took the law into his own hands. Hastings, who seems at this stage to have been more concerned to exclude the Woodvilles from government than with the precise nature of the constitutional arrangements, initially backed him.

In the short term, the seizure of power at Stony Stratford secured control of the government for Richard and his allies. In the longer term, even if Richard's thinking extended no further than the immediate present, it created more problems than it solved. He could not postpone the coronation indefinitely. It would be difficult to hold it without the king's mother, brother, sisters, half-brothers and other uncles present. Yet by his action at Stony Stratford he had created implacable enemies in Rivers, Sir Richard Grey and the rest of their family who were either in captivity, sanctuary, hiding, or exile. Whatever their relationship before 30 April, there can be no doubting the animosity between Richard and the Woodvilles thereafter. After the coronation the king's wishes could not be completely overlooked. He would have been likely to have wanted his mother's family restored. One option open to Richard was to buy time by extending the protectorate, and therefore the government excluding the Woodvilles, after the coronation. This he may have proposed, but have encountered conciliar opposition, even from Hastings who might have considered that his own ends had already been achieved. Even if it had been accepted it could only have been a short term expedient. If the *coup d'état* at Stony Stratford had been carried out only to make himself protector, it was a very

The seal of the mayoralty of Calais, which carried an emblem of a boar similar to Richard III's badge with, above it in a tree, a leopard waiting to pounce

short-sighted and ill-considered act which had made his position less, rather than more, secure.

Six weeks after becoming protector, Richard became king. The crisis which was resolved by his accession to the throne on 26 June began with the execution of Hastings on 13 June. Hastings and the other arrested councillors were accused of plotting against him. The accusation was given substance many years later by Polydore Vergil who described how Hastings began to suspect Gloucester's intentions after the violent seizure of power at Stony Stratford.[10] It is difficult to substantiate Richard's allegation of a conspiracy against him. No contemporary, independent evidence of it exists. It is also inherently unlikely that Hastings would have plotted with the Woodvilles; in April he had taken the lead in council in moves to exclude them. On the other hand he, Stanley and Bishop Morton may have begun to have second thoughts about Richard, whose ambitions they might have begun to fear. Mancini noted that Richard had 'sounded their loyalty' and had 'learnt that they sometimes forgathered in each other's houses'.[11] He himself had already, three days earlier, called for troops from the north to protect him, so he claimed, 'as it is now openly known' from a new plot by the queen to murder him.[12] It is difficult to see how the queen in sanctuary still represented a serious threat and strange, if the plot were openly known on 10 July, that he had not dealt with the conspirators then. The only plausible explanation is that Richard invented this conspiracy to justify the step he was about to take. If there were any substance to the charge of a Hastings' plot, it is likely to be that he and his allies had wind that something was afoot and were considering in their meetings what precautions to take. Either way, the most likely explanation is that the arrests and execution on 13 June were intended to pre-empt opposition before Richard made his own claim to the throne.

It is of course possible that Richard only advanced his own claim to the throne after he was informed by a deeply troubled Bishop Stillington that Edward V and his brother were illegitimate. It is possible, but highly implausible. The case finally put together concerning the bastardy of the princes, and enrolled in a parliamentary statute of January 1484, is theologically sound. It was that Edward IV had entered a pre-contract of marriage with Eleanor Butler before he had married Elizabeth Woodville and that this rendered his children by her illegitimate. Under canon law, had Edward IV entered a pre-contract of marriage with Eleanor Butler, all the children born of a later union, before or after Eleanor's death, even if Elizabeth Woodville had been ignorant of the previous liaison, would have been illegitimate. In this respect the fact that Edward IV and Elizabeth Woodville had married clandestinely

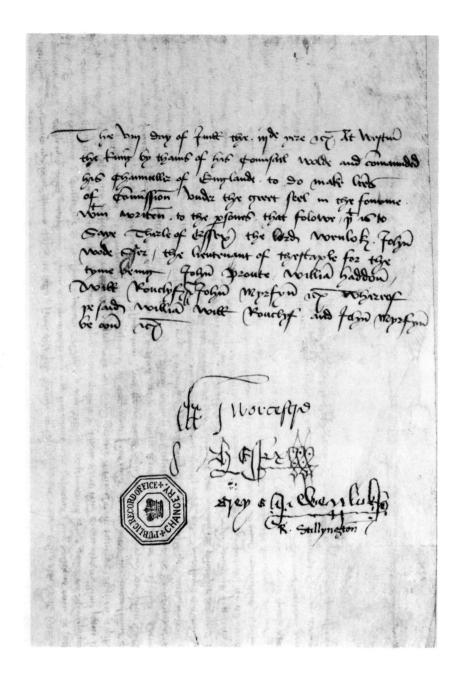

The signature of Bishop Robert Stillington lies at the foot of this document dating from the days when he was one of Edward IV's councillors. It is possible that resentment at his loss of office and influence led him to side with Richard III in 1483 and opportunely to reveal the secret of Edward IV's precontract of marriage which he had kept hidden for almost twenty years

made matters worse. Moreover, it was perfectly acceptable in law to raise objection on these grounds several years after the event. The pre-contract story, in its final form, presented a strong legal case.

There are, however, several sound reasons for doubting its truth. While it is the case that parliament was a proper body to adjudicate on matters of inheritance that resulted from illegitimacy, in England in the later-fifteenth century an ecclesiastical court should have heard the original charge. And if it were true, why was it not

put before such a court so as to remove all doubts? Moreover, even if
it had been proved that Edward V and his brother were illegitimate,
deposition was not the only course open to the protector. The stain
of illegitimacy could have been removed by the ritual of coronation.
Edward V, like Elizabeth I later, could have been declared
legitimate and all doubts removed. Above all, the revelation of the
princes' bastardy was so timely and convenient as to leave little
doubt in the minds of contemporaries that it was but the colour for
an act of usurpation.

There is, too, a suspicious degree of confusion over the precise
detail of the charge of illegitimacy as it was first advanced in June.
Mancini's account of the sermons and speeches hints at a change in
the story. At first the charge appeared to be that Edward IV himself
was a bastard; two days later it seems that the princes were. The first
official government statement appears in a letter dated 28 June to
the captain of Calais informing him that his oath of loyalty to
Edward V was no longer valid. Many people, he was assured, had
made similar oaths in ignorance of Richard III's true title which had
been shown and declared in a petition presented by the lords
spiritual and temporal and the commons on 26 June, a copy of
which was to be sent to Calais for publication.[13] Unfortunately that
copy has not survived. The earliest surviving version is, therefore,
that transcribed as part of the parliamentary act settling the throne
on Richard. This purports to reproduce that petition verbatim, but
doubts have been cast on its veracity. It is possible that the final,
official version, had been subsequently amended. Even so, there is
no reason to doubt that the substance of the original petition of
26 June was the same as that reproduced in January: namely that 'all
the issue of the said King Edward been bastards'.[14]

It is difficult to avoid the conclusion that Richard III usurped the
throne in June 1483. Perhaps in retrospect what happened appears
more controlled and more deliberate than was in fact the case. We
tend to favour a conspiratorial view of the past, where often a
'cock-up' theory might be more applicable. Did Richard III
mastermind a brilliantly conceived and skilfully executed *coup
d'état*? Or did it all happen in confusion, ignorance and fear?
Richard might well have had a plan to take the throne by one
means, but found that he had to change it as events developed. For
instance, it is not clear why Richard called for northern troops on
10 June when he did not in the event need them. But might it have
been his initial plan to stage a parliamentary 'election'; a plan
abandoned when Hastings and others found out what was going on?
Was 13 June, therefore, unplanned? Was everything brought
forward in a rush once the cat was out of the bag?

We should not assume that the usurpation was conducted

Part of Richard's case against the legitimacy of the princes lay in the idea that the marriage polluted by adultery could not be a true marriage. Here, the consequence of adultery, committed frequently enough by Edward IV, is shown as a warning to the irresolute in a copy of Gratian's Decretals, *the standard codification of canon law in the later Middle Ages*

according to a timetable; but there are nevertheless several observations that can be made with some certainty. The first is that Richard took and never surrendered the initiative. It is hard to sustain the idea that he was forced into usurpation by circumstances or by his rivals' actions. He did not need to seize Rivers and his companions at Stony Stratford; he did not need to execute Hastings on 13 June. On both these occasions experienced politicians walked unsuspectingly into a trap. None of Richard's victims in the summer of 1483 anticipated the fate awaiting them. In modern jargon, Richard was proactive, not reactive. The second observation is that Richard acted with unprecedented ruthlessness. His enemies were executed without trial. They were not in arms against their sovereign; they were not taken after battle and slain even under the colour of the law of arms. There was no pretence of lawful process. They were murdered in cold blood. The third observation is that Richard faced little opposition. Potential opposition was removed by pre-emptive strikes. The fourth observation is that he deposed a boy of twelve, his nephew, who on his own insistence had been placed in his trust. The magnitude of what he did should not be played down. Edward V was not of an age to have caused personal political offence. He could not be accused of tyranny, like Richard II, or gross incompetence, like Henry VI. He had begun to reign, but he had not yet ruled. The usurpation of 1483 was of a fundamentally different order to those of 1399, 1461, or even 1485. Those, whether justifiable or not, were acts of the last resort. In 1483, uniquely, deposition was used as a weapon of first resort.[15]

What motivated Richard in 1483? The most frequent defence in mitigation is that he was forced into it for his own survival. In particular, it is argued that if he had not taken the throne, he would himself have been destroyed by the Woodvilles. It cannot be denied that throughout the late spring and early summer of 1483 Richard justified his actions at every stage of his seizure of power by attacking the Woodvilles, whom he accused of ruining the kingdom as well as Edward IV's health and plotting to destroy him and all the old nobility of the realm. This was effective propaganda because the queen and her relations were unpopular, being considered grasping parvenus by many who resented the high favour they had enjoyed in Edward IV's later years. The ease with which Richard disposed of them suggests, however, that they had no great independent power on which to call. And as has been seen there is no evidence of conflict and animosity between Richard and members of the queen's family before 1483. We have only Richard's word for their plotting against him. In reality Richard III invented a Woodville scare as a screen for his own conspiracy.

Edward IV himself has been blamed for creating the situation

This portrait of John Howard, created duke of Norfolk by Richard III, was taken from a stained-glass window in his birthplace, Tendring Hall in Suffolk. Howard was an early supporter of Richard because Edward IV had denied him and his duchess their share of the Mowbray inheritance

which allowed Richard to take the throne in 1483. Firstly he made, or allowed Richard to make himself, an overmighty subject. Secondly, he alienated powerful figures such as the duke of Buckingham or Lord Howard who were prepared to support Richard so as to gain what Edward had refused them. Thirdly, it is suggested that he did not take adequate precautions against the eruption of feuding which engulfed his dynasty after his death.[16] But these criticisms are harsh. Yes, in retrospect, it was unwise of Edward to allow Richard to become so powerful. Yes, in retrospect, the small group on whom he relied had little in common except their personal loyalty to him; but he had no reason to believe that they would, in the event of his early death, behave any differently from the adherents of Henry V who had been prepared to sink their differences in the greater cause of ensuring that Henry VI grew to enjoy his inheritance. That Gloucester, Hastings and Rivers would jostle for position after his death was predictable; but how could

Edward have foreseen that his brother Richard, of all people, would use his power and authority to destroy his son and heir?

Personal ambition, awakened after Edward IV's death, was prominent. It is the one common strand that would make sense of all Richard's actions. But there were almost certainly other elements. He may have believed that he alone had the ability as well as the right to rule England during the minority. He may also have had deep-seated fears about his future if he once lost royal favour. In this respect Richard's weak title to his northern estates is germane. Royal favour became critical to him after the death of George Neville on 4 May 1483. At a stroke his title to the Neville estates was reduced to a life interest. It was essential for him to hold power at least so as to prevent others from undermining his position and at most so that he could secure legislation to amend his title in his favour. Indeed he may well have known that George Neville was dying before he seized power on 30 April. Richard could not afford to take the chance of allowing others to rule because he stood to lose his hard-earned place as a great northern magnate. In this respect, therefore, not against the Woodvilles, but because of his own vulnerability, self-preservation may have been a powerful motive. By going all the way and making himself king, even if he did not initially set out with this goal in mind, Richard resolved the question of his title to his northern estates once and for all.

Nevertheless, deposing his nephew was an extreme, and indeed risky, solution to such a problem. What is striking is the lengths to which Richard would thus appear to have gone to protect himself against what was still only a potential danger. Thus, we come back once again to the central point that Richard dictated events, deposed Edward V and made himself king; and, moreover, that he did so to the utter amazement of his contemporaries. 'An insane lust for power', secretly nurtured and disguised, biding its time and awaiting its opportunity, seemed to some contemporaries to offer the only explanation.[17] How else could the figure of such probity as Richard of Gloucester be matched to the figure of such treachery as Richard III?

The enigma still remains. Nine out of ten men in Richard's position would have played by the rules. They would first have employed the usual arts of persuasion, the levers of patronage, even the threat of force to get their own way. His father and his father-in-law before him had exhausted all other means before they resorted to deposition. Perhaps he had learnt a lesson from their history; that normal political behaviour had got them nowhere. We cannot tell what passed through Richard's mind as he made his way south to meet his new king at Stony Stratford in April 1483. He may already have decided to take the throne; or he may as yet have had no clear idea of what he would do. He may have coldly calculated how best to take the throne for himself; or alternatively he may have acted on impulse and so set himself on a course from which he found the only way forward was to take the throne. Whichever, he acted with a decisiveness and ruthlessness which completely wrong-footed his rivals and carried all before him. Thus it was that on 6 July, with great pomp and circumstance, Richard, the third of that name was crowned king of England.

The coronation was a splendid occasion well attended by the lords spiritual and temporal and leading gentry of the kingdom. This does not necessarily mean that Richard's accession was rapturously received. For many attendance was politic, especially as they had already come up to Westminster for another coronation. Of course there was a good turn out of the king's own committed supporters, many of whom had recently arrived from the north. Prominent among those present were: the duke of Buckingham; John Howard, duke of Norfolk; Edward, Viscount Lisle and William, Viscount Berkeley – all three promoted in reward for their recent support; the bishops of Durham, St David's, Lincoln and, of course, Robert Stillington of Bath and Wells; a crop of men, several lately members of Edward IV's household, created knights of the Bath in the traditional pre-coronation ceremony; and many gentlemen and ladies in personal attendance on the new king and queen who had long served them in the north. But the unprecedented military presence, the ostentatious welcoming of Sir John Fogge out of sanctuary to grace the occasion and the very noticeable absence of the archbishop of Canterbury from the banquet following the ceremony revealed the underlying political reality.

Richard was probably not deceived by the attendance of a number of his brother's erstwhile servants at his coronation. He knew that his usurpation of the throne had caught them by surprise and that they were still in disarray. He therefore sought to capitalize immediately on his advantage to win their more committed support. He could exploit the desire of men in royal service to stay in favour and could appeal as a crowned monarch to their allegiance before God to his office if not his person. Continuity was, therefore, his watchword. He presented himself as the true heir to Edward IV politically as well as genetically, desiring only to govern as before. Thus there was no great redistribution of royal patronage. A few changes had to be made: Viscount Lovell became chamberlain of the household in place of Hastings; John Kendall became king's secretary and Thomas Metcalfe, chancellor of the duchy of Lancaster. In general, however, Richard's own close associates received few immediate rewards; and some, such as the installation of Sir John Conyers as a Knight of the Garter, cost little. The king hoped that

*After hand of John Conyers a hardy [...]
[...] which D.D. the Erle of Salisbury
[...] Warwick goods [...] in the [...]
of Scotland and in other place for he
greatly [...] a great housholder and
wel beloved in his county and beloved
man wherefore he is [...]*

This copy of an entry in Writh's Garter Book records that Sir John Conyers, Richard III's principal northern retainer, succeeded to Earl Rivers's place in the Order. But the biographical note carefully avoids reference to the assistance given by this 'hardy knight' in the usurpation of the throne. Instead it concentrates on his service under the earls of Salisbury and Warwick against the Scots and the high regard in which he was held 'in his county'

the local ruling elites in the southern counties, by whom he was little known, would be reassured to find that little change was intended as a result of the usurpation.

Two weeks after the coronation the king set out, accompanied by a magnificent entourage which included five bishops and several lords, to show himself to his subjects. His route took him up the Thames valley, over to Gloucester, and then north-east through Warwick, Coventry, Leicester, Nottingham and finally York, whither he arrived on 29 August. It was, as intended, a triumphal progress. It impressed even that hostile critic John Rous, who grudgingly attested that on his route the king 'by popular request disafforested a great area of country which King Edward IV had annexed and incorporated in the forest of Wychwood under forest law, against conscience and to the public damage'. At the same time Rous noted, 'the money which was offered him by the peoples of London, Gloucester and Worcester he declined with thanks, affirming that he would rather have their love than their treasure'.[18] In this Richard seems to have anticipated Elizabeth I. As a letter by John Kendall to the city of York reveals, the progress was a carefully orchestrated piece of propaganda, in which pageants and ceremonial entries designed to royal order were staged at every opportunity. York was to put on a particularly impressive show 'for there come many southern lords and men of worship with them, which will mark greatly your receiving their graces'.[19] Southern opinion needed to be wooed. An equally hard-headed calculation lay behind the choice of route which enabled the king to consolidate support in the upper Thames valley where the new chamberlain of his household, Viscount Lovell was influential; in the west midlands where he controlled the estates of the earldom of Warwick (the

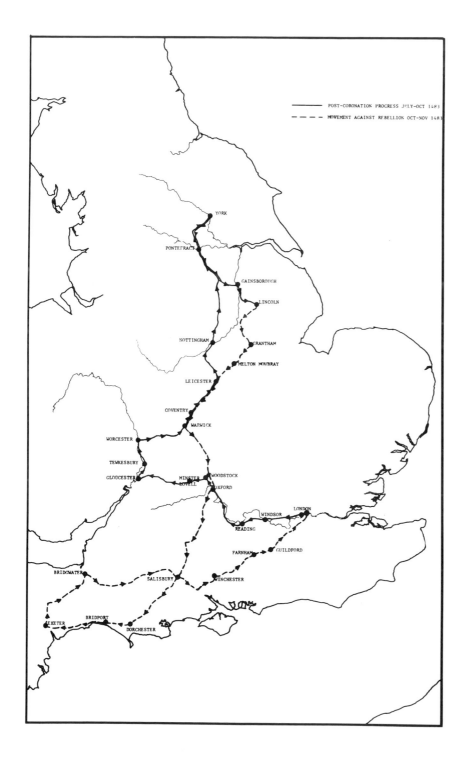

POST-CORONATION PROGRESS JULY-OCT 1483

MOVEMENT AGAINST REBELLION OCT-NOV 1483

YORK

PONTEFRACT

GAINSBOROUGH

LINCOLN

NOTTINGHAM

GRANTHAM

MELTON MOWBRAY

LEICESTER

COVENTRY

WARWICK

WORCESTER

TEWKESBURY

GLOUCESTER

MINSTER LOVELL

WOODSTOCK

OXFORD

LONDON

WINDSOR

READING

FARNHAM

GUILDFORD

BRIDGWATER

SALISBURY

WINCHESTER

EXETER

BRIDPORT

DORCHESTER

The itinerary of Richard III –
July to November 1483

young earl, Clarence's son, was also in the party); and the north-east midlands where Hastings had managed the duchy of Lancaster interest on Edward IV's behalf. But the climax was Richard's return in triumph to York which he entered on 29 August. His entry was marked by the shows and pageants ordered by John Kendall along the route followed by the Corpus Christi procession and culminated at the Minster where the king himself led a service of thanksgiving.[20] He stayed in the city for over three weeks. On 8 September his son and heir Edward was invested as Prince of Wales. The only fly in the ointment was the unwillingness of the archbishop, Thomas Rotherham, now free again, to participate. But the city was rewarded for its enthusiastic backing by the concession of the long-desired reduction in its fee farm.

These three and a half weeks in York, the climax of Richard III's political honeymoon, were to be the high-water mark of the reign. Never again was he to enjoy such triumph. Even as he heard solemn mass in the great minster and feasted in the archbishop's palace, trouble was stirring in the south. Not long after he left London a plot to rescue the princes from the Tower, where they had been held since June, had been discovered and thwarted. At the same time an attempt was made to smuggle their sisters out of sanctuary in Westminster to safety abroad. At the end of August, Buckingham, who had left the royal entourage at Gloucester to go on to his Welsh estates, was appointed to head a judicial commission to try treason in London and several south-eastern counties. By late September a conspiracy for risings throughout southern England aimed at the restoration of Edward V, in which Margaret Beaufort, countess of Richmond and mother of Henry Tudor was deeply involved, was well advanced. The king, who set out on a leisurely return from York on 20 September, seems to have been aware of what was afoot. He had surely anticipated that his enemies, whom he had so comprehensively outmaneouvred in the summer, would attempt a counter-revolution; the Crowland Chronicler reported that the whole conspiracy was known to him through spies.[21] It was at this

A wooden effigy head, almost certainly from a death mask, of Thomas Rotherham, Archbishop of York. Rotherham was unwilling to endorse Richard III's seizure of the throne and pointedly absented himself from the celebrations held in his palace and minster at York in September 1483

This letter, sent by the king from Minster Lovell on 29 July 1483, orders the trial of certain persons that 'as of late had taken upon themselves the fact of an enterprise', and who were then held in prison. The enterprise in question is generally taken to be an attempt to rescue the princes from the Tower

The earliest known portrait of Margaret Beaufort hangs in St John's College, Cambridge, the second and favoured of her two foundations at the university. A formidable opponent of Richard III, inveterate conspirator and dedicated promoter of her son's cause, she is appropriately portrayed on this occasion as a model of piety

time that the rumour spread that the princes were dead. Whether in reaction to the rumour, or following more certain intelligence, the conspirators turned instead to Henry Tudor, who, according to the Crowland Chronicler, they asked to marry Elizabeth of York, Edward IV's eldest daughter, and with her at the same time take the throne. At this late stage too, the duke of Buckingham threw in his lot with Richard's enemies, suborned it would seem by his prisoner, John Morton, bishop of Ely, himself in the thick of it. According to *Crowland* too, the king also discovered Buckingham's planned treachery and kept a careful watch on him.[22] He lingered at Pontefract until 8 October preparing to meet the uprising, but astutely waiting for the rebels to declare themselves.

On, or just before 10 October the rebellion finally broke. There were risings in Kent, spreading westward to Wiltshire by 23 October and the far south-west by early November. The risings were poorly coordinated and occurred as a series of chain reactions as the initial rebels in Kent, quickly dispersed by the duke of Norfolk, retreated westwards. The king himself marched via

On 12 October 1483, after the outbreak of rebellion, Richard sent an order to his chancellor, John Russell, bishop of Lincoln to deliver the great seal to him at Grantham. He scribbled a postscript to the official letter in his own hand in which he urged the bishop to act promptly and denounced the treachery of the duke of Buckingham

Nottingham and Oxford to Salisbury, where he arrived at the beginning of November, but sent troops to cut off Buckingham, who found that he could raise little support in Wales and that his crossing of the Severn was hindered by floods. He sought to flee, but was captured and brought to the king at Salisbury where he was promptly executed on 2 November. The king then pushed westward, reaching Exeter by 8 November. Henry Tudor arrived off Plymouth, but was too late to be of any assistance and so turned back to France. Many rebels submitted, but several managed to escape from west country ports to join Tudor in exile. The rebels were routed before they were able to bring their full force together. It is unlikely that they realized that the king had infiltrated their conspiracy and was aware of their plans. This would explain the speed and certainty with which Richard himself acted once the uprising began and its rapid collapse as he moved against it. It may even be that he deliberately dawdled in the north in September to entice the rebels into action.

The list of those ultimately attainted for treason in the parliament of January 1484 shows that, the duke of Buckingham and countess of Richmond apart, there were no peers involved. The leaders were men who had been prominent in Edward IV's household, men such a Sir John Fogge, Sir John Cheyney, Sir Giles Daubeney, Sir Richard Guildford, Richard Haute and William Brandon whom Richard had endeavoured to bring round to his side. In essence it was the rebellion of the loyal Edwardian Yorkists who

Sir Richard Guildford, one of the leaders of the rebellion in October 1483, ended his days on a much publicized pilgrimage to Jerusalem. He is here represented in a woodcut from the printed account of his journey

had not been able to oppose the usurpation itself, had regrouped and now belatedly attempted to strike back. Buckingham's participation is harder to fathom. Vergil, thirty years later, argued that it was because Richard had gone back on his promise to grant the duke his share of the Bohun inheritance.[23] In this, however, he was wrong, for the process of transferring the title had already begun when Buckingham rebelled. Vergil himself discounted the popular view current in his day that the duke had his eye on the throne and sought to use the rebellion to advance his own claim. Yet, this is

The frontispiece to a book of prayers owned by Margaret Beaufort, mother of Henry Tudor, commissioned after he became king, shows her arms (England with a Difference), with the page surrounded by a decorative border including her badge of the portcullis and Margarites, and with the eagle foot badge of her husband, Lord Stanley, just discernible in the initial letter

not impossible, if one allows that the duke had lost all sense of political reality. He did have a remote claim, which in Henry VIII's reign contributed to his son's undoing. Alternatively he may have jumped too soon on to what he judged to be the winning side. It is curious that Thomas, Lord Stanley, arrested by Richard in June and rightly suspected because of the involvement of his wife, the countess of Richmond, in the conspiracy eventually sided with Richard. One explanation might be that he originally intended to raise the north west on his son-in-law's behalf, but on hearing that Buckingham had thrown his hat into the ring, led the troops he had mustered to support Richard rather than to attack him. There was no love lost between the two men, and Stanley was the principal beneficiary in north Wales from Buckingham's fall. In this scenario Buckingham, by joining the rebellion, virtually sealed its fate.

In the event both the north and the midlands stood by the king. To this extent the royal progress proved to be a success. Rebellion was restricted to the southern counties from Essex to Cornwall. In one respect the king was stronger after rebellion than before: his enemies had declared their hand and had been routed. His victory confirmed the short-term success of the usurpation. But in another respect he was weaker. He had lost the support of his principal ally and had failed to win over the greater part of Edward IV's household in the south. Nevertheless, the issue had been clarified: to secure himself firmly on the throne, all he had to do was to destroy the makeshift alliance of die-hard Lancastrians and Edwardian Yorkists who had gathered around Henry. Once he enjoyed unchallenged possession of the kingdom, he could begin to make good the damage done to his reputation by the manner in which he had made himself king and which was now being inflicted by the persistent rumours that he had already done away with the princes.

Chapter 5

The Fate of the Princes

Sir Thomas More told a heart-rending story of the murder of the Princes in the Tower, which was the inspiration of Shakespeare and nineteenth-century painters, and which is still deeply embedded in the collective memory. It is perhaps one of the most potent images of English history. The passage is deeply moving, but it is almost certainly a literary creation:

Sir James Tyrell devised that they should be murdered in their bed, to the execution whereof he appointed Miles Forest, one of the four that kept them, a fellow fleshed in murder before time. To him he joined one John Dighton, his own horsekeeper, a big broad, square, strong knave. Then, all the other being removed from them, this Miles Forest and John Dighton about midnight (the sely children lying in their beds) came into the chamber and suddenly lapped them up among the clothes so bewrapped them and entangled them, keeping down by force the featherbed and pillows hard unto their mouths, that within a while, smored and stifled, their breath failing, they gave up to God their innocent souls into the joys of heaven, leaving to the tormentors their bodies dead in the bed. [1]

More claimed that it was 'very truth' and 'well known' that Sir James Tyrell, facing death for treason against Henry VII in 1502,

The Princes

There are four contemporary or near-contemporary representations of Edward V, one of his brother Richard. None is a likeness. In the illustration of Anthony, earl Rivers presenting a copy of the *Dictes of the Philosophers* to Edward IV, the young prince of Wales is shown in a family group.

He is portrayed in glass at Little Malvern Priory.

In the royal window in Canterbury Cathedral he is represented at prayer, alongside his younger brother the duke of York.

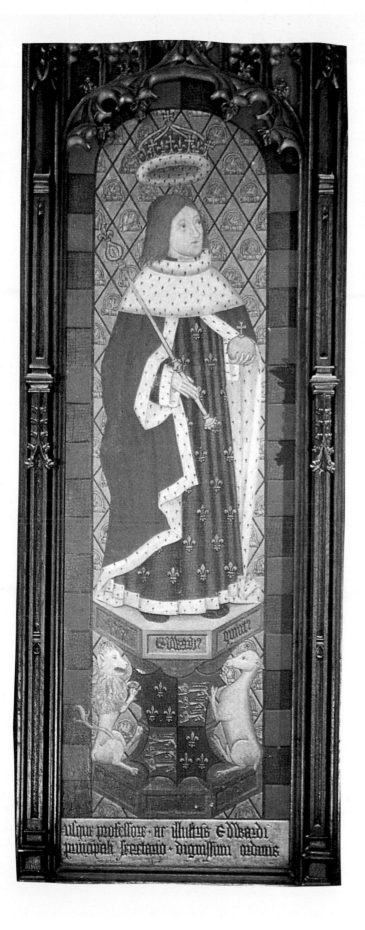

pierre varbeck natif de Tournay supposé pour Richard
Duc d'Yorck second fils d'Edouard IV roy d'Angleterre l'an 1492.
fut pendu à londres sur la fin de l'an 1499

A good likeness has survived of the would-be Richard IV, Perkin Warbeck.

It has been
ingeniously argued,
however, that the real
Richard of York
survived into the reign
of Henry VIII under
the protection of Sir
Thomas More and is to
be seen in Holbein's
family portrait.

According to this
theory Richard
was living under the
cover name of the
physician Dr John
Clements, and was
portrayed standing at
the back on the right-
hand side of the group.

confessed to the murder in the manner he described.[2] Two other early sixteenth-century historians, both writing after 1502, Vergil and the author of *The Great Chronicle* of London, repeated that Tyrell was or might have been the murderer. Neither cited a supposed confession; and indeed *The Great Chronicle* suggested alternative fates.

> Of their death's manner was many opinions, for some said they were murdered atween two feather beds, some said they were drowned in malmsey, and some said they were sticked with a venomous poison. But how so ever they were put to death . . . Sir James Tyrell was reputed the doer. But other put that wight upon an old servant of King Richard.[3]

No actual confession by Tyrell has ever been found; More alone assured his readers that the confession was made; historians have subsequently supposed that Henry deliberately put out the story at a time when his own dynastic prospects were looking bleak. However, this supposition is based entirely on More's unsubstantiated remark that Tyrell confessed: it was possibly just his own invention. The clear similarities even in More's tale to the story of the *Babes in the Wood*, especially in the manner in which one of the murderers subsequently confessed, powerfully suggest a literary rather than factual inspiration.

In essence, More's story is an elaboration of one of several circulating accounts. In particular, it bears striking resemblance to Jean Molinet's colourful story written in or around 1500 that the princes were smothered about five weeks after they were imprisoned and that they were then secretly buried in the grounds of the Tower.[4] In so far as More wrote that the murders were committed in late July or August 1483 and that the bodies, first buried 'at the stair foot', were subsequently re-interred in a more fitting place 'as by the occasion of his death which only knew it, could never since come to light',[5] he recorded no more than the general knowledge that the princes disappeared from sight in the summer of 1483 and were never seen again, dead or alive. Many versions were offered over the subsequent years as to what actually happened to them. Since no official enquiry was conducted or pronouncement made, before or after the accession of Henry VII, rumour ran rife and spread throughout Europe. Thus the Spanish merchant, Diego de Valera took home with him in 1486 the story that Richard poisoned them even while Edward IV was alive;[6] and in 1500 the Dutch chronicle known as the *Divisie* recorded the story that Richard starved them so that he could become king.[7] But no one really knew what had happened to them.

Unlike the princes, an earlier prisoner in the Tower, Charles, duke of Orleans, was allowed to live in comfort and came out alive. This late fifteenth-century illustration made for Edward IV shows the Tower much as it was in 1483

Any modern investigation must start with the well-attested disappearance of the two boys in 1483. Dominic Mancini explained how, even before he left London in mid-July, the ex-king and his brother 'were withdrawn into the inner apartments of the Tower proper and day by day began to be seen more and more rarely behind the bars and windows, till at length they ceased to appear altogether'.[8] A similar report later found its way into several versions of the London Chronicle. *The Great Chronicle*, for instance, recorded that 'the children were seen shooting and playing in the garden of the Tower by sundry times' before November 1483; and then, it is implied, they were seen no more.[9] Rumours of their deaths circulated rapidly. Indeed George Cely heard that Edward V might be dead not long after 13 June, and certainly before Richard claimed the throne.[10] John Argentine, dismissed from the king's household at about this time, told Mancini that the poor child, 'like a victim prepared for sacrifice', believed that death awaited him. Mancini also told his readers that he had seen 'many men burst forth into tears and lamentations when mention was made of him after his removal from men's sights, and already there was a suspicion that he had been done away with'. But he scrupulously noted six months later that he had not been able to find out whether the boy had been murdered or by what means.[11] It is clear, however, that there was great anxiety over the fate of the two princes in late June and July; that word quickly spread of their disappearance; and that the general expectation was that they would be killed.

The Crowland Chronicler, putting his memories down on parchment in the spring of 1486, recalled how the rumour arose in September 1483 that 'the princes, by some unknown manner of destruction, had met their fate'.[12] Some early reports went further and categorically stated as fact that the princes were by then dead. Robert Ricart, recorder of Bristol, entered in his *Kalendar* under the year ending 15 September 1483 that 'in this year the two sons of King Edward were put to silence in the Tower of London'.[13] A London citizen compiling historical notes before the end of 1488 entered the information that 'they were put to death in the Tower of London' in the mayoral year ending November 1483.[14] John Rous, writing in 1489, confidently stated that Richard killed the princes within three months of welcoming Edward V at Stony Stratford on 30 April: 'He received his lord king Edward V blandly, with embraces and kisses and within about three months or a little more he killed him together with his brother'.[15] Word to the same effect possibly reached France, if one late report is to be believed, even before Louis XI's death on 30 August. And in a speech to the Estates General at Tours in January 1484 the chancellor of France, Guillaume de Rochefort, reminded his audience how, as they knew, after the death of Edward IV, his sons were murdered and the crown was given to the murderer.[16]

Many early reports imply or state, as did Rochefort, that the princes were murdered first and then Richard took the throne. This too is how Caspar Weinreich of Danzig noted it in a near contemporary record of current events; so also did Jan Allertz, recorder of Rotterdam, who died in 1489.[17] The same is categorically stated in a generally overlooked English source, an entry in the Anlaby family cartulary in which a scribe, writing after 1509, confidently states that Edward V died on 22 June 1483. While this man mistook the year in which Edward IV died, he not only gives correctly the days and months of the births, accession and deaths of all other kings, but also the correct birth and accession dates of Edward V himself.[18] Such a source is by virtue of its late composition suspect, but in the light of continental reports, George

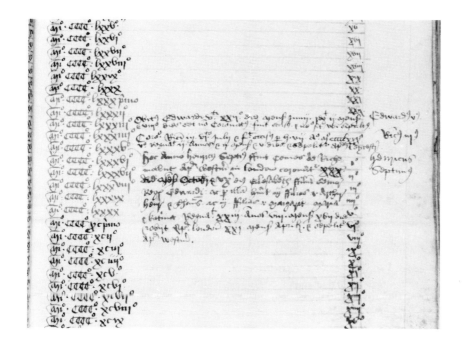

These entries in the Anlaby Cartulary noting the dates of successive reigns begin with the confident statement that Edward V died on 22 June in 1483. They end with the note that Henry VII died in London on 21 April in the twenty-fourth year of his reign. The author was not necessarily well-informed about what had happened over twenty-five years earlier

Cely's rumour and Rous's assertion, it is, to say the least, suggestive.

Thus, there is an impressive array of evidence dating from before 1500, some very early, which points to the boys meeting their deaths at Richard's hands in 1483. The reports are, however, muddled, contradictory and inconclusive. Philippe de Commynes, for instance, in his *Memoirs* completed in about 1500, managed to give three different stories. He first of all said that Richard had his two nephews murdered and then he made himself king (in that order); then, in a later passage he reversed the sequence of events, and finally he assured his readers that the duke of Buckingham murdered them.[19] Buckingham's possible implication in the murders has aroused considerable interest. Other contemporaries carried the same story. Molinet had heard it, but added that it was believed mistakenly that he had murdered the children to advance his own claim to the throne. *The Divisie Chronicle* likewise recorded, but without giving it much credence, that 'some others will say' that the duke was responsible.[20] Two earlier English sources, a fragment among the Ashmolean manuscripts in the Bodleian Library and the historical notes of a London citizen of 1488, both implicate the duke. The Ashmolean fragment records the rumour that Richard first took Buckingham's advice before killing the princes,[21] and the historical notes state that Richard killed them by the 'vise' of the duke. 'Vise' has alternative meanings – either advice or device, but whichever meaning is ascribed, it is unlikely that the author

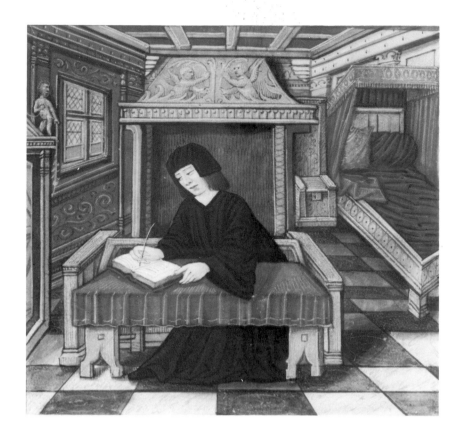

An early illustration of Philippe de Commynes at his writing desk. He heard different stories about the fate of the princes, which he repeated at different points in his memoirs

intended the reader to understand that the murders were committed without Richard's knowledge.[22] Thus a small group of near contemporary writings implicate the duke of Buckingham. It is entirely plausible that he was an accessory, as he was to a series of attested unlawful killings in 1483. However, the evidence is hardly strong enough to support the hypothesis, much favoured in recent years, that he murdered the princes without the king's authority.

Equally, while all the contemporary and near contemporary evidence, based on hearsay, gossip and rumour, is founded on an assumption that Richard was responsible for the deaths of the princes in 1483, none of it proves his guilt. For this reason the potential forensic evidence of the bones discovered in the grounds of the Tower of London in 1674 is of great importance. Two skeletons of children were found ten feet deep during the demolition of a staircase leading to the chapel in the White Tower. Contemporaries immediately leapt to the conclusion that they were the remains of Edward V and his brother. Four years later the remains, or what purported to be the same remains, were interred in a magnificent urn in Henry VII's chapel in Westminster Abbey. The fact that they were found in a spot which uncannily matched More's description of their initial burial 'at the stairfoot, meetly deep in the ground',

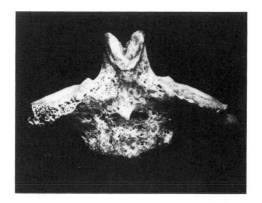

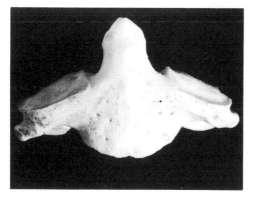

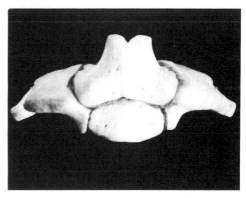

powerfully influenced speculation on the identification of the bones. But then, and more recently, historians have overlooked More's subsequent statement that they were moved to a secret and 'better place'.[23] In other words, if one chooses to believe More's highly improbable story, the skeletons *cannot* have been those of the princes; for according to him their final resting place was elsewhere. It is important to remember too that there was a reported earlier find of two similar skeletons in an old chamber that had been walled-up. These, too, could equally well have been the princes' remains. The fact is that there are many skeletons in the Tower's cupboard. One, of an iron-age youth, was found during an excavation in the Inner Ward in 1977. A burial site ten feet deep, an extraordinary depth to which to dig even a secret grave, could well be much older than the fifteenth century.

It was because there were so many question marks hanging over the bones interred in Westminster Abbey that they were exhumed and examined in 1933 by Lawrence Tanner, then the archivist of the Abbey, and William Wright. Professor Wright, one of the leading anatomists of his day, with the assistance of George Northcroft, president of the Dental Association, submitted the remains to a modern scientific analysis (modern, that is, in 1933). The conclu-

The bones: interpretations based on evidence from photographs and reports written over fifty years ago are fraught with difficulty. One dispute over the age of the skeleton of the elder focuses on the axis, or second cervical vertebra (above). The tip is not ossified and rounded. This normally happens by twelve or earlier, as in the example of a modern eight year old (below left) compared with a modern unossified five year old (below right)

sion was reached that the urn did indeed contain the bones of two children identifiable with Edward V and Richard of York and that there was a reasonable possibility that the story of suffocation told by More was in its main outline true. In recent years, however, considerable doubt has been cast on the reliability of the Tanner and Wright report.

The first major criticism is that the investigation was conducted and the report written on the profoundly unscientific assumption that the bones did belong to the princes. Wright set out to look for evidence that the bones were those of children between the ages of eleven and thirteen. Moreover, it was taken for granted that both sets of bones were of males – no attempt was made to determine their gender. Instead, effort was concentrated on speculating whether the skulls showed signs of death by suffocation. Even without the benefit of techniques and knowledge available in the last decade of the twentieth century, the investigation was sadly inadequate.

Tanner and Wright's report has been subject to the scrutiny and appraisal of several later medical scientists. At least four reassessments have been made of their conclusions since 1955, the two most recent of an extremely detailed and technical kind. Modern conclusions vary. Consensus exists, however, that the statements made by Wright concerning the skeletons, the lengths of certain bones and teeth are consistent with the age of the princes and moreover that the age differential between the two sets of bones would appear to be approximately correct. In all respects large margins of error are nevertheless allowed. It cannot, however, be ruled out that these are the bones of two children of the right age. Disagreement exists as to whether the information recorded by Wright can now be relied upon to show that the two skeletons were related. Whether it is the question of hypodontia (congenitally missing teeth) or the phenomenon of bilateral large wormian bones (whatever they are), opinions differ as to whether consanguinity is a strong possibility or impossible to tell. There is no question, however, that Wright left no information to deal with the vital issue of gender.

The forensic evidence of the bones is, therefore, likely to remain indecisive. Modern techniques, if applied, could advance our knowledge further. Analytical chemical means now exist to establish gender and blood relationships and to help date the age of skeletons at death. Radiocarbon dating can also now provide a date of death within an accuracy of plus or minus sixteen years. In the future these techniques may well be refined even further. But until it can be proved that the remains are those of the sons of Edward IV (potentially possible if Edward IV's remains at Windsor as well as the bones in Westminster Abbey were exhumed) and demonstrated that the bones are of two children who met their deaths either before or after 22 August 1485, little advance can be made. Even then we would be no further forward as to the precise manner of, or responsibility for, the deaths. Even if it could be shown that these were the remains of the princes and that they died before 22 August 1485, that would still not prove that Richard III murdered them; it might make that conclusion more likely, but it would not be proof.

Essentially the bones are a red herring. They cannot settle the question of whether Richard III murdered the princes. It is not surprising, therefore, that in the light of the continuing uncertainty over the fate of the princes other culprits than those implicated in the contemporary sources have been advanced. John Howard, duke of Norfolk, Margaret Beaufort (Henry VII's mother) and even (in jest?) Jane Shore (Edward IV's mistress) have been accused. None deserve serious consideration. The problem with all these accusations is that they beg the question of access to the Tower without Richard's knowledge and overlook the fact that Richard was responsible for the safekeeping of his nephews. If not a murderer, then he would still stand guilty of criminal negligence. It has been argued that Richard gave way to pressure not just from Buckingham but additionally, in an improbable unholy alliance, from Margaret Beaufort to dispose of the boys in August 1483 so as to clear the path for her son, Henry Tudor.[24] It is hard to believe that Richard, the man who had so comprehensively outwitted his rivals to take the throne, would have been so stupid as to fall for this. Besides it still leaves him an accessory and culpable.

The only plausible alternative to Richard III is Henry VII himself. It is the case that Henry issued no completely unequivocal proclamation condemning his predecessor. In the act of attainder passed in the autumn parliament of 1485, Henry called to mind 'the unnatural, mischievous and great perjuries, treasons, homicides and murders, in shedding of infants' blood, with many other wrongs, odious offences and abominations against God and man' done by Richard, late duke of Gloucester, 'calling and naming himself, by usurpation, King Richard III'.[25] It is a ringing condemnation and the subtext is transparent: Richard had committed an unnatural abomination against God and man in shedding the blood of children. The only infants anyone had in mind were Edward V and Richard of York. Yet he went no further than this slur, which, true or false, was a piece of propaganda.

Why was Henry VII not more specific? Why did he not conduct and publish the result of a thorough investigation? One reason might have been that he could not find the bodies or anyone to tell him where they were and how they had got there. Another is that he

ELIZABETHA · VXOR
HENRICI · VII ·

*Elizabeth of York who was but
a pawn in the game of dynastic
politics between 1483 and 1485*

had good reason not to raise the whole issue as to who was the true
successor to Edward V. In 1485 he took the throne by conquest in
his own right alone. While he may have initially hinted in 1483
that he would be willing to rule jointly with Elizabeth of York
(to take 'with her, at the same time, possession of the whole
kingdom', as the Crowland Chronicler put it),[26] by August 1485 he
had long since rejected any such idea of a joint monarchy on the
Iberian model (Ferdinand and Isabella then ruling jointly the
kingdoms of Aragon and Castile). The promised marriage did not
take place until 18 January 1486. In fact, according to a brief

continuation to the *Crowland Chronicle*, there was discussion in that first parliament in the autumn of 1485 about the marriage to Elizabeth of York 'in whose person, it seemed to all, there could be found whatever appeared to be missing in the king's title elsewhere'.[27] 'All' may be an exaggeration, but it would seem that a body of influential opinion initially favoured a joint monarchy to strengthen Henry's right to the throne. This he clearly rejected. Indeed Elizabeth was not to be crowned herself as consort until 25 November 1487, almost two years after the king's coronation, after the birth of their first-born son and heir, Arthur, and after the victory at Stoke in June 1487 had immeasurably strengthened Henry's hold on the throne.

Henry was determined that no question of his queen's claim to the throne would be raised once he had become king. Perhaps it was for this same reason that he also avoided any direct refutation of her illegitimacy. No act was passed repealing Richard III's title to the throne in which the illegitimacy of Edward IV's children had been declared. A discreet veil was drawn over the whole issue of the legitimacy and fate of the princes. Indeed, had Henry opened this Pandora's box, not only would he have had to contend with the argument that Elizabeth of York had a better claim to the throne, but he would also have had to ward off the alternative claim of Edward, earl of Warwick, the duke of Clarence's son who was the alternative male heir to Edward V. Thus Henry's watchword, having taken the throne for himself alone, might well have been 'least said, soonest mended'.

A third reason for Henry VII's silence might, of course, have been that he had found the princes alive and had himself ordered their deaths. Two pieces of evidence have been drawn upon to suggest that the princes might have been alive when he came to the throne. In the ordinance regulating the king's household in the north, dated 24 July 1484, arrangements were specifically made for the 'children' at breakfast time.[28] The children, it is suggested, were the princes. But there were other children likely to have been living in the northern household: at least two of Edward IV's younger daughters and the earl of Warwick who were living at Sheriff Hutton. Secondly on 9 March following, a warrant was

A record of payment to Richard III's illegitimate son, John of Gloucester, for the wages of the garrison of Calais. John was also known as the Lord Bastard

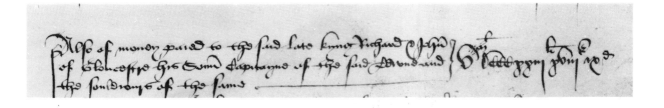

issued for clothing to be issued to the 'Lord Bastard'.[29] This has been interpreted as a reference to one of the princes. It is more likely, however, that the lord bastard in question was Richard's own bastard son, John, who was so styled on at least one other occasion.[30] Neither of these two references can therefore be relied upon as positive evidence that even one of the princes was still alive in 1484 or early 1485.

Sir Clements Markham took the idea of Henry VII's guilt further and argued that certain developments in 1486 and 1487 demonstrate that the princes met their deaths then. At the heart of the argument lies the withdrawal of the queen mother, Elizabeth Woodville to a convent in February 1487, linked with the issue of two pardons to Sir James Tyrell on 16 June and 16 July 1486. On the basis of this evidence Markham surmized that Tyrell committed the murder, as he later confessed, but in the summer of 1486 not 1483 and that Elizabeth was put away so that she should not discover the secret. This is the 'truth' discovered by Josephine Tey's ingenious sleuths in her popular novel, *Daughter of Time*.[31] It is, however, highly speculative. Many others beside Tyrell who had served Richard III found it advisable to purchase more than one pardon in the uneasy summer of 1486; and early in 1487 not only Elizabeth Woodville, but also her fickle son Thomas Grey, marquess of Dorset came under suspicion of involvement in the developing Lambert Simnel conspiracy. There are more plausible explanations of the evidence that Markham believed pointed to Henry's guilt. Indeed if the Woodvilles were becoming disenchanted with Henry, it is far more likely to have been connected with his unwillingness to accord his queen the status of joint monarch and his failure, as yet, to accord her the honour of a coronation.

It is, therefore, very difficult to construct a convincing case against Henry VII. Indeed any such case has to rest on the assumption that the princes were still alive when he came to the throne, and any argument based on his motive has to recognize that Richard III before him had exactly the same reason for getting rid of them. Henry VII's reticence about the fate of the princes is more likely to have stemmed from political calculation than personal guilt.

Yet another possibility is that at least one of the princes survived even beyond Henry's accession. In other words Perkin Warbeck may truly have been Richard of York. His letter to Queen Isabella of Castile appears to be the source for all later ideas that Richard survived. In it Perkin said that he was nearly nine years old (the wrong age) when his brother Edward was killed, but was himself spared by the murderer who took compassion and smuggled him

The signature of Perkin Warbeck as 'Rychard off England', from a letter sent from Edinburgh in 1496 to a hoped-for supporter and the father of one of his attendants

abroad after making him swear not to reveal his identity for several years.[32] It surely lies behind the comment in the *Divisie* that 'some say' that Buckingham spared one of the children and had him secretly abducted from the kingdom. There can be little doubt, however, that Warbeck was an imposter and that not only Henry VII knew this, but also those manipulating him knew it. Curiously Molinet reported that Henry's ambassador to Margaret of York, duchess of Burgundy offered in 1493 to show any envoy she cared to name the chapel in which the real Richard was buried.[32] He was probably bluffing, but confident that his bluff would not be called by Margaret since by then she had taken the imposter under her wing.

Warbeck's tale of his escape from the Tower seems to underlie the most inventive and imaginative solution yet offered to the mystery of the disappearance of the princes; the idea that Richard of York survived to reappear in Sir Thomas More's household and there to be painted by Hans Holbein in 1527. Jack Leslau's disentangling of the iconography and rebus of this painting, whereby he claims to show that the physician John Clements was really Richard of York in disguise, is breathtakingly ingenious. 'Hans Holbein', he concludes, 'concealed a message for posterity in this group portrait of the More family together with a portrait of Richard, duke of York, thus "proving" that he was alive in 1527 and living under . . . the protection of Sir Thomas More'. For good measure, Edward V is also said to have survived and to have been disguised as Sir Edward Guildford in another Holbein painting. Furthermore More's vivid account of the murder of the princes in his *History* is discovered to have been a 'smokescreen'. That Holbein was a master of symbolism and created pictures to be read by their owners is not open to doubt. And no doubt many of the objects in this portrait, just like the objects in the much studied *Ambassadors*, have an intended meaning for the sitter and his family. But Leslau has been quite unable to offer a shred of external or forensic evidence to support the idea that Richard of York, let alone Edward V, survived, incognito, into the reign of Henry VIII.[34] Until such evidence is forthcoming, the argument based on a highly individualistic reading of one painting must remain a brilliant flight of fancy.

At bottom, the difficulty facing all arguments to the effect that someone other than Richard III was responsible for the deaths of the princes, is the assumption that they were still alive on the morning of 22 August 1485. As an assumption this is less tenable than the assumption that they were dead by then. In circumstances in which no definitive evidence is available, one can only fall back on the balance of probabilities. The weight of contemporary opinion and belief, as much before Henry VII came to the throne as afterwards, both in England and abroad, was that Richard had them killed. 'After Easter', the author of *The Great Chronicle* remembered of 1484, 'much whispering was among the people that the king had put the children of King Edward to death'.[35] The ceaseless rumour to that effect can be supplemented by an analysis of political behaviour.

The initial purpose of the rebellion of October 1483 was to restore Edward V. At least one attempt to rescue him and his brother had already been made, but shortly before the uprising began, in reaction to what must have been persistent rumour that Edward V and his brother were dead, the rebels shifted their allegiance to Henry Tudor. He was probably the 'new and false king' in whose name, according to the official enquiry, rebellion was raised in Cornwall on 3 November.[36] On Christmas Day, in Rennes Cathedral, Henry 'upon his oath promised that as soon as he should be king he would marry Elizabeth, King Edward's daughter'.[37] His oath was the culmination of negotiations which had been begun in London, secretly, through the respective mothers, Margaret Beaufort and Elizabeth Woodville and their agents, especially the Welsh physician Lewis, 'who because of his science became a messenger between them . . . without any suspicion'.[38] The only conceivable reason for Elizabeth Woodville being party to these negotiations was that she, like Margaret Beaufort, believed her two sons by Edward IV to be dead.

Elizabeth's later conduct, when in 1484 she came to terms with Richard III, has dismayed historians. But Elizabeth was experienced in the volatile politics of the late fifteenth century. By negotiating a return to court for herself and her daughters on 1 March 1484, with a solemn promise on oath to guarantee their safety from 'ravishment or defouling contrary to their wills' and their freedom from imprisonment 'within the Tower of London', to support them according to their estate and to find honourable marriages for them, Elizabeth was taking out an insurance policy against Henry Tudor's defeat and death in battle against the king.[39] Again such a course of

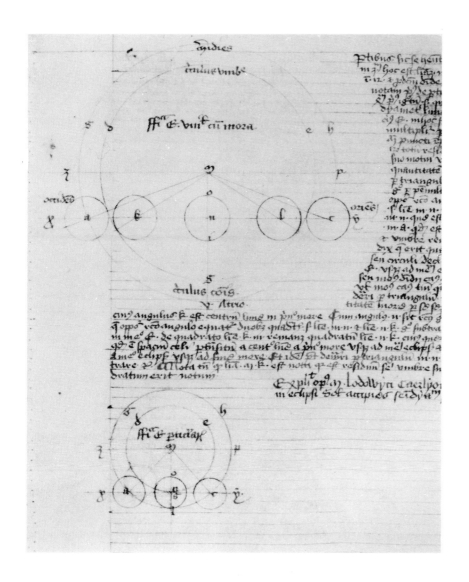

Part of an astronomical treatise by Lewis Caerleon, the physician who acted as the negotiator between Elizabeth Woodville and Margaret Beaufort in 1483

action would have been unthinkable had she believed her sons still to be alive. In this respect the reference to imprisonment in the Tower is particularly pertinent. Her submission was a piece of pragmatism. A year later the proposal that Elizabeth of York should marry the widowed king was seriously discussed. Politically, for Richard such a marriage would have damaged Henry Tudor's appeal; for Elizabeth Woodville it would have facilitated her full rehabilitation at the centre of events. But such a marriage would again have been unthinkable had Elizabeth of York not been universally considered the eldest surviving child of Edward IV. Elizabeth Woodville's behaviour might be considered heartless and unnatural (but how long should she have mourned?). More to the point, playing one contender to the throne off against another was

The seal of the monastery of Bermondsey to which Elizabeth Woodville retired in 1487, having finally lost her struggle to wield influence at the court of Henry VII

Elizabeth Woodville, whose attempts in 1484–5 to play one side off against the other to the advantage of herself and her daughters proved self-defeating

too transparently devious and in the end self-defeating (as she found after Henry VII became king). Whether one approves of Elizabeth Woodville's behaviour or not, it was surely based on a conviction that both her sons by Edward IV were dead. It is the unsentimental political realism displayed by Elizabeth which leads one to the conclusion that it was not only common rumour but also inside, informed opinion that Edward V and Richard of York were no longer alive.

The balance of probability is, therefore, that Richard III did indeed order the killing of his nephews before the middle of September 1483. Other explanations of their deaths during his reign which have been offered, such as that they died of natural causes, are based on nothing but speculation. A defence of Richard could be offered on the grounds of reasons of state. Having usurped the throne it was sound policy to put the king and his brother to death. Alive, they were bound to become the focus of dissent; dead, the king faced only a pretender with a transparently weak title. It would have been sound policy to leave it to rumour, maybe even inspired by an 'official leak', to suggest that the princes were dead; uncertainty in the autumn of 1483 might have added to the rebels' difficulties. But such a defence leaves unanswered the charge that by deposing Edward V in the first place, Richard had destroyed him and doomed him to death. When contemporaries, who were not absolutely certain of the manner of the young king's death, wrote that he had 'destroyed' or 'suppressed' him, they wrote with finely judged ambiguity.[40] He had certainly ruined him and his brother. After that there was little point in keeping them alive, and every reason for seeing them dead.

It is no defence either to argue that killing the princes was no worse a crime than other political crimes commonly committed in the fifteenth century. Yes, it was a violent and unscrupulous age (although one wonders if it was any more so than the twentieth century with its record of genocide). Yes, many men had been summarily executed by their enemies; but most until 1483 had been tried in military courts under the law of arms, after they had unfurled their banners in defiance of the king. The executions may have been summary, but they were not illegal. Hastings, Rivers, Vaughan and Grey, on the other hand, were executed without proper trial in what were simply political murders. Even though these killings were exceptional, the case of the princes was unique. They were not adults responsible for their actions but children in the care, and under the protection of the uncle who it was believed killed them. They were innocents, in the same sense as in the twentieth century we talk of innocent women and children. There was a powerful sense of outrage that innocent children had been so abused. According to Mancini men were moved to tears when they thought that an innocent child had been or was about to be murdered so that Richard III could make himself king. A marginal heading in the *Crowland Chronicle*, reads in its latin original, '*Fama de morte puerorum*', rumours of the deaths of the children.[41] A parallel marginal note in *The Great Chronicle* of London reads, '*Mors innocentium*', the death of the innocents.[42] Henry VII's condemnation, while it is vague on detail, is strong in emotion concerning

The bravery of Herod. Several commentators likened the fate of the princes to the Massacre of the Innocents. Here one of the first-born of Israel is being slaughtered in his mother's arms. The word 'Innocents' is prominently displayed

the shedding of infants' blood. There are, of course, powerful biblical associations conjured up by these phrases. They are made explicit in the condemnation made by the Welsh bard, Dafydd Llwyd ap Llewelyn in 1486:

> a servile boar wrought penance upon Edward's sons in prison . . . Shame on the sad lipped saracen that he slew Christ's angels. By the miracles of Non (St David's mother) he caused disgrace, the bravery of cruel Herod.[43]

'The bravery of Herod' sums up with magnificent irony the association between Richard's attributed crime and the Massacre of the Innocents.

The point has been well made that, contrary to certain influential sociological theories, children were as cherished and loved in medieval times as in any other. The sense of grief at the loss of a child was touchingly evoked in several versions of the Abraham and Isaac play in the Corpus Christi play cycles. Medieval emotion about children perhaps found its most moving expression in the narrative poem, *Pearl*, a parable of Christian love and suffering built on the experience of a man's grief at the loss of a two-year-old daughter. The death of a child, even if more commonly experienced in the later middle ages than in late twentieth-century Britain, was no less a heart-rending event. The Church too had encouraged the idea of the child as an innocent; not innocent, of course, from original sin, but innocent from all other. There was a special limbo for the souls of children in purgatory. Moreover, in secular life children up to the age of fourteen at the earliest were considered to be dependent on their parents or guardians. They could neither hold office nor be answerable at law. Hence a king under age, as a minor, was a king in name alone. The responsibility for what was done in his name lay elsewhere. By all the conventions of their day Edward V and Richard of York were free of fault; they were innocent victims. Here lay the true horror of what Richard was generally believed to have done. He was held to be a child murderer.

It cannot be proved that Richard III murdered the Princes in the Tower. It is not known when, where, by what means and by whose hands they met their deaths. It is probable, however, that they were killed with the knowledge of the king before the middle of September 1483. At best Richard was culpable for failing to protect their lives; at worst he himself was directly responsible. Equally important as the probable guilt of Richard III is the certainty that, well before his downfall two years later, he was generally believed to have killed the children. This belief was every bit as important as the truth of the matter itself; indeed in the circumstances it was the

An illustration from the unique manuscript of Pearl, *showing the grieving father separated by sin from his deceased daughter, who has been transfigured as a queen in paradise. The poem draws upon contemporary feelings about the innocence of children and the normal distress suffered when children die. Similar emotions were aroused by the fate of the princes*

perceived truth not the actual truth that was of decisive political significance. Because he had deposed his nephew, usurped his throne, shut him and his brother in prison in the Tower and took no steps whatsoever to demonstrate to the world that they were still alive, Richard was believed to have killed them. Because they were innocent children, not adults who had offended, his crime was judged to be even worse. Political murders, executions and assassination were not unknown in fifteenth-century Europe; the killing of innocent children was exceptional. It was believed that, by killing the princes, Richard had stepped beyond the normal bounds of political behaviour. For this he was condemned by many of his contemporaries. Such condemnation probably had a direct bearing on the unwillingness of many of his subjects to accept him as king of England. Hostile rumour, protest and dissent characterized the rest of his brief reign and the belief that he had murdered his nephews seriously handicapped Richard's efforts to secure himself on the throne he had usurped.

Historical Paintings of the Princes

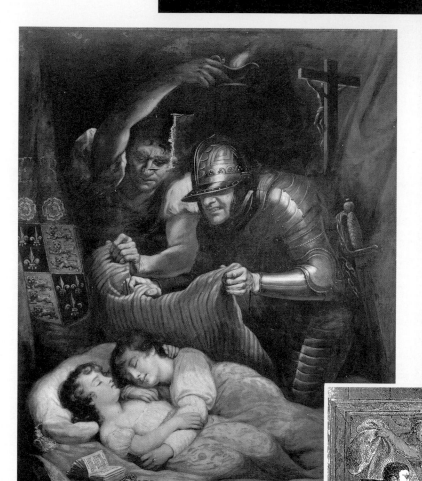

Our perception of the fate of the princes has been moulded by the late eighteenth-century and nineteenth-century vogue for paintings of dramatic or poignant historical moments. The deaths of the princes, as described by More, struck a chord with Victorian sensibility to the vulnerability of innocent children. Several versions sought to capture the moment when the two innocents were about to be smothered by the pillows.

The model was created by James Northcote . . .

Northcote's image of the moment of death was taken up with variations in numerous engravings and book illustrations such as this from Cassell's late-Victorian *Illustrated History of England.*

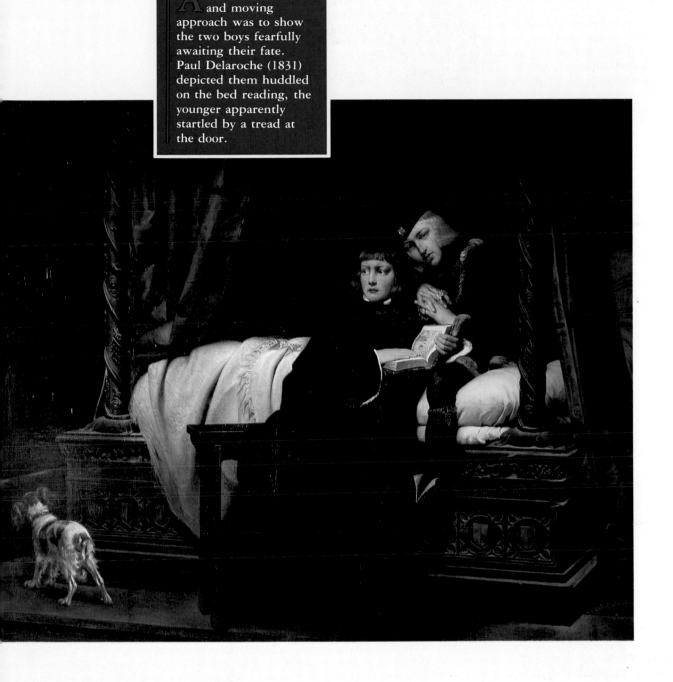

A more subtle and moving approach was to show the two boys fearfully awaiting their fate. Paul Delaroche (1831) depicted them huddled on the bed reading, the younger apparently startled by a tread at the door.

Millais (1878) placed them at the foot of a forbidding stair afraid as much of the dark as of what might happen to them.

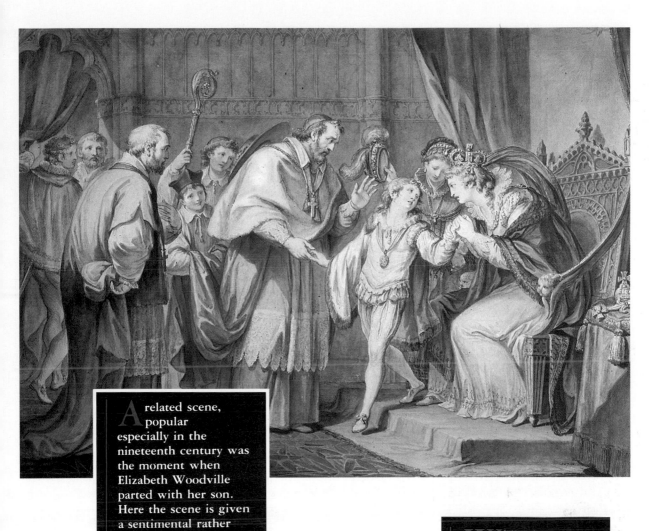

A related scene, popular especially in the nineteenth century was the moment when Elizabeth Woodville parted with her son. Here the scene is given a sentimental rather than a dramatic treatment.

While the vogue for historical paintings died out at the end of the nineteenth century, illustrations were still in demand for children's books. The influence of Delaroche and Millais is all too apparent in 'G.M.''s illustration for a mid-twentieth-century *Nursery History of England*.

Chapter 6

The Reign, 1483–5

Having regained control of the southern counties in the aftermath of rebellion, Richard III returned to London on 25 November 1483. His immediate priorities were to reformulate his regime so as to be secure of the dissident south, to convince still doubting subjects that he had a right to the throne, and to deal once and for all with the threat of Henry Tudor. If he could achieve all this he would be able to look forward to the hope of a long and successful reign. It was not an impossible task. The first two or three years of a usurper's reign were always the most difficult and uncertain, but both Henry IV and Edward IV before him had survived and triumphed: so might he reasonably have hoped. The prospect always existed that time and a benificent rule would remove the doubts surrounding his accession to the throne.

Richard's first and most important task was to establish his own personal authority in the southern counties. Captains of the king's army which had suppressed the rising were immediately appointed to the offices of sheriff and constable of strategic castles. The same men headed the judicial enquiries which were established in selected centres to indict the principal rebels. A considerable number submitted and threw themselves on the king's mercy, but nearly a hundred were finally attainted for treason in parliament in January 1484. Before the formal process of enquiry, indictment and conviction was completed, royal officers began to confiscate and occupy the estates of the condemned and the king himself started to redistribute them to trusted followers. Thus was instituted, even before the act of attainder was passed, the notorious plantation of northerners in the south.

It was the Crowland Chronicler, writing in the spring of 1486, who characterized Richard's settlement of the south as a plantation of northerners. Commenting on the January attainders, he emotionally declared:

> What great numbers of estates and inheritances were amassed in the king's treasury in consequence! He distributed all these amongst his northerners whom he planted in every part of his dominions, to the shame of all the southern people who murmured ceaselessly and longed more each day for the return of their old lords in place of the tyranny of the present ones.[1]

The tyranny in mind was not so much the actual behaviour of the new 'lords', but the transgression of the fundamental notion that the local communities should be ruled by their own native elites, men with deep roots in the districts, who regarded the occupation of royal office and the benefits of royal patronage to be theirs almost by right.

Some of the Crowland Chronicler's emotional condemnation can be substantiated. In the eighteen months following the October rebellion approximately three dozen northerners of Richard's household, a large number Yorkshiremen, were brought in to fill offices, sit on the commissions of the peace and array, and enjoy the lands of attainted rebels. Their declared task was to supervise the government of the counties in which they settled. A typical example was John Hutton (or Hoton) of Hunwick in County Durham. He was in his own society a member of the middle ranking gentry, and he had no previous connections with southwest Hampshire where he became the king's chief agent. As early as 11 December 1483 he was first appointed constable of Southampton Castle for life and granted the manor of Bisterne (now Bisterne Close) on the edge of the New Forest, confiscated from Sir William Berkeley of Beverstone, specifically in reward for his good service in the king's accession and against the rebels. In the following February he was charged by the king with the collection of the revenues from seven more of Berkeley's Hampshire manors. He was subsequently granted all these estates, the income from which was estimated as £66 13s. 4d. per annum for which he paid a token annual rent of £5 to the Crown. Hutton seems to have taken up residence in Hampshire by June 1484 at the latest. On 29 June he was additionally appointed constable of Christchurch castle, steward of Christchurch and Ringwood, and keeper of the New Park in the New Forest (from which, presumably, was taken the buck presented by him to the mayor of Southampton in July). He was made a JP for the county, a commissioner to raise loans there and a commissioner of array. He brought his own retinue with him, the

This window, part of the medieval building, still stands at Hunwick Hall in County Durham. It was the home of John Hutton or Hoton, one of Richard III's northern household men, whom he 'planted' in the south after the rebellions of October 1483

members of whom were liberally rewarded with the grants of lesser offices in the New Forest. Hutton represented the plantation in this corner of Hampshire. Huttons were to be found throughout the southern counties: esquires or knights of the body acting on behalf of the king, defending the coast, controlling the militia and keeping a watchful eye on the local gentry.

However, the scale and impact of the plantation must not be exaggerated. Not only northerners were involved. King's servants from the west midlands and East Anglia were also deployed. Several of those promoted in the southern counties, even among the northerners (for example, Halnath Mauleverer in Cornwall and Sir Ralph Ashton in Kent), had existing connections either by marriage or inheritance with the counties in which they subsequently played a prominent role. Moreover, the incomers never formed more than a minority serving the king as the new ruling elite. The king, who after all had just crushed a rebellion and had the capacity to reward generously, was able to retain the service of most of the lesser peers across southern England (Lords Dinham, Ferrers of Chartley and Zouche, for instance, were enthusiastic supporters) as well as many of the resident gentry who had not been implicated. A glance at the composition of the commissions of the peace or of array in 1484 or 1485 shows that many local gentlemen, if only through fear or prudence, were willing to collaborate with the new regime. Indeed several rebels soon made their peace and were welcomed back. After 22 August 1485 a veil was discreetly drawn; it was in nobody's interest then to challenge the myth that they had all to a man longed for the return of their old lords.

Those planted in the south, from the north or elsewhere, had a specific role to play. They first of all replaced Edward IV's one-time esquires and knights of the body as the representatives of the king's household in the region. They had to hold the south against possible future rebellion and defend the coast against anticipated invasion. It is unlikely that Richard considered the 'plantation' as anything but a temporary measure until Henry Tudor had been destroyed and the old lords made their peace. Nevertheless, all reservations made, the measures taken to secure the south did indeed cause resentment. There was a steady trickle of further defections to Henry Tudor and a recurrence of plots, such as that associated with William Collingbourne in July 1484 whose doggerel:

> the cat, the rat and Lovell our dog,
> rule all England under a hog[2]

caught the popular mood. Indeed such was the scale of continuing disaffection in the south that in November 1484 more of the newly appointed sheriffs were drawn from the ranks of northern household men than in 1483, immediately after the rebellion. As time passed the king was driven to rely ever more overtly on those, primarily from his ducal retinue in the north, whom he knew he could trust. There was no disguising the fact that in the last resort Richard had

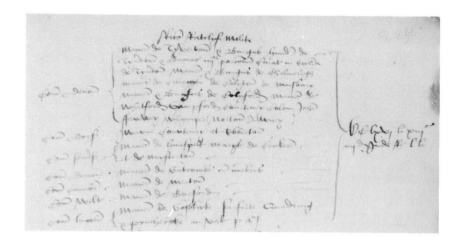

An official note made of the grants to Sir Richard Ratcliffe of lands in the south-west. They were valued, in round terms, at 1,000 marks (£666 13s. 4d.). In return he was to pay an annual rent of £50 to the crown

to depend on outsiders to retain control. Even though small in number, they were a constant reminder to the majority of local gentry that Richard was a king who had imposed his rule on them.

Elsewhere in England it was easier for Richard to establish his unchallenged authority. On the whole the peerage supported him. He relied particularly on the Howards (father and son) – John, duke of Norfolk, and Thomas, earl of Surrey – especially in East Anglia; on his chamberlain Francis, Viscount Lovell, a magnate of substance whose role extended, like Lord Hastings under Edward IV, beyond that of mere courtier; on his nephew, John de le Pole, earl of Lincoln, heir to the elderly earl of Suffolk; on William Herbert, earl of Huntingdon, his son-in-law (he married Richard's illegitimate daughter, Katherine) who was promoted to high office in south Wales after Buckingham's defection; and, in the north, on Lord Stanley, Ralph, earl of Westmorland and the earl of Northumberland. Stanley, the husband of Henry Tudor's mother, presented a dilemma. He had supported Richard in October 1483, yet was clearly not to be trusted. Moreover, there was a history of conflict between him and the king, his family and some of the king's retainers. But Richard appreciated that he could not afford to drive him into open opposition. In the immortal words of President Lyndon Johnson of the USA, it was better to have him inside the tent pissing out, than outside the tent pissing in. Richard did not face insurmountable opposition from the political elite of the kingdom. For their part, the magnates were above all political realists, unwilling to take unnecessary risks, especially after what they had witnessed in the summer of 1483.

The majority of the magnates accepted Richard III. So too did the majority of the bishops, who were accustomed to bend with the political wind. Some senior ecclesiastics were enthusiastic: Dudley of Durham (who unfortunately died in November 1483), Langton

The signature and garter stall plate of Francis, Viscount Lovell, who became chamberlain in succession to Lord Hastings. Lovell was both a personal friend of Richard III and a substantial magnate in his own right

of St David's, Redman of St Asaph, Russell of Lincoln, and, of course, Stillington of Bath and Wells. The two archbishops – Bourgchier of Canterbury and Rotherham of York – stood pointedly aloof, but in Rotherham's case leaving his senior diocesan staff to work enthusiastically for the king. Only Courtenay of Exeter, Morton of Ely, Woodville of Salisbury declared for Tudor. The episcopal bench, as the harmonious relationship between Langton and Morton representing the rival claimants in Rome in 1485 suggests, reached an understanding not to put political partisanship before duty to mother Church.

Richard III's committed support was drawn from the north. His own household, on which he primarily depended was largely, though not exclusively, northern in character. Neither William Catesby nor Sir James Tyrell were northerners, but Sir Richard Ratcliffe, Sir Robert Brackenbury, Sir Marmaduke Constable and many other intimates were. Once he became king, Richard was determined to retain, through his household servants, his personal interest in and control of the region. At first, like Edward IV in the Welsh marches, he used the household of the Prince of Wales, based at Middleham and Sheriff Hutton, as the body through which to rule. But tragically, in March 1483, the prince died. Since Richard himself spent May, June and most of July following in Yorkshire and Durham, he did not need to make alternative arrangements at once. However, when the king returned south he left a newly constituted council, composed of his principal northern retainers and the peers of the region, under the presidency of his nephew, the earl of Lincoln, to represent his authority. Its articles clearly

The tomb of a boy in Sheriff Hutton church traditionally said to be that of Edward of Middleham, Prince of Wales, whose death in April 1484 devastated his parents. It has been suggested, however, that the effigy is in fact that of a son of Richard Neville, earl of Salisbury

established that it existed first and foremost for the king's surety and the maintenance of his peace.[3] The council of the north that he thus instituted was the forerunner of the Tudor prerogative court; but in 1484 its purpose was primarily political rather than legal. Its establishment was a logical outcome of the possession of a substantial landed estate in the region. Indeed the revenues of these estates were immediately assigned not only to support the running costs of the new council, but also to reward with substantial annuities his new councillors.

The establishment of the council of the north may not have been anticipated by the earls of Northumberland and Westmorland (Ralph, Lord Neville succeeded his great uncle to the title in November 1484). Northumberland in particular had probably expected that the new king would surrender much of his personal interest in the region and allow him to step into his shoes. Westmorland too could have hoped for promotion: in June 1483 the king had promised that his support would be the making of him. While both earls were generously rewarded in terms of land and annuities, neither received any addition to their power. Northumberland was overlooked as president of the new council; and although he was given a grand new title as warden-general of the marches, in practice he continued as before as warden only of the east march. The king kept the office of warden of the west march in his own hands, making Lord Dacre his deputy. Neville, who might even have hoped for that office himself, also found that in the long vacancy following the death of Bishop Dudley, the government of the bishopric was kept firmly in royal hands through an episcopal council staffed by the king's men operating in a manner similar to the new council of the north. Richard kept tight political control. In so doing he avoided creating new overmighty subjects in the north who might in the future, just as he had done, threaten royal authority. As poacher turned keeper he knew well how to protect the game. But his policy ran the risk of alienating the magnates who had supported him in 1483, in part at least, in the very hope of becoming more mighty. It was no doubt the correct policy in the long-term, but in the short term it was risky.

Richard III made himself as politically secure as he could within England in 1484, but beneath the surface, he remained deeply unsure of his position. He faced a widespread scepticism about the validity of his title. His need to counter this underlay the first act of his first and only parliament. Parliament had been summoned to meet in November 1483, but it had had to be cancelled on 2 November because of the rebellion. On 9 December new writs were sent out summoning a meeting at Westminster on 23 January. The assembly was, understandably, pliant and subservient. The evidence has not

The tomb of the second earl of Westmorland in Brancepeth church, Durham. He was described by a contemporary as simple, and in his last years left the direction of family affairs in the hands of his heir, Lord Neville. As a boar emblem on his tomb shows, the family committed itself to Richard. But Lord Neville may have been disappointed not to be given a free hand in his native county

survived with which to determine whether the House of Commons was packed with the king's supporters; the election of William Catesby, the king's confidential servant, as speaker in the first parliament in which he had sat nevertheless strongly suggests that it was. According to the Crowland Chronicler, its principal legislation, an act ratifying Richard's title to the throne (Titulus Regius) and the act attainting traitors, was passed without opposition 'on account of the great fear affecting the most steadfast'.[4]

William Catesby, a lawyer and
the third member with Ratcliffe
and Lovell of Richard III's
notorious 'kitchen cabinet'

The Titulus Regius was passed, as it states for 'the quieting of men's minds' and for removing 'the occasion of all doubts and seditious language'. Its form is unusual, in that it purports to repeat the words of the petition presented in the name of the three estates of the realm to the king in June 1483 asking him to take the throne, so that by giving it the authority of a properly constituted parliament minds might be put at ease. Its significance lies not only in setting out the definitive version of Richard's claim to be the only man to have the right to the throne by inheritance (by virtue of his nephews' bastardy), but also in doing so in explicitly propagandist terms. It contrasts, in lurid detail, the moral and political corruption of the previous regime with his own matchless virtues. Under Edward the land was ruled by self-will and pleasure so that there ensued 'murders, extortions and oppressions, namely of poor and impotent people, so that no man was sure of his life, land nor livelihood, nor of his wife, daughter nor servant, every good maiden and woman standing in dread to be ravished and defouled'.

The beginning of the text of the Titulus Regius, showing half-way down the supposed transcript of the petition presented to Richard of Gloucester in June 1483 which the act of parliament itself re-affirmed

Richard, on the other hand, was known to possess 'great wit, prudence, justice, princely courage [and] great noblesse and excellence of birth'.[5] In short it was an act passed for public consumption.

The king's anxiety is revealed by two unusual steps taken during the session and immediately after parliament was dissolved on 22 February. Parliament was still in session when Richard called nearly all the lords spiritual and temporal and the leading members of his household together to swear 'a certain new oath undertaking to adhere to the king's only son, Edward, as their supreme lord, should anything happen to his father'.[6] Shortly after parliament was dissolved he summoned the leading members of the London companies together at Westminster, 'at which time the king's title and right was there published and showed'.[7] It would appear that Richard still faced an uphill struggle to convince the world of his right to the throne. These steps give eloquent testimony to Richard's lack of confidence. In modern parlance, he had a credibility problem, and he knew it.

Polydore Vergil had little doubt, a generation later, that Richard began to put on 'the show and countenance of a good man whereby he might be accounted more righteous, more mild, better affected to the commonalty and more liberal especially to the poor'.[8] The hostile tone is transparent, but Richard's historians will always have difficulty in determining how much the rest of the legislation of parliament and his other reforms arose out of a desire to provide good government, or from a need to restore his reputation by presenting himself as a monarch dedicated to the common weal. We know that Richard, as duke of Gloucester, had been concerned to administer impartial justice before 1483. He made public proclamation several times during his reign of his desire to see justice maintained: 'the king's highness is fully determined to see due administration of justice throughout his realm', he declared in November 1483.[9] He referred on more than one occasion to the profession of justice made by him at his coronation. He encouraged the clerk of his council, John Harrington, to discriminate positively in favour of petitions from the poor in an initiative which is seen as the first step towards the establishment of a court of poor requests. Several articles of the council of the north show a similar concern to maintain law and order; and the first enjoins the councillors not to be swayed by 'favour, affection, hate, malice or meed [reward], nor speak in the council otherwise than the king's laws and good conscience shall require, but be indifferent and no wise partial'.[10] As late as the summer of 1485 he convened a conference of senior judges to discuss certain difficult points of law raised by three recent cases. In the light of this well-attested interest, the legislation of his

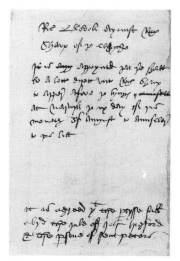

This unassuming document, preserved among the records of the court of requests, is one of a series of petitions presented to Richard III in the course of his progress in 1483. It contains an order to Roger Sharp to appear before the king at Warwick on 9 August to answer the charge made against him by Richard Bostok. The document confirms the report by Thomas Langton that he relieved the wrongs suffered by ordinary men who petitioned him, and shows his expressed desire 'to see due administration of justice' in action

The court of the King's Bench in
session at Westminster Hall.
Richard III is known to have
conferred with his judges over
particular points of law

parliament dealing with the administration of the law — allowing bail to prisoners, regulating juries and adjusting some finer points of land law — might indeed reflect a reforming zeal.

But there are reasons to hesitate before proclaiming Richard a great reforming king on the evidence of the public statutes of his parliament. One act, the abolition of benevolences (taxation in the form of 'gifts' from loving subjects without parliamentary consent), although remembered later as a good act made in his time, was equally a bid for popularity by condemning a much criticized expedient adopted by Edward IV towards the end of his reign. It is also difficult to see what personal interest Richard had in the remaining acts tidying up commercial law. Moreover, it is misleading to emphasize the legislation of the 1484 parliament in isolation and a misunderstanding of procedure to assume it was introduced by the Crown. Successive parliaments under Edward IV, Richard III and Henry VII dealt with inadequacies of the law concerning the conveyance and inheritance of land, the regulation of commerce and the administration of justice. They did so because the members of

A collection of Edward IV's hated benevolences which Richard III made illegal in his parliament

Legislation was enacted in Richard's parliament to tighten the regulations concerning the dyeing of cloth, here taking place. It is unlikely that the king himself had a personal interest in the matter

the House of Commons were drawn from the ranks of landowners, merchants and lawyers. Moreover, the normal course of such legislation was for it to be introduced in bills presented individually by members or collectively by the house. A meeting of parliament, whoever the king, whatever the political circumstance, was always an opportunity for routine amendment of the law. The king assented (and could veto), but he rarely initiated such legislation. There was nothing necessarily exceptional about the public acts of 1484. Richard III may well have taken seriously his coronation oath to maintain justice; he was almost certainly also aware of the advantages of presenting himself as a defender of justice. But in his parliament he may only have been exercising his conventional constitutional function.

In the administration of finance Richard had less room to make an impact than in the administration of justice. A king was expected to live within his means and not to tax his subjects excessively. Edward IV in his later years had achieved considerable success in this respect and was even rumoured to have died leaving a substantial treasure. If he did, little came into Richard's hands. In April 1483, after the coup at Stony Stratford, Sir Edward Woodville, Earl Rivers's brother may have made off with much of whatever treasure there was. In fact, surviving accounts of Edward V's reign show that government finances were under considerable pressure immediately after Edward IV's death. There was very little in the kitty when Richard became king. Thomas More famously castigated Richard for his profligacy: 'free was he called of dispense and somewhat above his power liberal; with large gifts he got him unsteadfast friendship, for which he was fain to pill and spoil in other places and get him steadfast hatred'.[11] This condemnation is compelling but unfair. Richard incurred heavy expenditure suppressing rebellion in 1483, fighting the Scots in 1484 and preparing to face invasion in 1485. There was little wanton liberality. In so far as he rewarded his friends generously this was largely out of the revenues of his ducal or confiscated estates. He paid close attention to the smooth running of the chamber system of finance inherited from his brother (the practice of supervising, collecting and spending through a household office rather than through the cumbersome bureaucracy of the exchequer). But this had only a marginal effect on his overall solvency. By 1485 he needed to resort to loans. Although the king's servants might have exerted pressure on potential lenders, these were not forced loans. A date in 1487 was set for repayment: it was hardly Richard's fault that he was unable to honour his obligation. Nevertheless the very resort to loans and the circumstance in which they were raised to withstand Henry Tudor's expected invasion, effectively counteracted whatever political advantage had been gained from the abolition of benevolences. By the end of his reign Richard was no longer able to present himself as a capable financial administrator, living off his own resources without need to appeal to his subjects for aid.

Richard's conduct of foreign policy after November 1483 was constrained and dominated by the need to neutralize the threat from Henry Tudor. However, when Richard came to the throne England was at war with Scotland and it appears that initially he sought to exploit success against the Scots to rally the kingdom behind him. Although he was unable to turn his attention to preparations for war in the early months of the reign, he soon made clear his intention to launch an attack on Scotland in the coming summer. On 18 February he wrote to Sir John Mordaunt and William Salisbury informing them that by advice of parliament he was determined 'to address us in person with host royal' towards Scotland by land and by sea. They were summoned to array by 1 May, and in a postscript, given until the end of the month to muster at Newcastle.[12] Preparations for war were under way in March. Richard himself left London on 7 March and made his way, via Cambridge to Nottingham. Here he was brought news of the death of his son, the Prince of Wales. The Crowland Chronicler, surely an eyewitness, remarked, 'You might have seen the father and mother . . . almost out of their minds for a long time when faced with sudden grief'.[13] Deep in mourning, the king and queen remained in Nottingham for over a month. The progress north was not resumed until 27 April and the king did not arrive in York until 1 May.

It is possible that the blow, both personal and dynastic, of the death of the Prince of Wales contributed to Richard's decision not to press ahead with an invasion of Scotland. Although he toured Durham and Yorkshire between 1 May and the end of July, the muster at Newcastle was cancelled. Instead he adopted the more modest strategy of victualling Dunbar which had been handed over to an English garrison by the dissident duke of Albany in the preceding year and sponsoring a raid by Albany and the earl of Douglas into the west march. Dunbar was successfully replenished, an English fleet breaking through an attempted Scottish blockade. However, the raid into south-west Scotland ended in disaster when Albany and Douglas were defeated at Lochmaben on 22 July. By the end of July Richard accepted that he was unable to make any headway in continued war against the Scots. The cost, and the need to concentrate all his efforts on Henry Tudor finally persuaded him to accept James III of Scotland's repeated overtures for peace. Negotiations were resumed with Scottish ambassadors. Richard, who had returned to Westminster on 4 August, travelled back to Nottingham at the end of the month, where on 11 September the Scottish ambassadors were received. On 14 September a three-year truce was concluded and a marriage agreed between the heir to the Scottish throne and Richard's niece, Anne de la Pole. The king stayed on in Nottingham until November when he returned once more to Westminster, where, with the exception of a brief visit to Canterbury, he spent the whole of the winter.

The truce with Scotland freed Richard, not before time, to devote all his diplomatic attention to Henry Tudor. Tudor had returned to Brittany after his attempted landing in the west country in November 1483. In his efforts to persuade the Bretons to hand him over, Richard was not helped by the volatility of Breton politics. Duke Francis was a weak ruler, unable to master faction at his court. Matters were made more difficult for Richard by the existence of two camps in and out of favour with the duke, one pushing for closer cooperation with France, the other for an English alliance to resist French ambitions. At first he sought to put

A portrait of Edward of Middleham, Prince of Wales, from the version of the Rous Roll completed during Richard III's reign, possibly before his son's death in April 1484 which is not recorded

Duke Francis of Brittany, the ineffectual ruler who gave shelter to Henry Tudor

pressure on the Bretons by stepping up a naval war. By the spring, when the anti-French faction was dominant, Brittany was more inclined to negotiate. A truce was reached in June and Richard agreed to supply a company of archers to assist the Bretons against France. In return the Bretons agreed to place Henry Tudor under arrest. But at the eleventh hour Tudor was forewarned, probably as a result of information being leaked from England, and in September he made a dramatic escape to France. By the end of the year his cause was being promoted by the French. Richard's diplomacy towards Brittany ended in complete failure. Henry Tudor was a far greater danger to him in France than he ever had been in Brittany.

There was factionalism in France too in 1484. During the minority of Charles VIII the government of the kingdom was in the hands of his aunt, the regent Anne of Beaujeu. It so happened that in 1484 and 1485 a group of anglophobic courtiers, alarmed by the apparent willingness of Richard to support Breton independence, exercised considerable influence. In the summer of 1485 substantial resources were put at Henry Tudor's disposal: a fleet was fitted out at Le Havre and part of the French army stationed in Normandy assigned to him. By this time there was nothing that Richard could have done to stop him. It is possible that had Richard not pursued his Scottish ambitions in 1484, he would have enjoyed more success in restricting Henry Tudor in Brittany, but circumstances in Brittany and France were largely beyond his control. Moreover,

Henry VII as a young man, before he became king and when his future looked anything but bright

Anne of Beaujeu, regent of France, to whom Henry Tudor fled in the autumn of of 1484 and whose government sponsored his invasion of England the following year

Henry had escaped his clutches because of treachery; someone in England, probably Margaret Beaufort, had tipped off John Morton in Flanders who had been able to send a messenger to him. In the last resort it was ill luck that Henry had arrived in France at precisely the time when a faction in power was prepared to give substantially more than lip-service to his cause.

By the spring of 1485 Richard knew that a French-sponsored invasion of England was imminent. He probably welcomed the prospect of dealing once and for all with the pretender and his fellow exiles. Henry had been a thorn in his flesh for almost two years. Not only had he inspired a resurgence of defections and disturbances in England, especially in the autumn of 1484, but also he had succeeded in undermining the loyalty of the Calais garrison, part of which had defected to him with their prisoner the earl of Oxford, in November. As early as December 1484, when Richard issued commissions of array, he had anticipated a landing. It did not materialize, but it had become clear, however, that Henry in France was steadily gaining strength. The sooner he landed in England, the sooner he could be crushed.

Richard did as much as he could to counter Henry Tudor's appeal in England. Once Queen Elizabeth Woodville and her daughters came out of sanctuary they were fêted by the king. The precedence given to Elizabeth of York at Christmas 1484, who pointedly wore the same clothes as the queen, shocked the Crowland Chronicler: 'it should not be left unsaid that during this Christmas feasting too much attention was paid to singing and dancing and to vain

Dancing and merry-making at court. Not everyone approved of the behaviour at Richard's court, which appears not to have been sober or decorous enough for one or two of his clerical contemporaries

exchanges of clothing between Queen Anne and Lady Elizabeth. . . The people spoke against this and the magnates and prelates were greatly astonished'.[14] The goings-on may have been misinterpreted by contemporaries; the display was perhaps designed to demonstrate that the Woodvilles gave their full backing to Richard, not Henry Tudor. Some success was achieved in winning back Woodville associates; Richard almost carried off the major coup of bringing the marquess of Dorset back to court, only to be foiled by Henry's men preventing his escape.

Another ploy was the flamboyantly staged removal of the body of Henry VI from Chertsey Abbey for reburial in St George's chapel, Windsor in August 1484. Henry Tudor claimed to represent the Lancastrian line and later expended considerable time and money in seeking his predecessor's canonization. Already in 1484 the late king enjoyed a flourishing cult. Edward IV had sought to suppress it. Richard pointedly reversed his policy by having Henry VI reburied alongside his brother. He also began to patronize Henry's foundation at King's College, Cambridge. By so publicly sponsoring the cult of the now venerable king, whose body was discovered to be 'for the most part uncorrupted', and whose sanctity, so Rous asserted, 'at once miracles abundantly attested',[15] Richard hoped to weaken Henry Tudor's appeal as the heir to Lancaster.

Henry VI as a saint. Although he played a part in Henry's death in 1471, thirteen years later Richard III sought to harness the growing cult of the martyred king to his cause

In other ways Richard sought to distance himself from his brother and to draw upon the reputation of the saintly Henry VI. He attacked the corruption of the previous regime. In the Titulus Regius he had emphasized his brother's immorality and the immorality of the court in general, picturing a society given over to lechery. He made a scapegoat of Jane Shore who was forced to do public penance for being a whore. In March 1484, in a circular to the bishops, he launched a campaign of moral rearmament, declaring:

> forasmuch as it is notoriously known . . . that there be many in the spiritual as well as the temporal party deliring [departing] from the true way of virtue and good living to the pernicious example of others and loathsomeness of every well disposed person.

Richard III made much of the immorality of his enemies. He would have approved of the message contained in this book illumination in which a devil, pulling back the bed hangings, reveals the adultery of a man and a woman between the sheets

He charged them to ensure that:

> all such persons as set apart virtue and promote damnable execution of sin and vices to be reformed, repressed and punished condignely after their demerits.[16]

In the same vein, the king's proclamations against his enemies in the service of Henry Tudor stressed that 'many be known openly as murderers, adulterers and extortioners contrary to the pleasure of God' and he castigated Tudor himself for his 'ambitiousness and insatiable covetousness' in usurping the title of king since he was 'descended of bastard blood, both of his father's side and his mother's side'.[17] There is an air of desperation about such intemperate character assassination, but the appeal to English prurience may have been based on calculation that an advantage lay in presenting himself to his subjects as a king in the mould of Henry VI. He may have personally held such prurient views; although it is worth remembering in this context that two contemporaries commented, somewhat critically, that his own court was not exactly dull: too much singing and dancing according to the Crowland Chronicler.

The climax to Richard's campaign to undermine Henry Tudor's appeal in England was his plan to marry his niece, Elizabeth, himself. In March 1485, after a short illness, Queen Anne had died. In the weeks before her death, Richard's apparent lack of concern, suggested by his unwillingness to visit her in her quarters, gave rise to the rumour that he had poisoned her. These were only intensified after her death by the speed with which he made known his intention to marry his niece. He was met, however, with the determined opposition of his closest associates, especially Ratcliffe and Catesby, who well understood that such a marriage would not only take the rug from under the feet of Henry Tudor but would also open the way for the pardon and restoration of rebels whose lands they, and many other loyal household men, held.

> These men told the king, to his face, that if he did not deny any such purpose and did not counter it by public declaration before the mayor and commonalty of the city of London, the northerners in whom he placed the greatest trust, would all rise against him, charging him with the death of the queen, the daughter and one of the heirs of the earl of Warwick, and through whom he had obtained his first honour, in order to complete his incestuous association with his near kinswoman.[18]

They may, as the Crowland Chronicler reported, have couched their opposition in terms of moral outrage at the prospect of such incest,

but their real concern was political. A full restoration of the Woodvilles and dissident survivors of Edward IV's household, necessary as it might now seem to the king for his survival, would have spelt the end of favour for many of his old ducal retainers who had sustained him in power for the last eighteen months. Faced by

In this illustration a man is being accused of having remarried within the prohibited degrees of consanguinity. Richard faced a similar accusation when he proposed his own marriage to Elizabeth of York

this threat Richard had no choice but to climb down and do as was demanded. And so, shortly before Easter (3 April), he appeared at St John's Clerkenwell and there denied before the mayor and aldermen, many lords spiritual and temporal and, significantly, 'the substance of all our household' that there was any truth in the 'rumours'. Furthermore, on 11 April letters were sent to many boroughs, including the city of York, ordering the corporations to do the same because, and the text is worth quoting in full:

> divers seditious and evil persons in London and elsewhere enforce themselves daily to sow seeds of noise and slander against our person . . . to abuse the multitude of our subjects and alter their minds from us, some by setting up bills, some by spreading false rumours.[19]

Richard III's increasingly desperate attempts to counter Henry Tudor's appeal in England back-fired on him. His credibility, already strained by the widespread belief that he had murdered his nephews, was dealt a further blow by the humiliation of having to deny rumours that he had poisoned his wife and planned to marry his niece. The whole sorry incident further served to undermine his attempts to present himself as a righteous and God-fearing king set upon restoring morality to public life. Moreover, it left him a virtual prisoner of the support from which he had now revealed he wished to distance himself.

As Henry Tudor busied himself in Normandy with his French backers making preparations for invasion, Richard fell back on the only hope for survival he had left – the destruction of his enemies on the field of battle. The south coast was well-defended, commissions of array set the county militias on their toes. On 11 May he left Westminster for the last time. He journeyed to Kenilworth and Coventry, finally arriving at Nottingham by 9 June. Here he made his headquarters, from which he could respond to a landing anywhere in England and Wales. Spies kept him informed of his enemy's preparations. As a precaution against treachery, he took Lord Stanley's son and heir, Lord Strange into his entourage as a hostage. It was a long and anxious wait. But eventually, on the evening of 7 August, Henry Tudor landed in Milford Haven.

Tudor set off on a measured march up the Welsh coast and then westwards through central Wales into Shropshire. Richard had word of the landing on 11 August when several of his knights and esquires were summoned to him. The duke of Norfolk knew by 14 August and was calling his men to join him at Bury St Edmunds on the sixteenth. Although the city of York seems not to have received a summons, themselves sending to the king to know how

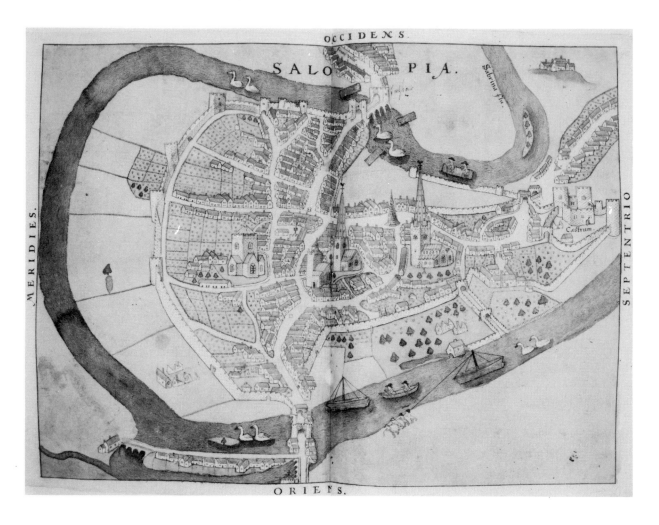

many men he might want, the earl of Northumberland was raising troops in Beverley. In the confusion and haste, it seems, not all the king's messages were delivered and not all his reinforcements raised. The king himself moved up from Nottingham to Leicester on 16 August or a day or two later. Tudor, meanwhile, had gathered strength in Shropshire and was moving east to Stafford on 17 August and Lichfield two days later, en route for London. At the same time Lord Stanley and his brother Sir William were converging with separate forces. A meeting almost certainly took place between Tudor and one of the brothers, who pledged family support. Cheshire might have already been raised by them in his cause. On 21 August Richard moved out from Leicester to intercept Henry as he marched down Watling Street. Hearing of the king's approach, Tudor turned to face him. The two armies engaged in the plain known as Redemoor, south of Bosworth Market on 22 August.

A sixteenth-century map of the town of Shrewsbury through which Henry Tudor marched on his road to Bosworth. The Welsh Gate which was opened to him is clearly marked

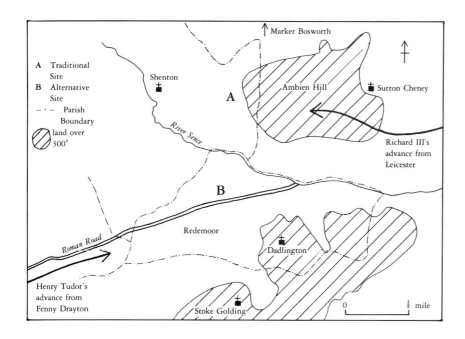

A Traditional Site
B Alternative Site
– · – Parish Boundary
land over 300'

Market Bosworth

Shenton

A

Ambien Hill

Sutton Cheney

River Sence

Richard III's advance from Leicester

B

Redemoor

Dadlington

Roman Road

Henry Tudor's advance from Fenny Drayton

Stoke Golding

0   ½ mile

Sites of Bosworth

The exact location and course of what was one of the most significant battles fought on English soil are the subject of controversy. Bosworth, for all its fame, is singularly poorly documented. Recent reconsideration of the site of the field has led to the plausible suggestion that it did not take place on the slope of Ambien Hill, as traditionally supposed, but half a mile to the south, on the plain below the village of Dadlington. Richard probably camped on Ambien Hill. On the morning of 22 August such was the confusion in the king's camp that the customary mass was not celebrated: an omission that was later interpreted as an ill omen. It is likely that he moved his men down to the plain to stand and await Tudor's army advancing up a Roman road from Fenny Drayton. Battle was first joined between troops under the duke of Norfolk, probably on the right flank of the king's army and the vanguard of Tudor's army, under the command of the earl of Oxford. After giving ground to the initial shock of Norfolk's charge, the professional French soldiers under the earl's command regrouped and counter-attacked. It would seem that Norfolk's men began to fall back. At this point the king, not yet engaged and seeing, as he supposed, Henry Tudor standing a little way off exposed and vulnerable, suddenly led his own men in a charge designed to end the battle quickly. But Richard had overlooked the lurking presence of Sir William Stanley, of whose treachery he was already aware, also standing to one side with his retinue. Once Richard was engaged in hand-to-hand combat, and the impact of

This grant of a royal licence to raise money for a chantry in the chapel of St James 'standing on a parcel of the grounde where Bosworth feld . . . was done' in the parish of Dadlington has been at the centre of the recent dispute about the site of the battle

A drawing of the presumed banner of Richard III at Bosworth in which the white boar was displayed along with the white rose in a sunburst of the house of York

his charge took him close to Henry, Stanley moved in for the kill from his rear. Trapped between the two forces, Richard and his men stood their ground and fought bravely to the end. Richard was finally overwhelmed and killed. As soon as the news of his death spread, the rest of his army broke and fled.

Richard III lost a battle he should have won. The sources, meagre as they are, agree that he outnumbered his enemies and suggest that he probably had the advantage of the land. Historians have debated the issue of what proportion of the peerage turned out for him. Some have suggested that only six were on his side and that at least three-quarters stayed away. On the other hand, it has been argued that at least twenty fought for him, almost half the adult and active number in 1485. Resolution of this issue is unlikely. Some, such as Lovell, Huntingdon, Audley and Dinham could not get there; others like Scrope of Bolton, Scrope of Masham, FitzHugh and Greystoke from the north may well have been present but in Northumberland's battalion. He probably was let down by some, but events moved so rapidly after Tudor's landing that, in spite of his preparedness, it was not possible to gather all his strength. In his anxiety to engage Henry before he won more recruits, Richard may have faced him before all his own men had come up. But in the light of his own experience in 1471, and any doubts he had about men turning out for him, this would have made sound sense.

However, the battle was lost on the field, not beforehand. The critical elements were his own fatal charge and the failure of the earl of Northumberland on his left wing to engage. Had Northumberland's northern levies fought, Richard would surely have carried the day. Yet as the Crowland Chronicler reported, 'in the place where the earl of Northumberland stood with a fairly large and well-equipped force, there was no contest against the enemy and no blows were given or received in battle'.[20] And, he added, many northerners in whom he put such special trust fled before coming to blows. It is not the case that no northerners fought on the day; several, including Sir Richard Ratcliffe, Sir Robert Brackenbury and probably John Hutton were killed. These were men of Richard's household who had answered, as they should as knights and esquires of the body, his call to fight by his side. They would have been with him in his last stand, not watching from the sidelines with Northumberland. It has often been argued, however, that Northumberland betrayed him. Four years later, when the earl himself was murdered during a tax revolt, it was suspected that his retainers, remembering the battle, were reluctant to defend him. It was said that the commons of the north 'bore a deadly malice against him for the disappointing of King Richard at Bosworth Field'.[21] There is even a suspicion that he was in communication

The memorial brass of John Sachaverel, a Derbyshire squire who fought and died alongside Richard at Bosworth

with Henry before the battle. Certainly, as we have seen, disappointment at not being given a free hand in the north could have given a motive for his standing aside and awaiting the result. Yet immediately afterwards both he and the earl of Westmorland were taken into custody by the new king and kept in prison until the end of November when they were released only under strict conditions of good behaviour. This, in contrast to the generosity shown to the Stanleys, was no reward for masterly inactivity. An alternative, and not implausible, explanation is given by Polydore Vergil:

> While the battle continued thus hot on both sides between the vanguards, king Richard understood first by espials where earl Henry was a far off with small force of soldiers about him; then after drawing nearer he knew it perfectly by evident signs and tokens that it was Henry; wherefore, all inflamed with ire, he struck his horse with the spurs, and runneth out of the one side without the vanguard against him.[22]

In other words, he charged recklessly and impulsively before Northumberland's men had been brought into action. A tactical blunder rather than betrayal may have cost Richard the battle, his throne and his life.

So Richard III's reign ended in disaster on 22 August. He had failed to win the confidence of his subjects. The means by which he made himself king, the belief that he had murdered his nephews, his over-reliance on his northern followers, his inability to stem further desertions to Henry Tudor and failure to discredit him meant that in the end all hung on the balance of this one battle. Had Richard won at Bosworth the lords and county gentry up and down the land, practised in the arts of time-serving, would probably have accepted the divine judgement of a decisive battle in his favour. Thus, had it been Henry Tudor's body, not Richard's, taken from the field, stripped naked and flung over a horse like the quarry after a hunt, he may well have succeeded in establishing his own dynasty on the throne. And since, as we are so often told, history is written by the winners, we would have had a different tale to tell of the first two uncertain years of Richard III's reign. As it is, it was Richard's body that was buried with little ceremony at the Franciscan Friary in Leicester. He was still only thirty-two; and he was the only usurper of four to fail in the fifteenth century.

English historians customarily assess the 'contribution' or 'legacy' of their kings; in particular, they like to establish the significance of their reigns for the development of the kingdom. They have difficulty with Richard III because his reign was so brief and ended

A Lancastrian rose as drawn on the roll of the King's Bench in 1500. Henry VII long continued to use the red rose as a symbol of his succession to Henry VI. In the final analysis, Richard III, by his actions, destroyed the house of York and opened the door to the Tudors

in such dismal failure. But it was not too short to have had an influence on the 'island story'. Its most obvious impact was negative. Richard III destroyed the house of York and by so doing opened the way for the Tudor dynasty. It can be argued that part of the responsibility for the failure of the Yorkist dynasty can be lain at Edward IV's door. It was he who established a regime based narrowly on the support of a handful of mighty subjects and therefore, it is suggested, it is he who must take the blame for the struggle for power which consumed his family after his death. However, while it is true that in hindsight Edward's policy was short-sighted, and was never likely in the long-term to provide a sound basis for the effective exercise of royal authority, Richard III's usurpation was hardly a consequence. Richard III's seizure of the throne arose out of the unpredictable ambition and opportunism of one man, ruthlessly exploiting the circumstances of an unforeseen minority. Thus Richard himself has to carry the ultimate responsibility for the destruction of his dynasty.

Were there more positive achievements? Historians have long looked for the contribution that kings made to the evolution of the English constitution. Richard's reign did its bit. He was the first king to be granted tonnage and poundage (customs duties) for life in the first parliament of his reign; a precedent to be maintained until the accession of Charles I. Richard's parliament passed the act abolishing benevolences, so reaffirming the principle that taxes could not be raised without parliamentary assent. Richard also pioneered the court of poor requests, which under the Tudors was to become an important avenue for the less advantaged. Much more controversially it has been claimed that by the means he adopted to authorize his accession to the throne he made a significant contribution to the development of parliamentary sovereignty in England. It is argued that since Richard called upon parliament as the supreme court to pronounce that he was the true king of England, he thereby established the principle that parliament had authority to determine the succession. However, this claim is based on a misreading of Titulus Regius in which Richard's supposed hereditary right was asserted, and overlooks the extent to which parliament in 1484 was deployed to ratify a *fait accompli*.

Historians have also debated for many years the extent to which the Yorkists laid the foundation for Tudor monarchy. Edward IV, who started the process of recovery of royal authority after the disastrous reign of Henry VI, initiated certain institutional reforms – summed up by the phrase household government – on which Henry VII and the young Henry VIII built. By household government is meant the direct management of affairs from within the king's own entourage rather than through the established

Vespasian, as here illustrated in a contemporary manuscript of Suetonius's Lives of the Caesars, *stood as the classical type for the constructive statesman and dynastic founder who rescued his country from anarchy. He is portrayed holding Rome in his left hand. Rous made use of the same image in one of his representations of Richard III. It is perhaps more appropriate for Henry VII, whom historians have seen in terms remarkably close to Suetonius's description of Vespasian, even down to the judgement that his one serious fault was avarice*

bureaucracy. Thus, the king's secretary deploying the king's own signet executed royal commands in preference to the slow and cumbersome procedure of the chancery; finances were managed and supervised through the king's chamber, bypassing the exchequer. Richard III had little time to contribute to this process. He tightened up the supervision of financial management in the chamber, but for the most part he was content just to use what his brother had instituted. Yorkist monarchy really means Edward IV's government. Richard III's only significant initiative in the government of the realm was the establishment of a council in the north as an extension of the royal council to rule a distant part of the realm. His primary purpose was political, to retain his own personal control of the region from which he came, not administrative or constitutional. Indeed the council did not survive his downfall. It was later re-established by Henry VII, but the connection with the longer-lasting Tudor Council of the North was tenuous and coincidental.

If Richard made any lasting contribution to the resurgence of monarchy at the end of the fifteenth century it was inadvertent, but ultimately of greater significance than any reforms he might have intended. By the very act of becoming king, Richard added a substantial northern estate to the crown lands. Before 1483 the Crown was territorially weak in the far north. This weakness had been a crucial factor in the inability of his predecessors, including Edward IV, to maintain a direct and effective control over the region. Time after time northern rebellions, led or inspired by northern magnates, had been at the bottom of civil disorder during the fifteenth century. The chief reason why the Crown had been unable to control the conflict between the Nevilles and Percys in the fifteenth century was that it had allowed both families, especially the Nevilles of Middleham, to amass too much power in the region. The war between the Nevilles and the Percys had also been a central feature of the Wars of the Roses. The Crown was unlikely to recover full control of the kingdom until it restored its authority over the far north. To do this it needed to break the power of the northern magnates. It had little chance to do so as long as it lacked a direct presence in the region. Edward IV had had an opportunity to rectify this in 1471, but he opted instead to entrust his brother Richard with the task of representing him.

In 1483 Richard made a decisive break with Edward's policy. He declined to rely on others in the north; by means of his new council he retained personal control. But the basis of his personal control was his landed estate and the royal affinity based upon it. After 1485 Henry VII continued where Richard had left off. He too kept Middleham (and his own lordship of Richmond), Sheriff Hutton,

Penrith and Barnard Castle in royal hands. He disbanded Richard's council; in its place he ruled directly through his own household men and councillors. He capitalized further by allowing the earls of Northumberland and Westmorland even less authority and power than Richard had ceded. If they did desert Richard in the hope that Henry VII would, in his innocence, allow them to rule the north, they miscalculated badly. In the north, therefore, Henry built on the foundations laid not by Edward but by Richard III; and in so far as the north had been a major arbiter of recent English politics, the absorption into the royal demesne of Richard III's northern estates was the decisive event in the extension of central authority over this distant region. 1483, not 1485, was the turning point in the history of the late-medieval north.

Yet, it was Henry VII and the Tudors who reaped the long-term benefit of Richard III's usurpation of the throne. It is anyone's guess as to what might have happened had Richard succeeded and had it been he who reigned until 1509. One can be fairly certain that he would have been a forceful king. In many ways he was not unlike Henry V; a man of chivalry, a benefactor of the Church, and enforcer of the law. The similarities are perhaps closer, weaknesses as well as strengths, than many recent admirers of Henry V would be willing to admit. Henry V, however, is renowned as the archetypal medieval hero king; Richard remains the controversial destroyer of the Yorkist dynasty.

Richard III's Saints

Some saints had national or regional significance. It is not surprising that a royal duke with chivalric leanings should venerate St George, here depicted in a mid-fifteenth-century mural in the parish church of St Peter and St Paul, Pickering.

St Cuthbert was the leading saint of northern England, to whose shrine in Durham Cathedral the duke and duchess were frequent visitors in the 1470s. They would also have known the early fifteenth-century glass representation of St Cuthbert holding the head of St Oswald in the south choir aisle of York Minster.

St Ninian was a more unusual choice, for his shrine at Whithorn in Galloway was a focus of Scottish veneration. However, he enjoyed a following in northern England and seems to have symbolized English ambitions over the border. He was thus an appropriate saint to be venerated by the warden of the west march. He is shown here from a Scottish book of hours.

St Anthony the Hermit appealed to those who sought by an ascetic life to triumph over the desires of the body. Richard's devotion to him may have echoed his own personal struggle (see also 'Pigs and Boars', p. 89).

Because she was considered to be the bride of Christ and was the greatest virgin saint after Our Lady, St Catherine enjoyed a widespread cult in the later middle ages. She was called upon to intercede with Christ by men and women of all classes. Many English alabaster images, of which this is one, were made of her in the fifteenth century.

St Barbara, whose symbol was the tower in which she was incarcerated by her cruel father, was a popular intercessor against sudden death. Here, in the Donne Triptych by Hans Memlinc, St Barbara presents Lady Elizabeth Donne (the sister of William, Lord Hastings who presumably did not enjoy the saint's protection in 1483) to the Virgin Mary. Sir John Donne was a prominent member of Edward IV's household who made his peace with Richard in 1484.

St Margaret, according to her legend, was by the power of her faith miraculously released from the stomach of a dragon who had devoured her. She was the intercessor for women in childbirth, and she is therefore likely to have been the duchess of Gloucester's choice.

Chapter 7

The Man

Five hundred years after his death, is it possible to understand the man who was Richard III? There are several almost insuperable difficulties. For a start almost all surviving contemporary or near-contemporary comment on his character was made retrospectively by people who were hostile. In this respect it is as difficult to see Richard the royal duke before 1483 as it is to see Richard the king. Contemporaries quickly applied hindsight to their interpretation of his character and motives before 1483, even those writing before 1485. Richard himself never put his personal thoughts on paper; or rather no personal letters, diaries or memoirs of his have come to light. No confessor in whom he confided, or companion-in-arms whom he inspired, subsequently extolled his virtues (as did John Blacman for Henry VI) or commissioned a panegyric (as did Humphrey of Gloucester for Henry V). Even those few comments passed in his favour during his lifetime have to be approached tentatively as the possible product of sycophancy.

Further clues to Richard's personality can be sought indirectly through his actions (both routine and exceptional), through his public declarations and through his known possessions. No two people are likely to agree as to what such evidence reveals; moreover, it has to be recognized that as a great royal duke and as king he performed on a public stage. A prince in the fifteenth century was not a private person. In all his acts he had always to be conscious of his standing, his reputation, his 'worship'. He was expected to live up to a code of behaviour enshrining certain commonplace ideals of nobility. The demonstration of these virtues for public consumption cannot necessarily be taken at their face value as revelation of the inner man. The man himself might genuinely have sought to live up to the highest ideals of his day; alternatively he might skilfully have played the part expected of him. The historian, living in so different a world so long afterwards, cannot easily discern between the actor and his role. Nevertheless, an examination as to whether Richard lived up to these ideals probably offers the most hopeful point of departure in an attempt to understand his character and personality.

We can begin fairly confidently in the knowledge that Richard knew his lines. He owned a copy in Latin of Aegidius Colonna's *De Regimine Principum* (The Conduct of Princes) which was one of the standard fifteenth-century 'mirrors' or advice books, in which a prince could find delineated for him the image of what he ought to be. He may well have been familiar with other works such as *The Declamation of Noblesse* published by Caxton in 1481, a debate on whether virtue was a personal or genetic quality, or the *Secretum Secretorum* (the Secret of Secrets) which advocated that the secret of success in the world lay in the cultivation of virtue and the shunning of vice. Such books were supplemented in the recommended reading for nobles by romances and histories which highlighted in literary form some of the same virtues: fortitude and largesse in romances; prudence in histories. Richard possessed copies of Chaucer's *Knight's Tale*, the *Destruction of Troy*, the *Seige of Thebes*, Geoffrey of Monmouth's *History* and an anonymous *Chronicle of English History*. In addition to the secular virtues, we can be confident that Richard was familiar with the Christian virtues expected of all men, but, because of their position and the example they set, considered essential in princes. He owned an English Bible, a copy of the *Visions of Matilda of Hackenborn*, a collection of Old Testament stories in verse and a book of hours. All noblemen and princes had their own libraries; it did not necessarily follow that they read their contents. Often the books, lavishly illustrated, were even then collector's items for show, but Richard's books were unadorned and well-thumbed. They passed through hands other than his, so there is no way of knowing how much use he personally made of them. But he did receive a conventional upbringing, so there is no reason to doubt that he was familiar with the model of virtue he was expected to follow. To what extent did he live up to it?

Pietro Carmeliano, who had come to England in 1480 and found employment as a chancery clerk, had few doubts in 1484 that Richard possessed all these virtues. He dedicated a copy of his life of St Catherine to Sir Robert Brackenbury and in his introduction sang the praises of his master.

If we look first of all for religious devotion which of our princes shows a more genuine piety? If for justice, who can we reckon

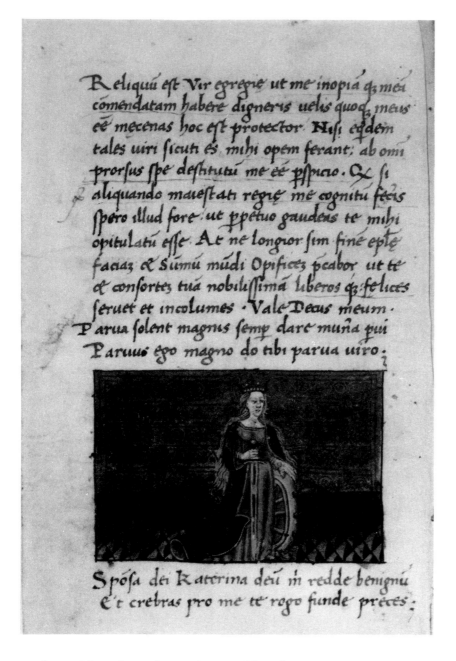

The image of St Catherine from Carmeliano's life of the saint which was dedicated to Sir Robert Brackenbury with an effusive eulogy of his king

above him throughout the world? If we contemplate the prudence of his service, both in peace and in waging war, who shall we judge his equal? If we look for truth of soul, for wisdom, for loftiness of mind united with modesty, who stands before our King Richard? What Emperor or Prince can be compared with him in good works or munificence?[1]

If Carmeliano is to be believed Richard was a paragon. However, when it is borne in mind that two years later he was one of the first to turn his pen against 'the murderous tyrant', it would be wise to approach Carmeliano's eulogy with caution. Was he merely a flatterer of princes, churning out the conventional praises on demand? Or did he, in 1484, write what he genuinely believed to be the case?

The four secular, or cardinal, virtues of fortitude, magnanimity, prudence and justice were classical in origin, but each had received a medieval gloss. Thus fortitude was bound up with the cult of chivalry. At the heart of chivalry lay the profession and practice of arms – fighting – in which the young nobleman was able to display his prowess and through which he won renown. Richard's chivalric credentials are impeccable. Fortitude was the one virtue even his enemies were prepared to allow him. Rous was constrained to say of his end, 'Let me say the truth to his credit: that he bore himself like a noble soldier and despite his little body and feeble strength honourably defended himself to his last breath'.[2] Polydore Vergil, following in the same tradition, stated of Bosworth that 'King Richard alone was killed fighting manfully in the thickest press of his enemies'.[3] His physical courage cannot be doubted. He had fought in two battles under Edward IV when he was eighteen. Perhaps it was the prowess shown in the first, Barnet, as much as his birth, which qualified him to command a division in the second, Tewkesbury. After 1471 he continued to exhibit a desire to win military fame. In 1474 he was reported to be planning a raid into Scotland, even though Edward IV was trying to complete a truce at the time. In 1475 his reluctance to honour the truce earned him a royal reprimand. Later in the year, according to Commynes, he was

The representation of Fortitude as a woman taming wild beasts, from a contemporary manuscript of the Game and Play of Chess. Few would question that Richard possessed this virtue

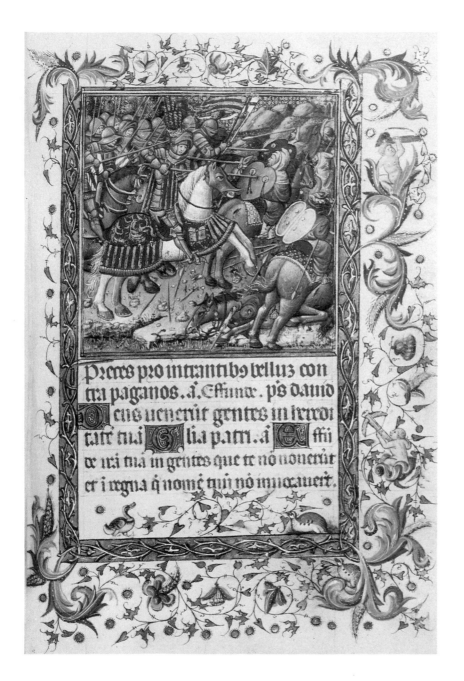

Alphonso V of Aragon doing battle with the Moors in Spain, and the beginning of a prayer for success against the heathen from that king's book of hours. Richard had a similar prayer entered into his own book. His only recorded thoughts are the comments he made to a German visitor to his court, von Poppelau, that he wished to make a crusade against the Saracens

the leader of a group of English captains in Edward IV's army which invaded France who objected to the treaty of Picquigny. He was, however, later brought round by Louis XI who 'gave him some very fine presents, including plate and well-equipped horses'.[4] He too had his price. After 1480, however, he was at long last able to slake his martial thirst against the Scots, which he did with apparent relish and some success. In 1482 he earned the plaudit of his brother

The hermit Ramon Lull, whose treatise was printed by William Caxton with an appeal to Richard III to revitalize English chivalry, here pictured instructing a would-be knight in a copy of The Order of Chivalry *made for Edward IV*

the king who wrote to the Pope that his 'success is so proven that he alone would suffice to chastise the whole kingdom of Scotland'.[5] In 1484 he, himself, in his only reported words, told Nicolas von Poppelau, 'I wish that my kingdom lay upon the confines of Turkey; with my own people alone and without the help of other princes I should like to drive away not only the Turks, but all my foes'.[6]

Richard's chivalric enthusiasm extended beyond personal feats of arms. From the age of seventeen he was constable of England, responsible for maintaining the discipline of chivalry, enforcing the law of arms, and supervising the heralds. He is reputed to have promulgated new ordinances for the heralds in 1478–80; and after he was king he issued a charter of incorporation for them and gave them a house for their headquarters; in effect he established the College of Arms. Richard's zeal seems to have been sufficiently well-known for both William Worcester and William Caxton to dedicate books calling for a chivalric revival to him. Caxton, in an

epilogue to his translation of Ramon Lull's *Order of Chivalry*, one of the standard treatises on chivalry, appealed to Richard as king to institute a programme of uplifting education and tournaments to lure the corrupt youth of the day away from the brothels and gambling dens of London.

> I would it pleased our sovereign lord that twice or thrice a year, or at the least once, he would do cry jousts of peace to the entent that every knight should have horse and harness, and also the use and craft of a knight, and also to tourney one against one, or two against two, and the best to have a prize, a diamond or a jewel, such as should please the prince.[7]

We may reasonably suppose that this epilogue tells us more about what Caxton thought the king would like to hear, than about his own attitude in these matters: he had a book to sell and hoped to

Two knights jousting in the way that would have met the approval of William Caxton. There is no evidence that Richard III, unlike Henry VII after him, did anything to encourage the pursuit of the martial arts through sponsoring tournaments

cash in on the king's campaign for moral rearmament. Chivalry itself appears to have been close to Richard's heart.

Magnanimity literally means greatness of soul. It is the same as big-heartedness or high-mindedness: 'loftiness of mind', as Carmeliano put it. It implied ambition to make the most of oneself and do as much as one could for the world. No one would accuse Richard of lacking ambition. But in the fifteenth century magnanimity also encompassed a more prosaic quality – largesse: open-handedness, generous hospitality, the maintenance of a magnificent estate. Largesse is suggested by the generous fees paid to his retainers and the rewards lavished on them after 1483; by the gifts he bestowed as he passed in his royal progress in 1483; and by his generous benefaction of religious houses. All this was tinged with policy, but whether calculated or not, it served to create a reputation for generosity. More personally one can occasionally get a glimpse of Richard, both as duke and king, in the role of 'magnificent housekeeper' as George Buck described him.[8] The magnificence of his life-style can be guessed from the jewels and silver vessels bought in 1473 from the goldsmith Jacob Faslard and charged to the account of the receiver of Middleham;[9] in the furs and other costly clothes bought for the duke and his 'most dearly beloved consort' on a Christmas shopping spree in London in December 1476, charged on this occasion to the account of his East Anglian receiver;[10] in the lavish celebrations of Christmas in 1484 of which the Crowland Chronicler disapproved; and in the remnants of a substantial feast literally unearthed at Barnard Castle. Richard did not stint on the conspicuous consumption demanded of one in his station. It took more lasting form in the extensive rebuilding he undertook at Middleham, Barnard Castle, Warwick and Nottingham; in Barnard Castle the carved white boars which marked his new works are still to be seen in castle and town.

Recently it has been suggested that Richard was over-lavish in his expenditure and that by 1483 he faced imminent financial collapse.[11] It is hard to prove this. The surviving, isolated estate accounts do not provide enough evidence to discover whether over several years he ran into substantial debt. Advice books to princes stressed that they should exercise prudence in balancing their expenditure against income, that they should not spend beyond their means. An awareness of this is suggested by Richard's employment of Thomas Metcalfe, one of the shrewdest accountants of his day, and his promotion to the position of supervisor of the administration of his northern estates. There is no evidence to suggest, however, that Richard himself took any interest in the minutiae of financial management; this, quite conventionally, he

A wood carving, on a misericord in Westminster Abbey, of a prostitute with a client who dips his hand into his purse. There were many prostitutes in Westminster, plying their trade in the neighbourhood of Caxton's press and no doubt benefiting from the throng of visitors to court

left to others. Improvidence is possible, but is not demonstrable.

The question of the prudence of Richard's service in peace, by which was meant not only his contribution to the common weal, but also good political judgement and the successful pursuit of his own interests, is altogether more complex. Of the loyalty of his service to his brother the king before 1483 there can be no doubt. It can be convincingly argued, too, that in these years he gave good service to the state. Loyalty seems to have reached its limit in 1483 and, as we have seen, the question of Richard's concern for the common good as king remains controversial.

The quality of his own political judgement is difficult to assess. Contemporaries commented on his decisiveness. The Crowland Chronicler remarked that he 'never acted sleepily, but incisively and with the utmost vigilance'.[12] Polydore Vergil heard that he was a

A late fifteenth-century representation of a feast held by Richard III gives an impression of the kind of event that took place from time to time in the great hall of a castle

man 'to be feared for circumspection and celerity' who had 'a sharp wit, provident and subtle'.[13] Intelligence, alertness and decisiveness are not much in doubt. The manner in which he outwitted his rivals in April 1483, tricked Hastings and others in the following June, and allowed Buckingham and other rebels enough rope to hang themselves in October reveals an astute mind. He was a master of political intrigue, but one has to wonder whether he was really so

A lord views building work going ahead on an extension to one of his houses. Richard III, as both duke and king, undertook several such projects

circumspect. Did he have the capacity to stand back and think coolly and impassionately about his long-term interests or the implications of his acts? Mancini commented that 'he rushed headlong' into the usurpation.[14] It has also been argued recently that both the usurpation and the reign provide little more than a story of one ill-considered expediency after another. Richard, it is suggested, 'moved from one unexpected crisis to the next, each time attempting to extricate himself from his immediate difficulties with a bold and decisive stroke'.[15] Giving little thought to the ultimate consequences of his actions, he was seriously limited in both political and human perception. This view is perhaps overharsh in substituting the impulsive fool for the scheming Machiavellian. Not only did he seize power in 1483 with ruthless self-confidence, but also, in presenting himself as intent on maintaining continuity with the previous regime while rooting out corruption and injustice, he demonstrated a shrewd grasp of politics and propaganda. There was a subtle mind at work in this.

Yet, overall, one cannot but question the wisdom of the usurpation itself. It was an act which led directly to his destruction rather than his preservation. It may have been a calculated and carefully staged seizure of power; or, alternatively, it may have happened unintentionally as one expediency led to another. But whichever way one sees it, the consequences were the same; he leapt from the frying pan into the fire. It is in this respect that Richard's political judgement can be questioned. Moreover, as the reign progressed, an air of desperation looms larger and larger. Where in 1485 is the man of 1483? Is the man who humiliated himself in April 1485 with the denial of his intention to marry his niece (the equivalent of a modern television broadcast to the nation assuring viewers that there is no truth in the rumours that he had been involved with a prostitute) the same as the man who in April 1483 ruthlessly seized control of his party? Perhaps his self-confidence and self-belief were undermined by the trials and tribulations of office, or by the personal tragedy of the death of his own son, or even, as later writers speculated, by remorse and guilt. His final months are marked above all by the ill-judged, inept and unrealistic pursuit of his plan to marry his niece, and an incapacity to do anything else but wait for Henry Tudor's landing. And at the final and long-awaited reckoning on the field of Bosworth, impulsive recklessness could well have sealed his fate.

Prudence in a medieval prince needed to be matched by justice. It is in relation to justice that we can begin to observe a disparity between Richard's public image and the inner man. As we have seen, as both duke and king, Richard maintained an avowed commitment to the administration of impartial and effective justice. His declarations and his acts demonstrate that he wanted the weak and the poor to have access to the law against the strong and the rich. It seems, too, that this commitment was known to others who appealed to him for help. However, his commitment to justice did not extend to his own personal interests. It was fine as a general principle applied to the world beneath him; but it had no bearing on his own life. In the division of the Warwick inheritance, in which his brothers as well as he were implicated, he showed no respect whatsoever for the rights of others or for natural justice. True heirs and possessors were disinherited to satisfy his ambition and self-interest. In particular the defenceless countess of Warwick was stripped of her inheritance. It is hard not to believe John Rous's claim that she turned to him for protection whereupon he locked her up for the rest of his life.[16] She did indeed go north in Richard's care in 1473 and she then disappeared from public view until 1485. More fully documented is the treatment of the countess of Oxford, threatened too with imprisonment in Middleham, who was bullied into handing over her estates to Richard in 1473. The importance of the harassment of these two dowagers lies in the revelation of the unscrupulous lengths to which Richard, barely aged twenty, was prepared to go to get his own way. It puts his treatment of his nephews, similarly vulnerable and defenceless in 1483, in a different light. It was not unprecedented or out of character. Respect for the principle of justice was the last thing on Richard's mind on these occasions.

One has further to question whether these were the deeds of a true Christian of genuine piety who was enjoined, among other commandments, not to covet his neighbour's house. However, Richard's acts of charity and declarations of faith were legion and well-attested. He endowed and patronized innumerable religious institutions. Some grants and gifts were small, such as the bell presented to the shipmen's fraternity of Hull; others like contributions to the restoration of the church at Barnard Castle, or the grant of the patronage of Cottingham to support the vicar's choral of York Minster, were more substantial. Some endowments resulted from inherited patronage. The lords of Middleham were the patrons of the nearby Premonstratensian abbey of Coverham. This was a sadly impoverished and lax house by the mid-fifteenth century. It was, therefore, an extension of his responsibility as patron to donate £40 for the repair of the church in 1472 and 1473 (a further £20 was donated in 1483) and to purchase and donate the advowson of Seaham in Durham, worth approxiamtely £15 p.a., in 1476. Richard's generosity as patron stands out in stark contrast to the neglect shown by his predecessors, the earls of Salisbury and Warwick. It is not to be dismissed lightly. It is sadly ironic,

All that is left of Coverham Abbey, near Middleham, the revival of which in the last decades of the fifteenth century owed much to Richard's patronage

therefore, that the credit for the revival of this house by 1500 was later given not to him but to a subsequent abbot. Patronage extended to the promotion and education of the clergy. He gave generously to both Queens' and King's Colleges, Cambridge. He took up and continued the promotion of a group of learned men advanced by George Neville, archbishop of York, notably Thomas Barowe, John Doget, John Gunthorpe, and above all John Shirwood, whom he nominated as bishop of Durham in 1484.

Richard's own foundations were lavish. In 1478 he secured licences to found two collegiate churches, one at Barnard Castle of twelve priests, the other at Middleham of six. These were to serve as

perpetual chantries, offering prayers for the souls of himself, his duchess and his family. In 1483, once king, he set in motion an altogether more ambitious scheme for a college of one hundred priests in York Minster. This project died with him, but work had begun on it and it has plausibly been suggested that it was intended to be his mausoleum, as St George's Windsor had been for Edward IV and Henry VII's chapel was to be at Westminster Abbey. In the event only the Middleham college was established, in 1480, the rector, William Beverley becoming its first dean.

The statutes of Middleham College reveal something of Richard's personal inclinations. Besides the Blessed Virgin Mary, devotion to seven saints was given prominence in the dedication of stalls and the special celebration of their feast days. They were St Anthony, St Barbara, St Catherine, St Cuthbert, St George, St Margaret and St Ninian. St George speaks for himself. Two of the three virgin saints, Barbara and Catherine, had a general appeal – Catherine as the mystical bride of Christ and Barbara as an intercessionary against sudden death; but Margaret, whose intercession was sought by women in childbirth, might have been chosen by his duchess. St Cuthbert was the principal northern saint. Richard was a frequent visitor to his shrine and from 1474 he and his duchess were members of the fraternity in the cathedral which entitled them to participate in divine service. St Ninian, the least well-known, was the principal saint of south-western Scotland based on his shrine at Whithorn in Galloway. He enjoyed a flourishing cult in northern England in the late fifteenth century and was a thoroughly appropriate figure for the warden of the west march to venerate. St Anthony is the most intriguing. His emblem, like Richard's, was a wild pig; in his legend it was the only beast that did not threaten him in the desert. The pig's rejection of evil came to symbolize the saint's triumph over the desires of the flesh. St Anthony's pig was also popularly associated with the runt of the litter. The fact that Richard as the last born was also said to be little is no doubt entirely coincidental.

The statutes of Middleham College also reveal a knowledgeable if conventional grasp of liturgy. While Richard would have relied heavily on the opinion of his spiritual advisers, he probably had the last word on the content. They specify in detail not only the daily round of divine service, but also the annual obits eventually to be celebrated for him and his duchess. There is nothing unusual in making such provision in advance, but the adoption of the liturgical Use of Salisbury (the religious ritual and ceremony more common in southern England), borrowed from Durham in a church in the diocese of York, and the reservation to the duke of the sole right to revise or interpret the statutes indicate a personal interest. His own concern might also be reflected in the injunctions that chaplains should be well educated, but should not 'haunt taverns or other unhonest places or persons at any time'.[17]

The preamble to the statutes emphasizes the idea that Richard was but 'a simple creature, nakedly born into this world, destitute of possessions and inheritances'.[18] Such sentiments lie in a long tradition of spiritual abasement and should not necessarily be read as a sign that he was a secret Lollard or highly conscious of his own personal circumstance as a younger son. It is exceedingly difficult to read states of mind into these documents. His acquired devotional works, a book of hours and the *Visions of Matilda*, copies of which were also owned by his mother, Cecily, duchess of York, who in her latter years was renowned for her piety, were used during moments of private contemplation and prayer. Their possession was conventional. In the book of hours, however, is transcribed a prayer which has given rise to much speculation.

On one page there is the rubric, or preamble to a prayer to

St Julian the Hospitaller, customarily invoked on the eve of a journey. There follows on the next page the body of a prayer in the name of Richard III. Until recently it was assumed that the text was all of one prayer. In fact a whole page is missing, including the body of the prayer to St Julian. They are, therefore, two separate prayers. Moreover, internal evidence establishes that the St Julian prayer was entered sixty years before Richard's reign. Any supposed link between St Julian, who committed a terrible crime in murdering his own parents before winning salvation by a life dedicated to holy works, and Richard III's state of mind is thus unfounded. What one is left with, therefore, is a prayer calling upon 'the most sweet lord, Jesus Christ, to keep me, your servant King Richard and defend me from all evil, from the devil and from all peril, present, past and to come, and deliver me from all tribulations, sorrows and troubles in which I am placed'.[19] The prayer itself was at least one hundred years old, but was adopted and adapted for Richard's needs. It recites how Jesus had relieved a whole army of Old Testament figures from their trials and tribulations including Lot from the city of Sodom, and Susannah from false accusation and testimony. Nothing too particular should be read into this: certainly as evidence for paranoia or even schizophrenia (on the grounds that the accusations were not false) it is wholly inadequate. Moreover it was not unique for a prayer of this kind, dwelling upon the machinations of one's enemies, to be entered into a book of hours; several of Richard's contemporary rulers had copies made for them. However, the unusual length, the exceptional number of biblical precedents and the fact that it was entered into the book only during his reign, suggest that this version existed for a man who felt he had a particular need for divine assistance. It is possible, but no more, that the prayer is another sign that Richard was finding it difficult to cope with the stress he was under.

There was much to Richard III's outward show of piety that was conventional for a man of his birth and station. There was nothing exceptional in being a generous benefactor of Holy Church, a patron of clergy, a founder of chantries, a devotee of his own chosen saints as intercessors, and the owner of devotional works. Perhaps the scale and lavishness of his patronage and foundations can be taken as evidence of more than conventional piety; but equally they might only reflect a desire to impress contemporaries. Impress them it did. Even John Rous, a chantry priest himself, but one of his most hostile critics, was constrained to praise him for his foundations about which he had accurate information. 'He founded a noble chantry for a hundred priests in the Cathedral of York, and another college at Middleham. He founded another in the church of St Mary

of Barking by the Tower, and endowed the Queens' College at Cambridge with 500 marks annual rent.'[20] And Richard's outward show seems to have been founded on a knowledge of liturgy, devotional practice and a need to find solace in prayer. He himself seems to have had few self-doubts and to have been convinced of his own genuine piety. Yet such conviction sits ill with some of his deeds.

In many ways Richard III lived up to contemporary ideals of virtue. Outwardly he was chivalrous, generous, just and pious. As Mancini observed, or was informed, in 1483: 'The good reputation of his private life and public activities powerfully attracted the esteem of strangers'.[21] Not just strangers. He inspired the devoted service of many who came into contact with him, especially those like Lovell, Ratcliffe and Brackenbury who came early into his life and career. Men were prepared to die for him. His tenant, Robert Morton of Bawtry in the far south of Yorkshire, made his will on 20 August 1485, which was shortly afterwards proved, as he was 'going to maintain our most excellent king Richard III against the rebellion raised against him in the land'.[22] A few days later the city fathers of York officially minuted news of Richard's death in famous terms: 'King Richard, late mercifully reigning over us . . . was piteously slain and murdered to the great heaviness of this city'. As late as October the city council still had the courage to refer to him as 'the most famous prince of blessed memory'.[23]

Richard's appeal went beyond the council chamber in York. The most persistent and committed resistance to Henry VII in the north after Bosworth was popular and plebeian in character. Most of the peers and gentry of the region came easily to terms with the new regime; after all they had adjusted just as well after Warwick's downfall in 1471. An ageing Sir John Conyers once more set an example in the art of prudent political accommodation. A few of Richard's closest surviving associates such as Thomas Metcalfe and William Beverley flirted with rebellion in 1486 and 1487. The rebels in 1487 deliberately made for Yorkshire where they believed they would attract widespread support, but they were bitterly disappointed: the north-eastern landed elite already considered the White Rose a lost cause. However, popular disturbances, especially in 1489 and 1491, had a Ricardian undertow. Richard had secured exemption from taxation in town and country and had used his influence to promote the well-being of the region. He was perceived as one who had been a friend of the commons. Sir Francis Bacon, a century or so later commented that Richard's memory 'lay like lees at the bottom of men's hearts, and if the vessel were once stirred it would rise'.[24]

Yet popular opinion, even in northern England, was divided.

(Left) A king, his queen, courtiers and staff of a chapel royal attend mass being celebrated by a bishop. The organist accompanies from the initial letter below. This is precisely the image of his piety that Richard III presented to his subjects

The city of York itself was split. Richard enjoyed the enthusiastic support of a faction with which Thomas Wrangwish, twice mayor and his annuitant, was chiefly associated. After 1485 Wrangwish's group lost control and their opponents, more amenable to Henry VII, took over. Wrangwish himself became involved in the rebellion of 1489 which led to the death of the earl of Northumberland. Even as early as 1482 a saddler in the city was brought before the council for having used seditious words against the duke of Gloucester. He was accused of remarking that the duke was doing little for the city except grinning at it; in modern parlance, one supposes, 'taking the citizens for a ride'.[25] As late as 1491 a quarrel erupted after a few drinks in a York house. A Ricardian, John Painter, gave his opinion that the late earl of Northumberland had betrayed the king. This prompted William Burton, the schoolmaster of St Leonard's Hospital, to launch into a diatribe against Richard III, calling him a hypocrite and a crookback, whom he for one had never loved, and who was deservedly buried in a ditch like a dog.[26] Passions still ran high in York six years after Bosworth. It seems that he was one of those charismatic public figures to whom people react strongly, either enthusiastically for or violently against.

The people of York, like most of his contemporaries, saw only the public figure and image of Richard III. They did not know the inner man who remains elusive to this day. His enjoyments seem to have been conventional. He retained groups of minstrels and players who toured the country as well as performing in his own court. While king he sought the best musicians for his chapel. He perhaps preferred hawking to the chase, for again as king he sent out orders for the best hawks to be found for the royal mews. It has been said by some that his personal life was beyond reproach. It was so only if one is prepared to overlook the fathering of two illegitimate children, John and Katherine, probably before he was married. We may perhaps accept the double standard that used to condemn premarital sexual intercourse by women, but condone the sowing of wild oats by men. But is it as easy to accept the other double standard by which Richard self-righteously castigated his enemies for themselves procreating or being descended from bastards? His marriage with Anne Neville was probably, like most marriages, a match determined by political and material considerations. It may, as is suggested by reference to his 'most dearly beloved consort' in such an unlikely place as an estate account, have blossomed into a relationship of affection. But such affection would seem to have run its course by 1485, for when Queen Anne lay dying his reluctance to visit and comfort her led to disapproving gossip and fed rumours that he had poisoned her.

(Right) A falconer rewards his hawk in a detail from one of the Devonshire Tapestries woven earlier in the century. It would seem that Richard himself preferred hawking to hunting

Minstrels with pipes and tabors, such as Richard III retained, entertain a court in which sensual pleasure appears to hold sway. The man in the centre seems to be particularly pleased to be dancing with his partner. The illustration is from a copy of the Romance of Gyron le Courtois

Richard made much of his desire to see a reformation of morals and a purge of licentiousness: 'our principal intent and fervent desire', he informed his bishops in 1484, 'is to see virtue and cleanness of living to be advanced, increased and multiplied and vices and all other things repugnant to virtue, provoking the high indignation and fearful displeasure of God, to be repressed and annulled'.[27] He blackened the names of his enemies for their moral transgressions and inadequacies. It is possible that this was a reflection of his own obsessive prurience; or it may have been the product of a calculated and cynical propaganda campaign. Independent evidence is hard to come by. On the one hand his statutes for

Middleham College enjoined the chaplains not to associate with 'dishonest persons' (prostitutes?) and his attachment to the ascetic St Anthony who triumphed over the temptations of the flesh suggest a puritan; on the other hand his court was considered too hedonistic by the Crowland Chronicler and in September 1483 Thomas Langton appears to have commented to his friend, the prior of Christ Church, Canterbury, that 'sensual pleasure holds sway to an increasing extent'.[28] Caxton, as we have seen, considered it commercially worthwhile to promote a book by appealing to Richard's known enthusiasm for chivalry and much publicized disapproval of houses of ill-repute. However, whichever way we look at it, Richard does not emerge in a particularly attractive light. Either he was a prig or he was a hypocrite.

In the final analysis there appear to have been profound contradictions in Richard's behaviour, and perhaps, therefore, in his personality. The antiquary William Hutton may well have been correct when he commented that he bore 'the greatest contrariety of

A contemporary image of a hypocrite feigning holiness reflects the view held by some, then and now, that Richard merely put on the show and countenance of piety

character'.[29] He was a complex man. But one should not assume that his personality never changed. In the early 1470s he seems to have behaved with the impetuosity and impatience of youth. After 1475 he seems to have settled down as he became more secure and confident in himself and his place in the world. Perhaps in 1483 all the old uncertainties and anxieties were reawakened and the impetuosity of his earlier years resurfaced. It is worth remembering that he was still only thirty when he usurped the throne. Yet, even if one allows for the impatience of youth, there remains an unsettling discordance between the public show of moral rectitude and the lack of apparent moral constraint in some of the things he did. It may well be that he was a man capable of extreme self-deception; that he was so confident of his own ability and morality that he was able to convince himself that he alone had the talent and right to rule in 1483; and that in ensuring this end he could do no wrong. Was he one whose conviction of his own superiority induced the belief that it was inconceivable for him to act basely and that, therefore, anything he did was, by definition, justified? Did he believe that his own virtue entitled him to be above the law? Did he delude himself that such flagrant disregard for the right of inheritance to the Crown would be welcomed by a grateful realm?

After 1483 Richard seems to have changed again. The self-confidence and assurance so apparent in that year apparently evaporated during 1484. It may be that he began to comprehend the enormity of what he had done. The devastating death of his son and heir in March 1484 may well have been interpreted by him, as well as by his contemporaries, as an act of divine retribution. 'How vain are the attempts of man to regulate his affairs without God', intoned the Crowland Chronicler when he told of the prince's death.[30] The blow might have shattered his confidence in his own invincibility. He lost, if he ever had held, the trust of his subjects. Bills were forever being posted and rumours circulated which challenged his right to rule. His enemies seized the initiative; he resorted to more desperate ploys to secure himself. His chosen prayer might suggest too that he was beginning to feel the strain. Eyewitness descriptions given later to Polydore Vergil that 'while he was thinking of any matter, he did continually bite his nether lip' and that he was constantly pulling his dagger in and out of its sheath, similarly suggest a state of high anxiety.[31] The survivors of Bosworth seem to have known of the restless and troubled night he spent before the battle which was duly recorded six months later by the Crowland Chronicler:

> The king, so it was reported, had seen that night, in a terrible dream, a multitude of demons apparently surrounding him,

A man tormented by demons lies on his bed as death strikes. Stories that Richard's last night on earth was disturbed by such a nightmare, and that he failed to celebrate mass before the battle, conjured up the image of a sinner going to his death unshriven

just as he attested in the morning when he presented a countenance which was always drawn but was then even more pale and deathly.[32]

Perhaps Thomas More had indeed 'heard by credible report of such as were secret with his chamberers that, after this abominable deed done, he never had quiet in his mind, he never thought himself sure'.[33] Was Richard in his last months beginning to crack under stress?

Richard III's Books

Richard III owned several books, mainly of a religious, chivalric or romantic nature. Most were unadorned and have been well-thumbed, which has led historians to suppose that they were for reading not display. One of the more richly illuminated pages in an otherwise plain book of hours was the Annunciation.

Like his mother, Cecily, duchess of York, Richard owned a copy of the *Visions of Matilda*, a popular devotional work. Many of the pages in the copy he owned were heavily annotated, but it is not known by whose hand.

de la cruaute de ceulz de biauuoisin et uint le re
gent sen vi de meaulz pour aler a sens.

En ce temps se montephcient mil
les gens de biauuoisins et le rsineu
rent et assemblerent pluss autres
en diuerses flotes en la terre de mont morency
et abatirent et ardirent toutes les maisons
et chasteaulz de montmorency et des autres ge
tilz homes du pais Et ainsi se firent autres af
semblees de telles gens en mucien et es autres
lieux denuiron. Et en ces assemblees auoit
le plus de gens de labour. Et si y auoit de riches
hommes bourgois et autres. Et touz getilz
hommes que ilz pouoient trouuer il tuoient
et si faisoient ilz gentilz femmes et pluss enfans
qui paroit trop grant foiseneue. En cel
temps le du regent qui estoit ou meurhe
de meaulz qui auoit fait enforcier et enforcoir
de iour en iour senparti et sen ala ou chastel
de monsterel ou fort dionne. Et asses tost aps
senparti et alla en la cite de sens en la quelle
il entra le samedi xe iour de uing ensui
uant au matin. En la quelle cite il fu receu
par les gens dicelle honorablement si come
ilz le deuoient faire come a leur droit seigne
apres le roy de france son pere. Et toutesuoies
auoit lors peu de villes cites et autres en la
languedoc qui ne feussent meues contre les
gentilz hommes tout en faueur de ceulz de paris
qui trop les haioient come pour le mouue
ment du peuple. Et neant moins il fu
rent receu en la dicte ville de sens a grant
paix et honorablement. Et fist le dit regent
en la dicte cite grant mandement de gens
darmes.

Cellui samedi meismes qui estoit
le xe iour du mois de uing lan
mil ccclviii pluss qui estoient par
tiz de la ville de paris iusques au nombre de
.cccc. ou enuiron. des quelz estoit capitaine
un apelle pier giles espicier de paris. Et enui
ron .v. qui sestoient assemblez a alli des quelz
estoit capitaine un apelle iehan baillant p
uost des monnoyes du roy et alerent a meaulz
Et la soit ce que iehan soulaz lors maire de
meaulz et pluss de la dicte ville en eussent
uire au dit regent quilz lui seroient bons et
loyaux et ne souffenroient aucune chose estre
faite contre lui ne contre ne contre son hon
neur neantmoins ilz firent ouurir les por
tes de la dicte ville aus diz de paris et de alli
Et firent mettre par les rues les tables et les
nappes le pain et le vin et les viandes sus
et beurent et mengierent se il uouldrent et
se rafreschirent. Et apres se mistrent en ba
taille en alant droit vers le moihne de la dicte
ville de meaulz ou quel estoit la duchesse de
normendie et sa fille et la seur du dit regent
appellee ma dame ysabel de france qui puis
fu femme du filz le sire de millan et fu contesse
de vertuz que le roy iehan son pere lui dona
en mariage. Et auec eulz estoient le conte
de foiez le seigneur de hangest et pluss autz

Richard Gloucestr

Comment ceulz de paris et de alli furent descõ
fiz a meaulz et de la mort du maire de la dicte
ville appelle Iehan solaz.

A copy of the early fifteenth-century English translation of Vegetius, *De Re Militari* was acquired by Richard as king. This page bears an initial decorated with the arms of his queen.

Richard's copy of *Tristan*, a chilvalric romance, was very plain. This simple decorated page was characteristic of many of Richard's books.

Most royal books were lavishly illustrated, suggesting that they were acquired for show as well as for reading aloud. Here, from a copy of Colonna's *History of the Destruction of Troy* acquired by the royal library by 1535, Hector, one of the great military heroes of the Middle Ages, goes into battle against the Greeks. Richard also owned an unadorned copy of this chilvalric work.

Richard III was a man of considerable ability, energy and attractiveness. His chivalry, in particular, in an age which highly valued such martial qualities in a young nobleman, warmly commended him to his contemporaries. He was also a man having to cope with the insecurity and uncertainty of being a younger son without his own inheritance, despite all his advantages of birth and favour. It was no doubt frustrating for a man of his restless ability to accept the constraints imposed by his circumstances. It was his tragedy that his ambition, and his sense of his own worth and importance, led him to disregard all law and right in the pursuit of his own interests. He did not hesitate to kill to make himself king. What he did in 1483 both surprised and horrified contemporaries not only because it was so unexpected of him, but also because it went beyond the bounds of contemporary political ethics. Richard lacked the moral courage to face fatefully and with fortitude the uncertainties and risks of the future in 1483.

We may speculate about Richard III's mental state, but precisely how he thought, why he did what he did, what 'made him tick' will remain speculation for ever. We will never know the inner man. Indeed one wonders whether any of his contemporaries ever knew it. Of this, however, we can be sure: he was not one-dimensional. He was neither a hateful child murderer, nor a paragon of contemporary virtue. He was a man who lived up to several of the ideals of contemporary nobility, yet one who when tested was found wanting. It is possible that he himself came to understand this and that the realization was the cause of great anguish. Nevertheless, he destroyed both himself and the high reputation he had gained as duke of Gloucester by the crimes he committed in order to seize a throne that was not his by right.

Chapter 8

Later Stories of Richard III

The literary dimension to writings about the subject of Richard III and the Princes in the Tower is as evident in the centuries after Shakespeare as it is in his age and earlier. The archetypal story of the wicked guardian established in the sixteenth century held sway, with only the occasional challenge, for a further three hundred years. Indeed at the end of the nineteenth century it was given a powerful endorsement in one of the first of the modern histories to take advantage of the opening up of the public records for research. James Gairdner declared in his *Life and Reign of Richard the Third*, published in 1898, that:

> the attempt to discard tradition in the examination of original sources of history is, in fact, like the attempt to learn an unknown language without a teacher. We lose the benefit of a living interpreter, who may, indeed, misapprehend to some extent the author whom we wish to read; but at least he would save us from innumerable mistakes if we followed his guidance in the first instance.[1]

Gairdner's tradition was the archetypal story. Not surprisingly, therefore, he reiterated the conviction 'that Richard was indeed cruel and unnatural beyond the ordinary measure even of those violent and ferocious times'.[2]

Gairdner has been followed in recent times by such eminent historians as J.R. Lander, Charles Ross and Rosemary Horrox. Lander suggested in 1980 that 'towards the end of his life he [Richard] had become in the highest degree schizophrenic, a criminal self-righteously invoking the protection of the Almighty'.[3] Ross softened Gairdner only to the extent of perceiving him to be no worse than his contemporaries: 'to put Richard thus into the context of his own violent age is not to make him morally a better man, but at least it makes him more understandable'. Taking a more cynical view of the world, he suggested that his failure was more the consequence of political miscalculation than of moral shortcoming.[4] But Dr Horrox in the most recent analysis of that political failure has argued that in deposing his nephew as an act of first resort Richard went beyond what contemporaries regarded as acceptable political behaviour. The deposition of Edward V was both political misjudgement and moral offence.[5] In these modern works, behind the trappings of modern historical scholarship and the front of contemporary political scepticism, Gairdner's tradition, the archetypal story, is still at work.

It is most flamboyantly visible in the pages of Desmond Seward's *Richard III: England's Black Legend* (1983) in which he mischievously claimed that his was 'the most hostile life of Richard III to appear for over a century'. Here is the story of 'the most terrifying man ever to occupy the English throne', an enthusiastic pupil at his brother's feet, who early mastered the art of murder for political ends. Two analogies are deployed to reinforce the image. On the one hand Richard III is likened to a tyrant of the Italian Renaissance, a grim precursor of the Machiavellian Prince; on the other he is a modern boss of organized crime, a Godfather taking over England with his northern 'mafia', employing 'hit men' to make offers which his contemporaries cannot refuse. The 'black legend' Seward asserts was the 'stark reality'.[6] As an up-dating of the archetypal ogre, his tale is nothing if not vivid, but it is hardly as new as the author himself claimed. Indeed, as we have seen, it is the oldest of all the stories of Richard III.

However, an alternative story, hinted at in one or two contemporary and near contemporary sources and occasionally told in the intervening years, has come to the fore in the twentieth century. This story is as follows. A noble young man, who loves his wife and is renowned for his honesty, piety and valour, finds out after the sudden death of his brother the king that his nephews are bastards. He has to choose between accepting an illegitimate boy as king, or reluctantly following the law to allow himself to be elected to the throne. He courageously and unselfishly takes on the burden of kingship. He maintains his nephews honourably as private subjects

*Marlon Brando as Don Corleone
in Francis Ford Coppola's film,*
The Godfather. *Recently
Richard has been likened by a
hostile historian to a mafia boss*

and seeks to rule justly for the common good. But he is surrounded
by corruption and self-seeking enemies. In the final conflict with
them he is betrayed by some of his own followers and dies bravely in
the thick of battle. It is another archetypal story, perhaps the most
common in western literature; the story of a martyrdom. He is a
hero, prepared to die for his principles, even if misunderstood by
many of his contemporaries and traduced by his enemies.

Hints of the story of the saintly brother are to be found in
contemporary sources. Thomas Langton, bishop of St David's,
wrote in September 1483 that 'he contents the people where he goes
best that ever did prince. . . . On my trouth I liked never the
conditions of any prince so well as his'.[7] The city of York, as we

have seen, lamented his 'murder' at Bosworth.[8] And even John Rous, who wrote so scathingly of his villainy after his death, wrote glowingly during his life that:

> the most mighty prince Richard . . . all avarice set aside, ruled his subjects in his realm full commendably, punishing offenders of his laws, especially extortioners and oppressors of his commons, and cherishing those that were virtuous; by the which discreet guiding he got great thank of God and love of all his subjects rich and poor.[9]

From these beginnings an alternative view of Richard III, liberated (it is said) from the malign influence of Tudor propaganda, has developed. It has been a slow and halting progress. The first 'defence' of Richard III by Sir William Cornwallis towards the end of Elizabeth I's reign was a 'paradox', a kind of rhetorical exercise in which the objective was to defend the indefensible. While a Tudor ruled England Richard III's villainy could not seriously be questioned. It was not until after Elizabeth I's death that a writer would dare challenge the established story. George Buck, whose history was first compiled in 1619, was the first to attempt a sincere rehabilitation of the last Plantagenet. He was motivated by a desire to exonerate his own lineage, for an ancestor was one of those attainted after Bosworth and his family had been ruined. Moreover, the Bucks had originally been of Yorkshire stock and George wished to present a different, northern view of Richard III. His work, however, did little more than deny allegations and assert that certain actions were justified by circumstances. There is no sustained attempt in its pages to develop a coherent alternative to the dominant story.

It was not until a century and a half later that the story of the wicked uncle was questioned again. In his *Historic Doubts* of 1768, Horace Walpole applied the philosophy of the Enlightenment to the topic. It was, he argued, unreasonable and irrational to suppose that any man could have behaved as unnaturally as Richard was supposed to have done. The evidence needed irrefutably to demonstrate it. 'All I mean to show', he argued, 'is, that though he may have been as execrable as we are told he was, we have little or no reason to suppose so'. Thus he proceeded to examine sceptically all the supposed evidence for the crimes imputed to Richard, suggesting in passing that Henry VII was 'so much worse and more hateful' that we may believe he invented the slanders against Richard and may well himself have been responsible for the death of at least one of the princes. 'It is perhaps as wise', he concluded, 'to be uncertain on one portion of our history, as to believe so much as is believed in all histories'.[10]

Horace Walpole, a child of the Enlightenment, who initially could not believe that anyone could be as evil as Richard III was traditionally painted, was one of the first to express doubts about the received picture

Walpole's scepticism of the reliablity of history was not particularly novel: a line can be traced back through Dryden and Sidney to Aristotle. Nevertheless his honest (and perhaps slightly tongue-in-cheek) doubts led to a heated private correspondence with Hume and others who seemed to misunderstand his purpose. Twenty-five years later even Walpole himself retracted. After the Terror in Paris he added a postscript in which he recorded his sorrow to have lived to find that in an age called enlightened such horrors could be displayed which he had supposed were impossible even in a dark age. He concluded, therefore, that he must now believe that any atrocity may have been committed by an ambitious prince of the blood aiming at the Crown in the fifteenth century.[11] Walpole's

Marie Antoinette on the way to punishment on the scaffold as sketched by J.L. David. It was the Terror in France in 1793, and the executions of the king and queen in particular, that convinced Walpole that crimes as savage as those attributed to Richard III could indeed be committed by mankind

retraction in an age of revolution has been less frequently noted than his original expression of doubts in an age of enlightenment. Despite it, he laid a path that others were to follow in both questioning the evidence and in shifting blame to Henry VII. However, he did little himself to advance an alternative story.

Indeed nobody until the nineteenth century took up the challenge of not merely doubting or denying, but positively rewriting the story of Richard III. This was left to Caroline Halsted, whose two-volume *Richard III as Duke of Gloucester and King of England*, published in 1844, can claim to be the first full-blooded telling of the tale of the saintly brother. She set out, she claimed, not to 'unduly exalt' her subject 'into a hero of romance', but to rescue his character as a prince 'from those unjust charges which alone derogate from the acknowledged superiority of his princely career'.[12] Nevertheless, despite her avowed intent, she did indeed exalt him. She waxes lyrical about 'his shining abilities, his cultivated mind, his legislative wisdom, his generosity, his clemency'. He did not usurp the throne; his rare talents and ability for government justified his accession to it. An earlier conclusion that it cannot be proved that he killed the princes is subtly transformed into a later assertion of 'his innocence as regards the great catalogue of crimes so long and so unjustly laid to his charge'. Confidently she concludes, 'the day is not far distant when truth and justice will prevail over prejudice'.[13] Romance as well as exaltation intrudes: in the form of a supposed love-match with his Duchess Anne ('the most imaginative mind could scarcely have desired a hero of romance to act a nobler and more chivalric part') and in the description of sublime landscapes as at Barnard Castle ('the situation of the fortress was one of surpassing beauty, embracing as it did some of the finest points of view connected with the wild and picturesque vale of Tees').[14] The tone as well as the narrative structure of the new story was set in these pages.

Caroline Halsted found at least one early convert in a Dr Daniel who in the week beginning 14 November 1859 addressed an audience in the booming new town of Middlesbrough (a not so picturesque part of the vale of Tees) in defence of Richard III. His talk inspired a ringing response from the editor of the *Weekly News*. 'The object of the lecture', the editorial comment of 19 November ran, 'appeared to be to clear away the popular belief, or prejudice as he would call it, with which that monarch's life and conduct is regarded'. But the *Weekly News* remained unimpressed:

> Dr Daniel has failed to adduce any evidence to controvert the facts of history and the character of Richard III remains, to excite the denunciations and reprobation of right-minded men. We are still of the opinion that Richard was one of the vilest among many other great criminals who have sat on the throne of England.[15]

In the last the paper revealed its republican leanings, but it is clear that the alternative interpretation of Richard III still cut little ice.

Indeed, it is only in the twentieth century that Halsted's work has been taken up and sustained. Sir Clements Markham, after a

lively dispute with James Gairdner, reiterated her views more bluntly and less elegantly in his *Richard III: his Life and Character* (1906). His Richard, not so much a romantic hero as a Great Imperial Statesman, who foresaw that feudalism was giving way to the modern world and who might even have solved the Irish Question,[16] was totally exonerated of the crime of murdering the princes. He had maintained them in honourable state until his death. It was Henry VII who stood in the dock and was found guilty.

After Markham there was no going back. His legacy was the foundation of the Fellowship of the White Boar in 1924 by S. Saxon Barton and friends, later the Richard III Society, dedicated to clearing his name. At first a small band of apostles, in recent decades it has expanded into a flourishing and respected historical society, committed to the propagation of research as well as to the clearing of Richard's name. The turning point in the society's fortunes came in the 1950s with the publication of two works:

J.M.W. Turner's watercolour of Barnard Castle, although it took some liberties, captured a similar sense of the sublime to that expressed by Sir Walter Scott in his Rokeby:

> *Old Barnard's towers are*
> *purple still,*
> *To those that gaze from*
> *Toller-hill;*

Caroline Halsted was also inspired by 'the surpassing beauty' of this stretch of the Tees

The face that launched a thousand novels. It was this somewhat anxious image from a late sixteenth-century copy of the standard Tudor portrait of Richard III that convinced Josephine Tey's Inspector Grant that Richard was innocent of the crimes attributed to him

Josephine Tey's, *The Daughter of Time* (1951) and Paul Murray Kendall's *Richard III* (1955).

The Daughter of Time is in effect a dramatization and popularization of Markham. It is to him what Shakespeare was to Vergil. A hospital-confined Detective-Inspector Grant, intrigued by a reproduction of the National Portrait Gallery's picture of Richard ('really quite a nice face') is inspired to solve the mystery of the Princes in the Tower. Grant knows instinctively that the face in the portrait is not the face of a murderer. Assisted by a somewhat implausible American research student, he proves that Henry VII not Richard III committed the crime. That it is Markham's case is neatly acknowledged at the end when the sleuths discover that 'someone called Markham' had already come to the same conclusion years ago.[17]

The twentieth-century hero. James Butler's statue of Richard III in Leicester was commissioned by the Richard III Society and unveiled in 1980 by Princess Alice, Duchess of Gloucester. In a dedicatory message delivered on behalf of her son, Richard, Duke of Gloucester, she declared that the occasion marked not only the acknowledgement of a fine man's achievements but also confidence in the belief that the truth is more powerful than lies

    The Daughter of Time is 'fiction': Kendall's *Richard III* is 'history'. Kendall leans more towards Halsted than Markham. His subject is a romantic hero not a lost statesman. He stands for the honesty and simplicity of the country against the treachery and sophistication of the court. In the pages of this tale, moral rectitude is pitted against corruption and vice. The landscape of Richard's adopted Wensleydale symbolizes his virtue:

Wensleydale was less subdued to man than the softer country-side which Richard had known in the south: a land of scattered castles and abbeys, their villages and fields huddled about them amidst the great wild sweep of moor. . . The earth was gigantic, elemental; leading men's thoughts to God, teaching men the necessity of human ties; confirming men in their feeling for old ways and old things. The people were directly swayed by their instincts, quick to take arms in a quarrel, slow to shift loyalties, earnest in their convictions. Here young Richard, in those impressionable years between nine and thirteen, discovered the native country of his spirit, a country which half created, half affirmed the kind of man he was to be.[18]

The native country of Richard III's spirit is the romance of the knight in shining armour.

The impact of these two works – Josephine Tey's novel and Paul Murray Kendall's biography – can be seen in the publication of at

The moors above Middleham. The wild, 'elemental' grandeur of this landscape provided Paul Murray Kendall with a metaphor of Richard III's personality. It was, he wrote, 'the native country of his spirit'

 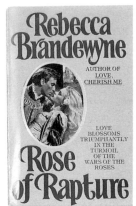 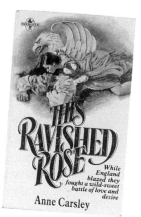

The covers of Ricardian novels encapsulate the popular, romantic nature of their content. They are modern Arthurian tales, woven around the figure of Richard III, a once and future king, standing for a lost world that never was and never will be

least forty novels on Richard, his queen and their household since 1960, thirty-four after 1970. Most seek to exculpate their hero. Romance often flourishes on the fringes of great events. Thus to take one example, Susan Bowden's *In the Shadow of the Crown* (1987) tells the story of Joissy Radcliffe who comes to the duke of Gloucester's household at Middleham as his ward. She loses her inheritance, but finds love with a young man who eventually finds a steady job as horse master at Jervaulx Abbey. Heroines lose more than inheritances in some of these bodice-ripping yarns which have proliferated in the last twenty years. In Rebecca Brandewyne's *Rose of Rapture* (1984), Lady Isabella Ashley escapes both rape and rabies before finding true happiness.

Over a longer period, twenty-four plays have been written for stage or radio, mostly to set Shakespeare straight, including one in which the bard is arraigned in Hell on a charge of falsifying history. One would have thought that the Devil would have approved. More inventively David Edgar's *Dick Deterred* (1974), a parody of Shakespeare, satirized Richard Nixon at the time of the Watergate scandal; and David Pownall's *Richard III: Part Two*, performed by Paine's Plough on the Edinburgh Festival Fringe in 1977, explored the idea through three time shifts (1948, 1984 and 1484) that we continually rewrite our history to justify the current political order.[19] Most recently, in November 1990, the BBC screened Andrew Davies' adaption of Michael Dobbs' novel *House of Cards* which cast the central character, Francis Urquhart, as a latter-day Richard III, confiding in the viewers as he plotted and murdered his way to 10 Downing Street.

As interest in the story of Richard III has intensified, a popular approach has been through the genre of murder mystery or court-room drama. Josephine Tey launched this; and her book is now published as a Penguin Crime Classic. Several books and plays have been produced as investigations into an unsolved murder mystery. Audrey Williamson's *The Mystery of the Princes*, for instance, won the Gold Dagger Award for the best non-fiction crime book in 1978. In 1979 the BBC broadcast a dramatized enquiry based on Elizabeth Jenkins' *The Princes in the Tower* which concluded that the circumstantial evidence against Richard III was strong. The same approach has been developed for the purpose of teaching history in schools. In 1974 Jon Nichol's *Richard III* provided a selection of sources and asked pupils to imagine that they too, like Detective-Inspector Grant, were conducting an enquiry into the disappearance of the princes. Two years later an influential Schools Council History 13–16 Project presented the mystery of the princes as an investigation for pupils who were asked to consider selected evidence for and against and finally decide a verdict of guilty, not guilty or not proven in the case of Richard III and the murder of the princes.

But the ultimate in court-room drama was a four-hour reconstructed trial produced by London Weekend Television in 1984: a kind of Rumpole and the Tower Murders. In a replica of Court Number Four of the Old Bailey, two eminent barristers cross-examined expert witnesses in front of a presiding judge, the late Elwyn Jones, and twelve jurors. The charge was that King Richard III, who was unable to appear in person, did in or about the month of August 1483, in the Tower of London, murder the two princes. The play-acting was unscripted and no one knew what the outcome would be, not even the performers, until the jury delivered its

Jeremy Potter, then chairman of the Richard III Society, convinces the court that Richard did not murder the Princes in the Tower in the London Weekend Television Trial of Richard III in 1984

Cartoons and Caricatures

The figures of Richard III and the princes have from time to time inspired humorous writing and comics. Since 1928, when C.W. Scott-Giles first advanced the hypothesis that *Alice in Wonderland* and *Alice Through the Looking Glass* were important lost sources for Shakespeare's history plays rediscovered by Lewis Carroll, attention has been drawn to the extent to which Carroll drew upon persons and events of the Wars of the Roses to inspire his whimsy. The duchess's baby that turns into a pig is thus identified as Richard III. As Alice remarks when this event occurs, 'If it had grown up, it would have made a dreadfully ugly child but it makes rather a handsome pig, I think'. Tenniel's portrait of the duchess, her dress patterned with white roses, suggests the duchess of York. However, Tenniel's model was the caricature of an old lady attributed to Quentin Massys hanging in the National Gallery.

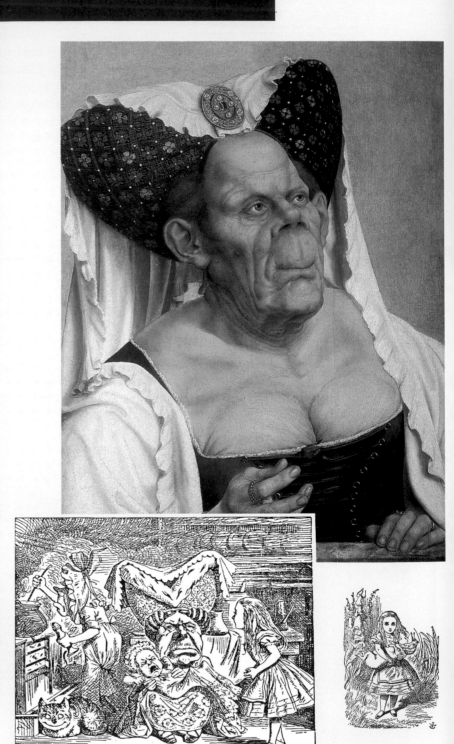

In 1987, *Winters of Discontent* told the story of how Jonny Quest, like Alice, is transported into a different world, but in his case the Tower of London in 1485. Here he found the princes (looking surprisingly like Millais's boys!) alone and well.

They are grateful to their uncle for looking after them so well, as they disclose during a wooden-sword fight.

DO YOU WANT TO SWORDFIGHT, JONIKWEST?

SOMETIMES WE PRACTICE SWORDS BEFORE WE GO TO BED, SO WE CAN SLEEP.

UM... NO THANKS, I THINK YOU'RE TOO GOOD FOR ME.

BUT...≥GASP≥... DOES YOUR UNCLE TREAT YOU... ≥PANT≥... WELL?

WAK!

YES, OF COURSE! WHEN OUR FATHER DIED, HE COULD HAVE THROWN US OUT. BUT HE'S TREATED US LIKE HIS OWN.

SKAK

WE DON'T SEE MUCH OF HIM. HE SPENDS MOST OF HIS TIME IN THE LIBRARY, READING OR WRITING LETTERS. HE SAYS EVEN A PRINCE SHOULD LEARN TO READ.

CAN YOU READ?

SOMETIMES HADJI AND I HAVE **PILLOW** FIGHTS. BUT YOU DON'T HAVE PILLOWS.

Jonny also discovers that there are no pillows in the Tower.

PILLOWS! OF **COURSE** WE DON'T! **NOBODY** SLEEPS ON PILLOWS, 'CEPT **LADIES** WHO ARE HAVING **BABIES**.

PILLOWS FOR SLEEPING ON! WHAT A THOUGHT!

I'VE GATHERED WHAT LOYAL FORCES I COULD. IF WE RIDE HARD, WE CAN STOP THE INVASION FORCE AT BOSWORTH FIELD, WITH LUCK.

BOSWORTH? BUT BOSWORTH'S WHERE SHAKESPEARE SAYS YOU...YOU...

YES, I KNOW. PERHAPS HE'S WRONG ABOUT THAT, TOO.

BUT IN CASE HE'S NOT, I'M HAVING THE PRINCES SENT AWAY TO FRIENDS OF MINE IN THE NORTH.

BUT WE WANT TO GO WITH YOU, SIRE! WE'RE WARRIORS!

Having saved the gentle and scholarly Richard from an assassination attempt, Jonny then helps the princes to escape while the king sets off to meet his fate at Bosworth.

DON'T STOP FOR ANYTHING! GET AWAY! **RUN!**

KILL ME THAT INTERFERING SPROUT!

Anne Stanyon's *Prove It!* is a lively school text book which explores through comic strip several historical mysteries, including the Princes in the Tower. A 'presenter' sets the question.

Alternatives are put. On the one hand the discovery of the bones seems to confirm More's story.

On the other hand the princes may have survived.

verdict. Mr Dillon for the defence, skilfully turning expert witnesses inside out, triumphantly pulled it off, convincing the jury that it could not convict even on a balance of probabilities.[20]

In the late 1980s Richard III was put into comic strip. Anne Stanyon inventively presented several historical mysteries in this form in her schools' text book, *Prove It! Interpretations in History* (1988). In this a trendy television presenter leads the reader/viewer through a did-he-or-didn't-he investigation. The most original treatment is to be found in *Winters of Discontent*, Jonny Quest, number 10, published by the Comico Company, Norristown PA in 1987. In these pages Richard III receives the *Back to the Future* treatment as executed by Hanna-Barbera. Jonny, who has just seen a performance of Shakespeare's play, is transported back to 1485 by a time machine. Here, to his amazement, he finds a gentle and studious Richard ('Taste steel, milksop', cries a would-be assassin), whose nephews are grateful for the kind way he has treated them. Jonny has arrived just in time to help them to escape death at the hands of Richard's enemies ('I'm having the princes sent away to friends of mine in the north'), before Richard himself goes off to meet his doom at Bosworth.[21]

The comic strip is a characteristic late twentieth-century genre in which to retell the stories of Richard III. *Winters of Discontent* picked up another recent feature, found in conventional historical writing, which was to equate a regional division between north and south, as perceived to have existed in Thatcher's England, with a similar divison then in Yorkist England. It was Kendall who reminded his readers that Richard was a man of the north. It is a well-established and well-documented association running back to the city of York's much quoted eulogy. Tudor historians were conscious of it. Edward Hall remarked in passing that the people of the north entirely loved and highly favoured him;[22] the idea found its way into Bacon's history of Henry VII; and Buck, in more effusive terms, repeated that he was 'generally well beloved and honoured of all the northern people, his countrymen, not only for his greatness and allies, but also (and chiefly) because he was a valiant, wise and a bountiful and liberal prince'.[24] Later northern historians tended to be embarrassed by this close association, being either puzzled by the evidence or seeking to deny it. Not until 1859 was a northerner, James Raine jun. (perhaps converted by Dr Daniel on his lecture tour) prepared once more to be fulsome in his praise: 'rarely if ever has there been a prince in the north so universally beloved as Richard III'.[25]

In recent historical writing the northern connections of Richard III have been given their full weight, especially as a political factor in his career. Larger theories have been advanced that England in the fifteenth century was deeply divided. 'Then as now', Jeremy Potter suggested in 1983, 'England was two nations, and the events of Richard III's reign are best seen through the perspective of north versus south'.[26] A year later Professor Frank Musgrove explained the miners' strike of 1984 partly in those terms. 'The conflict between north and south', he argued, had 'its roots deep in medieval history'. For instance, 'in the time of Richard of Gloucester (who later became Richard III) Wensleydale was the centre of political power'.[27] Professor Musgrove's remarks were very much in accord with the views of many political commentators who perceived in the 1980s a deep division between a dominant south and an unregarded north held in contempt by a home-counties political establishment. Then as now, perhaps, the story of the wicked uncle was the story of the south-eastern political elite; the story of the saintly brother was the story of the north.

There are thus two stories of Richard III in circulation in the late twentieth century. They have an appeal today as great as at any time in the last five hundred years, but their fundamental attraction lies in their being cast in archetypal moulds. It is because history is a form of story-telling and because two conflicting archetypal stories have been created around the lives and deaths of Richard and his nephews that the same stories will continue to be told and retold. There is no escaping the conditioning of centuries. The modern historian may try to insist that his story is genuinely independent and objective, but his readers will soon discover where he stands.

As the story has been unfolded in these pages, as readers will have observed (some with dismay), it has more closely fitted the archetype of the wicked guardian than the pattern of the saintly brother. But perhaps there is a third story, as yet untold, which might offer a way of reconciling conflicting views. This story is that told by Shakespeare in *Macbeth* of a tragic hero destroyed by irresistable ambition. Richard's life *was* a tragedy. So much promise and potential was ruined by a ruthless disregard for the rights of others in the pursuit of power. And like Aristotelian tragedy the stories of both *Macbeth* and Richard III can strike fear and pity in the beholder. The fear lies in the realization that a man is capable of such acts as were committed to seize power (the killing of a king who is a guest or the destruction of the nephews who are wards); the pity lies in the awareness that men of such honour and renown, so admired and respected, could do such things. Perhaps it is the pity, the shame of it, that remains above all; that a man of such apparent virtue as Richard should have destroyed both himself and so many others to satisfy his ambition.

This story, too, is hinted at by a contemporary, who, appropriately, might have the last word. Robert Fabyan was a London draper of almost exactly the same age as Richard. He was in London and an observer of the dramatic events of the summer of 1483. Some twenty-five years later, in his continuation to the *Great Chronicle* of London, he wrote down, in sadness more than anger, his considered assessment of the infamous king who had been Richard III:

> Had he suffered the children to have prospered he would have been lauded over all; whereas now his fame is darked and dishonoured as far as he is known.[28]

A bedesman prays for the soul of the departed at the foot of the effigy of Edward Redman (one-time retainer of Richard III) in All Saints', Harewood, West Yorkshire

Appendix: Selected Documents

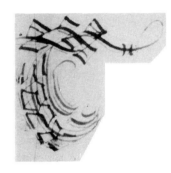he first of these three hitherto unpublished documents illustrates one aspect of Richard, duke of Gloucester's 'good and benevolent' lordship in the north – his offering his services as an arbitrator of local quarrels. The text of the arbitration made by Gloucester of differences between Richard Clervaux of Croft and his neighbour Roland Place of Halnaby is preserved in the Clervaux Cartulary, a book containing copies of title deeds and related documents compiled by Richard Clervaux himself. Neither Clervaux nor Place was a retainer of the duke at the time, but they lived in the district he dominated and Clervaux was in fact a distant kinsman. The quarrel in Croft may have derived in part from the recent grant of the right of free warreny (the privilege to hunt lesser game such as foxes and hare) which might have brought him rapidly into the conflict with his neighbour referred to in one of the clauses. The award did not immediately settle all differences between the two. Two years later the guarantors were called in to decide on the ownership and responsibility for the maintenance of a dyke that ran between their properties, but this is the last recorded matter of dispute. It has been suggested that a lasting reconciliation between the two was marked by their jointly building a new porch to the parish church, for the arms of Clervaux and Place with the initials 'R C' and 'R P', now set in the tower, were before reconstruction in 1878 set over the door. Visitors to the church will also note that the

descendants of Clervaux and Place still keep to the sides of the church agreed in 1478. Richard Clervaux's vast tomb stands in the Clervaux chapel in the south aisle and the north side of the nave is dominated by a seventeenth-century family pew installed by the Milbanks, successors to the Place family at Halnaby. For further information see my 'Richard Clervaux of Croft: a North Riding Squire in the Fifteenth Century', in *The Yorkshire Archaeological Journal*, 50 (1978). I am grateful to Mr William Chaytor for permission to publish the text.

The second document, a letter from Richard of Gloucester to Sir Robert Claxton of Horden, Co. Durham, gives substance to Richard's reputation as the champion of the weak against the strong. Not only was Claxton one of the county elite, but he was also the father of one of Gloucester's retainers (his illegitimate son, Lionel) and the father-in-law of another (Richard Conyers of Ulshaw). The tone of the letter is peremptory and high-handed, and the confidence with which Richard offers his own independent remedy reveals the extent to which by 1480 he dominated the politics and government of the county palatine, nominally ruled by its bishop, William Dudley. Furthermore the reference to the duke's learned counsel (his lawyers) meeting at Raby gives an early indication that he had already acquired, by means and in circumstances as yet unknown, a foothold in the possessions of the old and infirm earl of Westmorland and his family. The matter at issue between Claxton and Randson may well have been the possession of a messuage and eighty acres of arable land at Burntoft in the county. In the autumn of 1482 Claxton granted this property to Randson. The deeds were witnessed by two of Gloucester's local retainers. This might represent the final settlement of the dispute in Randson's favour. For further discussion see my 'St Cuthbert and the Hog: Richard III and the County Palatine of Durham, 1471–85', in R.A. Griffiths and J.W. Sherborne, eds., *Kings and Nobles in the Later Middle Ages* (Gloucester, 1986), esp. p. 120. I am grateful to Geoffrey Wheeler for supplying me with a photocopy of the document and for his advice on the dating.

The third and last document is one which was overlooked by James Raine in his selection of letters for publication from the letter book of the Priory of Durham. This is probably because it was undated and not because it concerned Richard III towards whom he showed a strong antipathy. However, it is clear from internal evidence that it dates from the first year of Richard's reign. The king to whom Sir Richard Ratcliffe was so close could have been none other than him; and Robert Ebbchester died on 24 June 1484. The letter gives powerful and otherwise unsuspected testimony to the influence exercised by Ratcliffe in the county palatine ('our country'), as well as confirming the close relationship that had existed between Richard as duke of Gloucester and Ebbchester's predecessor, Richard Bell. Regrettably the principal record of the administration of the palatinate, the patent roll of its chancery, is missing for the years 1483–90, so it is not possible to establish what official role Ratcliffe came to play in its affairs. The bishop seeking promotion for his man was Richard Redman, bishop of St Asaph, himself close to the king. He would fully have appreciated the force of Ebbchester's argument. I have not, as yet, discovered whether William Brown did eventually receive preferment from the priory. See my 'St Cuthbert and the Hog', loc cit, for further discussion. I am grateful to Pat Mussett of the Department of Palaeography and Diplomatic at the University of Durham for a photocopy of this letter.

Editorial Note

The original spellings in the documents have been retained except with v and u, i and j. Abbreviations and contractions have been expanded. Modern punctuation has been introduced where it has been judged necessary to clarify the meaning.

1) *Arbitration Award by Richard of Gloucester, 12 April 1478.*

Richard duc of Gloucestre, Great Chamberlayn, Constable and Admirall of England to all maner of men to whom this our present awarde indented shall cum, greting. Know ye that, where Richard Clervaux squier on the one parte and Roland Playce squier on that other part by there seilett obligations bering date the xxth day of Marche the xviii yere of the Reigne of kyng Edward the iiiith ben and stand bounden un to us either in c li. sterling upon condicon that if they and either of them and all other them belongyng fro hensfurth be of gude bering and also stand, performe and fullfyl our doome, ordenance and awarde of and upon all maner actions, sutes, quarelles, trespasses, offences, dettes, debates and demandes betwene them before the date of the sayd obligacions hadde done, caused, hanging, moved or sturrid so that our sayd dome, ordenaunce and awarde be made and geven by us the sayde duc to thame on this syde the fest of the Nativite of Saint John Baptiste then next follwyng, as by the sayde obligacions and conditions more playnly may appere, we the saide duc tendiryng the peas and welle of the contre where the saide parties doue inhabite and also gladly willyng gode concorde, rest and frendly unite to be hadde fro hensfurth betwene the sayde partes, take upon us the charge of Arbetrement, ordenaunce and jugement of, in and upon the premises and for the fynale appeasing and cessing of the same, after ritht deliberation had, make owre awarde, ordenaunce and dome in maner and form follwyng: that is to say Furst we, the sayde duc, awarde, ordeyn and deme that all maters of compleynt and variance before the date of this our present awarde had and gevyn be, by both parties, clerly remitted and set aparte everich enens oyther forever, and that as welle the sayde Richard as the sayd Roland at all tymes after shall be of gude beryng and demenynit aither enens other and that nowder of thame shall brake nor cause to be broken the peas of the kyng oure soverayn lorde aneynst other. Allso we awarde, ordeyne and deme that as welle the sayde Richard as the sayde Roland betwyx this and pasch next comyng shall sufficiently ffence or make to be fenced with dike, qwyksalle, pale or heege the boundes of there severell groundes and pastures and meadowes and them from hensfurth to kepe and upholde so that the catall belongyng them or any their tenants come not into everich others grounde through defaute of closure. And if it happen in the mene seson the catall of the sayd Richard or hys tenands through the defaute of closure of the sayde Roland or hys tenandes come or breke in to hys grownde, the sayde Roland nor hys tenandes in no wyse shall pynde them nor take amends for the hurte but esely dryffe thame of hys grownde. And in lyke wysse yf it happyn in the mene seson the catall of the sayd Roland or hys tenaunts throughe the defaute of closure of the sayde Richard or hys tenaunts come or breke into hys grounde, the sayde Richard nor hys tenaunts in no waysse shall not pynde them nor take amendes for the hurte but easely dryve thame of his grounde. Allso we awarde, ordeyne and deme that ye sayde Richard Clarvaux frohensfurth shall hold hym content for ever with such land lyeng in Crofte as he has in exchange of the sayde Roland for landes lyeng in Jolby and in lyke wysse the sayde Roland Playce frohensfurth shall hold hym content forever with such landes liyng in Jolby aforsayd as he hath in eschange of the sayde Richard for the sayde landes liying in Crofte acordyng to the evydens of the sayde eschange made and true entent of the same. Allso we awarde, ordeyne and deme that the sayd Richard Clarvaux and hys wyffe from hensfurth shall holde thame content to sitt in there parishe churche chaunsell on the southside in such places as he and hys ancestics and theire wyffes heretofore have allways used to sitte and none other wysse attene to make their syttynge within the sayde church or chaunsell. And in lyke wysse the sayde Roland and hys wyffe from hensfurth shall holde thame content to sitt in the sayde parish church chaunsell on the north syde in such places as he and hys ancestres and thaire wyffes hertofore have allweise usyd to sitt and none other wyse to attene to make there syttyng within the sayde church or chaunsell. Allso we awarde, ordyne and deme that the sayd Richard in nowyse fro hensfurth shall beleve, take to his service or reteigne to do hym service any servaunt or tenaunt belongyng to the sayd Rouland or dwellyng upon the grounde, landes and tenementes of the sayd Rouland or of any other mens ground, landes and tenementes where of the sayde Rouland hayth or shall have the rule and governance. And in lyke wyse the sayd Rouland in nowysse from hensfurth shall beleve, take to hys service or reteigne to do hym service any servaunt or tenaunt belongynge to the sayde Richard or dwellyng upon the grounde, landes or tenementes of the sayde Richard or of any other menes grounde, lands and tenements where of the sayd Richard hayth or shall have the rule and governans. Allso we awarde and ordeyn and deme that the sayde Richard in nowyse fro hensfurth shall hunt, hawke, fishe or foule the severell grounds of the sayde Rowland beyng warren withoute hys wylle and licence. And in lyke wyse the sayd Rouland in nowysse from hensfurth shall hunt, hawke, fysshe or fowle the severell ground of the sayd Richard being warren withowte hys wylle and licence. And if it happyn any of the hundes of the sayde Richard hereafter to be caste of or let ronne within hys awne grounde to any game and in the folowyng the same come in to the severell grounde of the sayde Rouland, the sayde Richard shall not passe hys awne grounde in folowyng hys sayde hundes but strake and blaw for thame enlesse he be licenced by the sayde Rouland to follow them. And if the sayd Rouland fynde the hundes of the sayd Richard so folowynge the game upon his grounde he shall rebuke thame and no noder hurt ne damage do thame. And in likewysse if it happyn any of the hundes of the sayde Rouland hereafter to be cast of or lett renne within hys awne grownde to any game and in folowyng the same come in to the severell grounde of the sayde Richard, the sayde Rouland shall not passe hys awne grounde in folowynge hys sayde hundes but strake and blaw for thame enlesse he be lycencyd by the sayde Richard to folow thame. And if the sayd Richard fynde the hundes of the sayde Rouland so folowyng the game upon hys grounde he shall rebuke thame and no noder hurt ne damage do thame. Allso we award, ordeyne and deme that in case hereafter any contravension, offence or unkyndness happyn to falle betwene the sayde partes than we wolle that the parte so fyndynge hym grevyd shall shewe hys greffe fro tyme to tyme to Thomas Mountfort, William Burght squires, Sir William Pudsay parson of Bolton and Thomas Franke squier by us indeferently named to here, examyne and fynally to determyne the same as ofte as the case so shall require. And if the sayde greffe be of such weight that thai in no wysse can nor may appeasse the same, than thai show unto us the cause why they ne so can do to the intent and effecte that we thereupon may determyne the same wych we wolle that they shall reste upon as ofte as the cause so shall require thes premisses and everich of thame truely to be observyd and kept by the said partes and aither of theme upon payne of forfaiture of their sayde obligacions. In wyttenes where of to ayther parte of this our present awarde, ordenance and dome indented we have set our seale and signe manuell, gevyn at our castell of Meddelham the xiith day of Aprile the xviii yere of the Reigne of Kynge Edwarde the iiiith.

(North Riding County Record Office, Clervaux Cartulary, ZQH 1, fos 155–6)

2) *Richard of Gloucester to Sir Robert Claxton of Horden, 12 August 1480*

The Duc of Gloucester, Gret Chamberleyn, Constable and Admirall of England.

Right welbeloved we grete you wele. And merveille gretly that according to oure lettres to you late direct for one John Randson ye have not peasibly sufferd him to maynure and occupie suche lyvelode to him of right appertaining as is by you ayenst all right and conscience from him witholden as by his pitueuse complaint to us shewed we be enformed; nor also have comen your self or have sent unto us and our lerned counsell to Raby suche your counsell with your evidence as we might have bene assertened of the trough of your title therof according to our desire, but by meanys and excuses delaith the said John therof as he seith. We moved of pite gladly willing him to have according to his right woll therfore and eftsones advise you all excusaciones and delaies laide apart that now at this next sessione to be holden at Duresme ye in your owne persone or suche other as ye trust be afore our lerned counsell ther with your evidence as in like wise the said John for his part shallbe. Where that at right woll shalbe duly mynystered unto you without delaie not failing therefore therof as ye entend to do unto us singuler pleasure. And so demeane you herin that we have no cause to provide his lawfull remedy in this behalve. Yoven under our signet at our castell of Barnard Castell the xiith day of August

(Washington DC, Library of Congress, Thatcher, 1004)

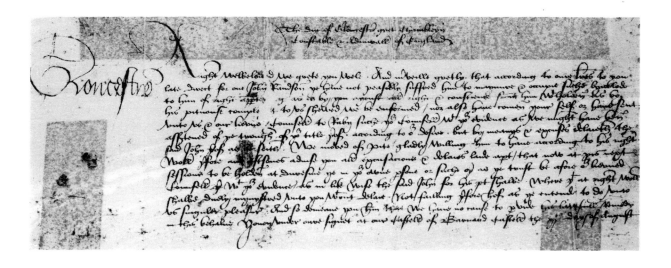

3) Robert Ebbchester, Prior of Durham to Richard Redman, Bishop of St Asaph, c. 1483–4

Littera missa Domino Episcipo Assenense

Right reverent fader in God and my especiall good lord with my most humble reverence I recommend me to your goode lordship praing youre goode lordshipe that ye wull stond als goode and tendre lord to my bretheren and me as ye have doon aforetyme. And whereas ye wrote to me for the next avoydance of the vicariage of Meryngton being of patronage to the behofe of master William Browne youre lordship shal understond that Sir Richard Ratcliffe shewyd to me with witnesses therupon how that he had a graunt therof by my predecessore afore desiryng of me to ratify the same wheropon with advise of my bretheren considering the gret rewll that he berith under the kynges grace in oure cuntrey maid a graunt to hym of the sayd vicariage if the [*] that he shuld propose to us were found able and so in this matter I may not please youre goode lordshipe. I will shew to the seyd master Wyllyam in tyme comyng more speciall favores to help to his provissyon as sone as I may conveniently certain of myne own frendes provydyd fore. And Almyghty God have youe in his most blessyd kepyng.

(Durham, Dean and Chapter Muniments, Reg. Parv. III, fo. 188 v)

* A word is missing here, but from the sense of the passage it is clear that the author refers to Ratcliffe's nominee.

Sources

Abbreviations

Crowland	*The Crowland Chronicle Continuations, 1459–1486*, Nicholas Pronay and John Cox, (eds.) Richard III and Yorkist History Trust, Gloucester, 1986
Great Chronicle	*The Great Chronicle of London*, A.H. Thomas and I.D. Thornley (eds.), 1938
Harley 433	*British Library Harleian Manuscript 433*, R.E. Horrox and P.W. Hammond (eds.), 4 vols, 1979–83
Mancini	Dominic Mancini, *The Usurpation of Richard III*, C.A.J. Armstrong (ed.), 2nd edn., Oxford, 1969
More	Sir Thomas More, *The History of King Richard III*, R.S. Sylvester (ed.), Newhaven, 1976
Rot Parl	*Rotuli Parliamentorum*, J. Strachey and others (eds.), VI, 1777
Rous	'John Rous's account of the reign of Richard III', translated from *Historia Regum Angliae* in Alison Hanham, *Richard III and His Early Historians*, Oxford, 1975, pp. 118–24
Vergil	*Three Books of Polydore Vergil's English History*, H. Ellis (ed.), Camden Society, 1844
YCR	*York Civic Records*, A. Raine (ed.), I and II, Yorkshire Archaeological Society, Record Series, 98 (1939) and 103 (1941)

Chapter 1 *(pp. 1–22)*

1 Sir Philip Sidney, *An Apology for Poetry*, G. Shepherd (ed.) (Manchester, 1973), p. 105.

2 J.O. Halliwell, *Letters of the Kings of England*, Vol.1 (1846), p. 161.

3 YCR, I, p. 125; *Rot Parl*, p. 276.

4 Crowland, p. 183.

5 *Christ Church Letters*, J.B. Sheppard (ed.) (Camden, New Series, Vol. 19, 1877), p. 46.

6 Mancini, p. 57.

7 Ibid., pp. 61, 63, 83, 95.

8 P. Tudor Craig, *Richard III*, 2nd edn. (National Portrait Gallery, 1977), p. 95.

9 Rous, p. 120.

10 Vergil, p. 227.

11 More, p. 9.

12 Crowland, p. 181.

13 More, p. 89.

14 Vergil, p. 226.

15 Rous, p. 121.

16 *YCR*, Vol. II, pp. 71–3.

17 More, p. 8.

18 Mancini, p. 137.

19 Sir George Buck, *The History of King Richard III (1619)*, A.N. Kincaid (ed.) (Gloucester, 1979), Appendix A, pp. 319–21.

20 William Shakespeare, *King Henry VI, Part Three*, Act 3, Scene 2.

21 Ibid., Act 5, Scene 6.

22 Thomas Percy, *Reliques of Ancient English Poetry*, H.B. Wheatley (ed.), Vol. 3 (1885), pp. 172–6.

23 Ibid., p. 175.

24 Shakespeare, *King Richard III*, Act 4, Scene 3, ll. 4–11.

25 Percy, *Reliques*, 3, p. 174.

26 Shakespeare, *King Richard III*, Act 1, Scene 3, ll. 347–8.

27 C.A. Halsted, *Richard III as Duke of Gloucester and King of England*, Vol. 2 (1844), pp. 389–400.

28 D. Seward, *Richard III: England's Black Legend* (1983), p. 112.

29 *The Cely Letters, 1472–1488*, Alison Hanham (ed.) (Early English Text Society, 1975), pp. 184–5, 285–7.

4 Mancini, p. 137.

5 James Gairdner, *History of the Life and Reign of Richard the Third*, (Cambridge, 1898), p. 5.

6 *Registrum Abbathiae Johannis Whethamstede*, H.T. Riley (ed.), Vol. 1 (Rolls Series, 1872), p. 345.

7 Jean de Waurin, *Anchiennes Cronicques d'Engleterre*, E. Dupont (ed.), Vol. 3 (1863), p. 184.

8 John Warkworth, *A Chronicle of the First Thirteen Years of the Reign of King Edward the Fourth*, J.O. Halliwell (ed.) (Camden Society, 1839), pp. 25–6.

9 John Leland, *Collectanea*, Thomas Hearne (ed.), Vol. 6 (1774), pp. 2–14.

10 *York City Chamberlains' Account Rolls, 1396–1500*, R.B. Dobson (ed.) (Surtees Society, 192, 1980), p. 126.

11 *The Chronicle of John Hardyng*, H. Ellis (ed.) (1802), p. 1.

12 *Calendar of Close Rolls, 1468–76*, p. 138.

13 Michael K. Jones, 'Richard III and the Stanleys', in *Richard III and the North*, Rosemary Horrox (ed.) (Hull, 1986), p. 35.

14 Vergil, p. 152.

15 *English Historical Documents: vol.4, 1327–1485*, A.R. Myers (ed.) (1969), p. 314; *Historie of the Arrivall of Edward IV*, J. Bruce (ed.) (Camden Society, I, 1838), p. 30.

16 *Arrivall*, p. 38.

17 Warkworth, *Chronicle*, p. 18.

18 Crowland, pp. 29–31.

19 More, p. 9.

20 Shakespeare, *King Henry VI, Part Three*, Act 5, Scene 6.

Chapter 2 (pp. 23–59)

1 Rous, p. 120.

2 More, p. 8.

3 John Rous, *The Rous Roll* (Gloucester, 1980), cap 56.

Chapter 3 (pp. 60–89)

1 *Paston Letters and Papers of the Fifteenth Century*, N. Davis (ed.), Vol. 1 (1971), p. 447.

2 *Rous Roll*, cap 56.

3   M.A. Hicks, 'The Last Days of Elizabeth, Countess of Oxford', *E(nglish) H(istorical) R(eview)*, CIII (1988), p. 91.
4   British Library, Cotton MS, Vespasian C.xvi, fo. 126.
5   Buck, *Richard III*, p. 21.
6   *YCR*, I, p. 52.
7   North Yorkshire County Record Office, The Clervaux Cartulary, ZQH 1, fo. 155.
8   Library of Congress, Thatcher Collection, 1004.
9   *Rot Parl*, p. 38.
10 *YCR*, I, p. 54.
11 Mancini, p. 63.
12 More, p. 9.
13 Mancini, p. 65.
14 *YCR*, I, p. 136.
15 C.E. Morton, 'A Local Dispute and the Politics of 1483', *The Ricardian*, VII (1989), pp. 305–7.
16 *YCR*, I, pp. 2–3.
17 (P)ublic (R)ecord (O)ffice, King's Bench 9/349.

ed. J. Raine (Surtees Society, XXXV, 1859), pp. 210–12.
21 Crowland, p. 163.
22 Ibid.
23 Vergil, p. 193.

Chapter 5 (pp. 115–143)

1   More, p. 86.
2   Ibid., pp. 88–9.
3   *Great Chronicle*, pp. 236–7.
4   Jean Molinet, *Chroniques*, J.A. Buchon (ed.), Vol. 2 (1828), pp. 402–3.
5   More, p. 88.
6   E. Nokes and G. Wheeler, 'A Spanish Account of the Battle of Bosworth', *The Ricardian*, II (1972), pp. 1–3.
7   M. Lulofs, 'Richard III: Dutch Sources', *The Ricardian*, III (1974), p. 13.
8   Mancini, p. 93.
9   *Great Chronicle*, p. 234.
10 Hanham, *Cely Letters*, pp. 184–5.
11 Mancini, p. 93.
12 Crowland, p. 163.
13 R. Ricart, *The Maire of Bristowe is Kalendar*, L. Toulmin Smith (ed.) (Camden, New Series, V, 1872), p. 46.
14 R.F. Green, 'Historical Notes of a London Citizen, 1483–88', *EHR*, LXXXXVI (1981), p. 588.
15 Rous, pp. 120–1.
16 *Journal des Etats-generaux de France tenus a Tours en 1484*, J. Masselin (ed.) (Paris, 1835), p. 38.
17 L. Visser-Fuchs, 'English Events in Caspar Weinreich's Danzig Chronicle', *The Ricardian*, VIII (1986), pp. 317, 320, n28.
18 C.F. Richmond, 'The Death of Edward V', *Northern History*, XXV (1989), pp. 278–80.
19 Philippe de Commynes, *Memoirs: the Reign of Louis XI. 1461–83*, translated with an introduction by Michael Jones (1972), pp. 354, 396, 397.
20 Lulofs, *Ricardian*, III, p. 13.

Chapter 4 (pp. 90–114)

1   More, p. 10.
2   Mancini, p. 77.
3   *YCR*, I, p. 74.
4   Crowland, p. 153.
5   Mancini, p. 73.
6   Crowland, p. 153.
7   Mancini, p. 75.
8   Crowland, p. 155.
9   Mancini, p. 91.
10 Vergil, p. 175.
11 Mancini, p. 91.
12 *YCR*, I, p. 73.
13 *Harley 433*, III, p. 29.
14 *Rot Parl*, p. 241.
15 Rosemary Horrox, *Richard III: a Study of Service* (Cambridge, 1989) p. 328.
16 Charles Ross, *Edward IV* (1974), pp. 424–5.
17 Mancini, p. 91.
18 Rous, pp. 121, 122.
19 *YCR*, I, p. 78.
20 *The Fabric Rolls of York Minster*,

21 Bodleian Library, Ashmolean MS, 1448, fo. 287.
22 Green, *EHR*, LXXXXVI, p. 488.
23 More, p. 88.
24 Helen Maurer, 'Whodunit: the Suspects in the Case', *Ricardian Register*, XVIII (1983), pp. 22–3.
25 *Rot Parl*, p. 276.
26 Crowland, p. 163.
27 Ibid., p. 195.
28 *Harley 433*, III, p. 114.
29 Ibid., II, p. 21.
30 P.W. Hammond, 'John of Gloucester', *The Ricardian*, V, p. 319.
31 Sir Clements Markham, *Richard III: his Life and Character* (1906), pp. 126, 236–7.
32 Gairdner, *Richard the Third* p. 279.
33 Molinet, *Chroniques*, 2, pp. 420–1.
34 J. Leslau, 'Did the Sons of Edward IV Outlive Henry VII?', *The Ricardian*, IV (1978), pp. 10–11. For further debate of the issue see *Ricardian*, V (1979), pp. 24–6, 55–60.
35 *Great Chronicle*, p. 234.
36 I. Arthurson and N. Kingwell, 'The Proclamation of Henry VII as King of England, 3 November 1483', *Historical Research*, LXIII (1990), p. 105.
37 Vergil, p. 203.
38 Ibid., p. 196.
39 *Harley 433*, III, p. 190.
40 Mancini, p. 61; Crowland, p. 185; see also the comments of Jeremy Potter, *Good King Richard? An Account of Richard III and his Reputation, 1483–1983* (1983), pp. 76, 85.
41 Crowland, pp. 162–3.
42 *Great Chronicle*, p. 236.
43 Craig, *Richard III*, p. 95.

Chapter 6 (pp. 144–181)

1 Crowland, p. 171.
2 *Great Chronicle*, p. 235.
3 *Harley 433*, III, p. 107.
4 Crowland, p. 171.
5 *Rot Parl*, pp. 240–1.
6 Crowland, p. 171.
7 Anne F. Sutton, 'Richard III's Tytylle and Right: a new discovery', *The Ricardian*, IV (1977), p. 2.
8 Vergil, p. 192.
9 *Harley 433*, II, pp. 48–9.
10 Ibid., III, p. 107.
11 More, p. 9.
12 Halliwell, *Letters*, 1, p. 157.
13 Crowland, p. 171.
14 Ibid.
15 Rous, p. 123.
16 *Harley 433*, III, p. 139.
17 *The Paston Letters*, James Gairdner (ed.), Vol. 6 (1904), pp. 81–4.
18 Crowland, p. 175.
19 Halliwell, *Letters*, 1, p. 159.
20 Crowland, p. 181.
21 *Great Chronicle*, p. 242.
22 Vergil, p. 224.

Chapter 7 (pp. 182–210)

1 Bodleian Library, Laud MS 501; translated by Craig, *Richard III*, p. 41.
2 Rous, p. 123.
3 Vergil, p. 224.
4 Commynes, *Memoirs*, p. 259.
5 *Calendar of State Papers, Venice: vol 1, 1202–1509*, R. Brown (ed.) (1864), p. 145.
6 Mancini, p. 137.
7 W. Caxton, *The Book of the Ordre of Chyualry*, A.T.P. Byles (ed.) (1926), pp. 124–5; reprinted in C.T. Allmand, *Society at War* (Edinburgh, 1973), p. 30.
8 Buck, *Richard III*, p. 21.
9 PRO, Duchy of Lancaster, 29/648/10485
10 Rosemary Horrox and Anne F. Sutton, 'Some Expenses of Richard Duke of Gloucester, 1475–7', *The Ricardian*, VI (1983), pp. 267–8.
11 M.A. Hicks, *Richard III as Duke of Gloucester: A Study in Character* (York, 1986), pp. 23–5.

12 Crowland, p. 163.
13 Vergil, pp. 200, 227.
14 Mancini, p. 91.
15 Charles T. Wood, *Joan of Arc and Richard III* (Oxford, 1988), p. 181. See also 'Richard III, William Lord Hastings and Friday the Thirteenth', in *Kings and Nobles in the Later Middle Ages*, Ralph A. Griffiths and James Sherborne (eds.) (Gloucester, 1986), pp. 161–3.
16 Rous, p. 121.
17 'The Statutes of Middleham College', J. Raine (ed.), *Archaeological Journal*, XIV (1857), p. 169.
18 Ibid., p. 160.
19 Lambeth Palace Library, MS 474, fo. 183, translated by Anne F. Sutton and Livia Visser-Fuchs, *The Hours of Richard III* (Stroud, 1990), p. 78. For the recent demonstration that the prayer was not addressed to St Julian see ibid, 60–2 and Anne F. Sutton and Livia Visser-Fuchs, 'Richard III and St Julian: a new myth', *The Ricardian*, VIII (1989), pp. 265–70.
20 Rous, p. 121.
21 Mancini, pp. 63–5.
22 Joseph Hunter, *South Yorkshire*, Vol. 1 (1828), p. 75.
23 *YCR*, I, pp. 119, 126 (lawfully corrected to mercifully).
24 Sir Francis Bacon, *The History of the Reign of King Henry VII*, J. Spedding et al (eds.) (Works, Vol. 7, 1858), p. 88.
25 *YCR*, I, p. 56.
26 *YCR*, II, pp. 71–3.
27 *Harley 433*, III, p. 139,
28 Hanham, *Early Historians*, p. 50.
29 Quoted by Charles Ross, *Richard III* (1981), pp. xix and 229, who himself disagreed with Hutton.
30 Crowland, p. 171.
31 Vergil, p. 227.
32 Crowland, p. 181.
33 More, p. 89.

Chapter 8 *(pp. 211–230)*

1 Gairdner, *Richard the Third*, pp. xi–xii.
2 Ibid., p. 1.
3 J.R. Lander, *Government and Community, England, 1450–1509* (1980), p. 330.
4 Ross, *Richard III* (1981), pp. liii, 229.
5 Horrox, *Richard III: a Study of Service* (Cambridge, 1989), pp. 327–8.
6 Seward, *Richard III*, pp. 15, 21, 54, 117, 154, 199.
7 Sheppard, *Christ Church Letters*, p. 46.
8 *YCR*, I, p. 119.
9 Antonia Gransden, *Historical Writing in England: vol. 2, c.1307 to the Early Sixteenth Century* (1982), p. 315, from BL Add MS 48976, No. 64 (see frontispiece).
10 Horace Walpole, *Historic Doubts on the Life and Reign of Richard III*, 2nd edn. 1768 with postscript of 1793, with an introduction by P.W. Hammond (Gloucester, 1987), pp. 12, 121–2, 127.
11 Ibid., p. 223.
12 Halsted, *Richard III*, 1, pp. xii, 15.
13 Ibid., 2, pp. 105, 485, 501.
14 Ibid., 1, pp. 252, 343.
15 Middlesbrough Central Reference Library, *The Middlesbrough Weekly News and Cleveland Advertiser*, 19 Nov. 1859. I am grateful to Mr David Abbott for drawing my attention to this piece.
16 Markham, *Richard III*, pp. 161, 162–3.
17 Josephine Tey, *The Daughter of Time* (1951), p. 179. An earlier reworking of Markham was Philip Lindsay's *King Richard III*, published in 1933, some passages of which disturbingly seem to conjure up a fascist Richard, a model of an idealized leader encapsulating 'the spirit that is England' to whom the English should turn 'in this moment of

See Potter, *Good King Richard?*, p. 237.

18 Paul Murray Kendall, *Richard III* (1955), p. 46.

19 This and the preceding paragraph are based on information from The Richard III Society, Barton Library Catalogue of Books, compiled by Carolyn Hammond, pp. 34–51.

20 Richard Drewett and Mark Redhead, *The Trial of Richard III* (Gloucester, 1984). This publication is a transcript of the original recording, not of the edited version broadcast on 4 November 1984.

21 *Jonny Quest*, No. 10 (Norristown, Pa, 1987).

22 E. Hall, *The Union of the Two Houses of Lancaster and York* (1809), pp. 426, 442–5.

23 Bacon, *Henry VII*, p. 88.

24 Buck, *Richard III*, pp. 20–1.

25 Raine, *Fabric Rolls*, p. 87 n.

26 Potter, *Good King Richard?*, p. 46.

27 *The Sunday Times*, 12 Aug. 1984.

28 *Great Chronicle*, p. 238.

Further Reading

This bibliography is intended as a guide to further reading, chapter by chapter and topic by topic. It is not comprehensive; indeed it is highly selective. It concentrates on the more scholarly recent works which support and amplify the main text. It is hoped that it also provides enough information to enable the reader to take up and pursue aspects of the subject which have not been fully developed.

All works are published in London unless otherwise specified.

General

There are several surveys of late fifteenth-century English history available. Up-to-date and sound introductions are to be found in C.S.L. Davies, *Peace, Print and Protestantism, 1450–1558* (1976); Anthony Goodman, *The Wars of the Roses: Military Activity and English Society, 1452–97* (1981), which, as its title indicates, concentrates on the fighting itself; J.R. Lander, *Government and Community: England, 1450–1509* (1980); A.J. Pollard, *The Wars of the Roses* (1988); and Charles Ross, *The Wars of the Roses* (1976). The principal modern academic monographs on Richard III are Charles Ross, *Richard III* (1981), which provides an excellent summation of research at that time, and Rosemary Horrox, *Richard III: a Study of Service* (Cambridge, 1989), which is founded on new research into politics and patronage. These works can be supplemented by the essays published in P.W. Hammond (ed.), *Richard III: Loyalty, Lordship and Law* (1986) and Rosemary Horrox (ed.), *Richard III and the North* (Hull, 1986). More popular works marking quincentenaries to note are Giles St Aubyn, *The Year of the Three Kings* (1983) and Michael Bennett, *The Battle of Bosworth* (Gloucester, 1985). Any reader wishing to explore many of the byways, as well as the main highways, of the subject of Richard III should consult *The Ricardian*, the journal of the Richard III Society, now with over 100 issues to its credit. A selection of articles published between 1975 and 1981 is to be found in J. Petre (ed.), *Richard III: Crown and People* (1985). R. Edwards, *The Itinerary of Richard III* (1983) usefully enables one to follow Richard's movements as king: a companion volume for his years as duke of Gloucester is in preparation.

The principal printed sources are listed above under 'Sources'. They can be supplemented by A.F. Sutton and P.W. Hammond (ed.), *The Coronation of Richard III: the Extant Documents* (Gloucester, 1983); by A.F. Sutton and L. Visser-Fuchs, *The Hours of Richard III* (Stroud, 1990); and shortly by a new edition of the York House Books edited by Lorraine Attreed to be published by the Richard III and Yorkist History Trust.

Selections from the sources are to be found in K. Dockray, *Richard III: a Reader in History* (Gloucester, 1988); J.R. Lander, *The Wars of the Roses* (2nd edn., Gloucester, 1990); P.W. Hammond and A.F. Sutton (ed.), *The Road to Bosworth Field* (1985); and Pamela Tudor-Craig, *Richard III* (National Portrait Gallery, 2nd edn., 1977). The last is a catalogue of an exhibition mounted in 1973 which also contains a detailed discussion of the surviving portraits.

Chapter 1

Analysis and discussion of the quality and reliability of the sources and of the early histories are to be found in G.B. Churchill, *Richard III up to Shakespeare* (Berlin, 1900; reprint Gloucester, 1976); Antonia Gransden, *Historical Writing in England: vol. 2, c. 1307 to the Early Sixteenth Century* (1982); Alison Hanham, *Richard III and His Early Historians, 1483–1535* (Oxford, 1975); Jeremy Potter, *Good King Richard? An Account of Richard III and his Reputation, 1483–1983* (1983); A.R. Myers, 'Richard III and Historical Tradition', *History*, XIII (1968); and Ross, *Richard III*, 'Introduction, The Historical Reputation of Richard III: Fact and Fiction'. For further discussion of the date and authorship of the Crowland Chronicle see the introduction to Pronay and Cox, *Crowland Chronicle Continuations* and the references therein; Daniel Williams, 'The Crowland Chronicle, 616–1500', in Daniel Williams (ed.), *England in the Fifteenth Century* (Woodbridge, 1987), pp. 371–90; and the debate in *The Ricardian*, VII, No. 99 (December 1987). For More's History see also the introduction by R.S. Sylvester to *The History of Richard III*, volume 2 of the Yale edition of the works of Sir Thomas More

(Newhaven, 1963) and Alistair Fox, *Thomas More: History and Providence* (1982).

The pioneering discussion of Shakespeare's vision of history was E.M.W. Tillyard, *Shakespeare's History Plays* (1944). This should be supplemented by R.H. Wells, *Shakespeare, Politics and the State* (1986) and John Wilders, *The Lost Garden: a View of Shakespeare's English and Roman History Plays* (1978). For the text and critical discussion of *Richard III* see the Arden edition, ed. Arthur Hammond (1981). Two recent explorations of the play in performance are J. Hanken (ed.), *Plays in Performance: Richard III* (1981) and R.C. Hassel, *Songs of Death: Performance, Interpretation and the Text of 'King Richard III'* (Nebraska, 1987).

Chapter 2

Besides the general works cited above, for mid-fifteenth-century government, politics and society see A.L. Brown, *The Governance of Late Medieval England, 1272–1461* (1989); Chris Given-Wilson, *The English Nobility in the Late Middle Ages* (1987); J.R. Lander, *The Limitations of English Monarchy in the Later Middle Ages* (Toronto, 1989); K.B. McFarlane, *The Nobility of Later Medieval England* (Oxford, 1973); D.A.L. Morgan, 'The King's Affinity in the Polity of Yorkist England', *Transactions of the Royal Historical Society*, fifth series, XXIII (1973); T.B. Pugh, 'The Magnates, Knights and Gentry', in S.B. Chrimes et al (eds.) *Fifteenth-Century England, 1399–1509* (Manchester, 1972).

York's career and the politics of the 1450s are to be followed in R. A. Griffiths, *The Reign of King Henry VI: the Exercise of Royal Authority, 1422–61* (1981), pp. 666–771 and P.A. Johnson, *Duke Richard of York, 1411–1460* (Oxford, 1988). For York's claim to the throne see R.A. Griffiths, 'The Sense of Dynasty in the Reign of Henry VI', in C.D. Ross (ed.), *Patronage, Pedigree and Power in the Later Medieval England* (Gloucester, 1979) and T.B. Pugh, *Henry V and the Southampton Plot* (Gloucester, 1988), pp. 134–5. The most complete documentation concerning Richard III's boyhood is to be found in M.A. Hicks, *False Fleeting Perjur'd Clarence* (Gloucester, 1980), pp. 15–26 and A.F. Sutton, 'And to be Delivered to the Lord Richard, Duke of Gloucester, the other Brother . . .', *The Ricardian*, VIII (1988).

Warwick the Kingmaker and the Nevilles have been studied in R.L. Storey, *The End of the House of Lancaster* (1966); R.A. Griffiths, 'Local Rivalries and Northern Politics: the Percies, the Nevilles and the Duke of Exeter, 1452–55', *Speculum*, XLIII (1968); C.D. Ross, *Edward IV* (1974); and, most recently, A.J. Pollard, *North-Eastern*

England during the Wars of the Roses: Lay Society, War and Politics, 1450–1500 (Oxford, Clarendon Press, 1990), chapters 10–12. The crisis of 1469–71 is elucidated in Ross, *Edward IV*, chapter 7. His account can be supplemented by Hicks, *Clarence*, chapter 2; A.J. Pollard, 'Lord FitzHugh's Rising in 1470', *Bulletin of the Institute of Historical Research*, LII (1979); and P.W. Hammond, *The Battles of Barnet and Tewkesbury* (Gloucester, 1990).

Hammond, *Barnet and Tewkesbury*, now provides in Appendix 2 the most comprehensive discussion of the death of Edward of Lancaster. For the death of Henry VI see W.J. White, 'The Death and Burial of Henry VI', *The Ricardian*, VI (1982).

Chapter 3

For northern England see R.L. Storey, 'The North of England', in Chrimes (ed.), *Fifteenth-Century England* and, for a fuller discussion (and slightly different view), Pollard, *North-Eastern England*, Part 1 and Conclusion. The authoritative statement on the settlement of the Neville inheritance is M.A. Hicks, 'Descent, Partition and Extinction; the Warwick Inheritance', *Bulletin of the Institute of Historical Research*, LII (1979). This is supplemented by the same author's *Richard III as Duke of Gloucester: A Study in Character* (Borthwick Paper, No. 70, York, 1986). I differ from Dr Hicks in my interpretation as to why Richard was left with a flawed title to his Neville estates. For Richard's treatment of the Countess of Oxford see Hicks, 'The Last Days of the Countess of Oxford', *EHR*, CII (1988).

Full details of Richard's retainers in the north can be garnered from Keith Dockray, 'Richard III and the Yorkshire Gentry', in Hammond (ed.), *Loyalty, Lordship and Law*, pp. 28–57; Horrox, *Richard III*, chapter 1 and *Richard III and the North*, pp. 82–107; A.J. Pollard, *The Middleham Connection: Richard III and Richmondshire, 1471–1485* (Middleham, 1983) and *North-Eastern England*, chapters 7 and 13; and Ross, *Richard III*, pp. 47–55. His relationships with the principal peers in the north are discussed by M.A. Hicks, 'Dynastic Change and Northern Society: the Career of the Fourth Earl of Northumberland, 1470–89', *Northern History*, XIV (1978); Michael K. Jones, 'Richard III and the Stanleys' in Horrox (ed.), *Richard III and the North*; and A.J. Pollard, 'St Cuthbert and the Hog: Richard III and the County Palatine of Durham, 1471–85', in R.A. Griffiths and James Sherborne (eds.), *Kings and Nobles in the Later Middle Ages: a Tribute to Charles Ross* (Gloucester, 1986), pp. 109–29.

Richard III's relationship with the city of York is explored in

Edward Miller, 'Medieval York', in P.M. Tillott (ed.), *The Victoria County History of Yorkshire: the City of York* (1961) and D.M. Palliser, 'Richard III and York', in Horrox (ed.), *Richard III and the North*. L.C. Attreed, 'The King's Interest: York's Fee Farm and the Central Government', *Northern History*, XVII (1981) concentrates on one particular cause in which Richard supported the city. His relationship with the clerical establishment is discussed by R.B. Dobson, 'Richard III and the Church of York', in Griffiths and Sherborne (eds.), *Kings and Nobles*, pp. 130–54. For Richard and Durham Priory see Mary O'Regan, 'Richard III and the Monks of Durham', *The Ricardian*, IV (1978) and Pollard, 'St Cuthbert and the Hog'.

Anglo-Scottish relations and the war of 1480–84 are most fully considered in Norman Macdougall, *James III: a Political Study* (Edinburgh, 1982). The English perspective is explored in Pollard, *North-Eastern England*, chapter 9. Hicks, *Clarence* and Ross, *Edward IV*, discuss fully the ambiguities of Richard's relationship with his brother George and his role in 1478. Doctors Hicks and Horrox have slightly differing views on the relationship between Edward IV and Richard, for which see Horrox (ed.), *Richard III and the North*, pp. 1–26. For the Woodvilles see M.A. Hicks, 'The Changing Role of Wydevilles in Yorkist Politics to 1483', in Ross, *Patronage, Pedigree and Power*; Horrox, *Richard III*, pp. 121–7; and D.E. Lowe, 'Patronage and Politics: Edward IV, the Wydevilles and the Council of the Prince of Wales, 1471–83', *Bulletin of the Board of Celtic Studies*, XXIX (1980–2).

Chapter 4

The outline of events can be fleshed out in almost any account. Ross, *Edward IV*, is harder on Edward in holding him responsible for what followed after his death than Horrox, *Richard III*. Colin Richmond, '1485 and All That, or What Was Really Going on at the Battle of Bosworth', in Hammond (ed.), *Loyalty, Lordship, and Law* takes the case against Edward further. Both Horrox and Ross, *Richard III* favour the conspiratorial interpretation of Richard's seizure of power. Charles T. Wood, *Joan of Arc and Richard III: Sex, Saints and Government in the Middle Ages* (Oxford, 1988), chapters 8 and 9 and 'Richard III, William, Lord Hastings and Friday the Thirteenth', in Griffiths and Sherborne (eds.), *Kings and Nobles*, pp. 155–68, tend to favour the 'cock-up' theory of history. My wife's view might be characterized as that of a cocked-up conspiracy. Recent discussion of the events has been befuddled by the debate over the date of Hastings' execution launched by Alison Hanham in

'Richard III, Lord Hastings and the Historians', *EHR*, LXXXVII (1972), finally brought to an end by C.H.D. Coleman, 'The Execution of Lord Hastings', *Bulletin of the Institute of Historical Research*, LIII (1980) which demonstrated beyond reasonable doubt that he did indeed die on 13 June.

The theological complexities of Richard's case that his nephews were bastards are skilfully delineated by R.H. Helmholz, 'The Sons of Edward IV: A Canonical Assessment of the Claim that they were Illegitimate', in Hammond (ed.), *Loyalty, Lordship and Law*, pp. 91–103. This authoritative essay supersedes Mortimer Levine, 'Richard III: Usurper or Lawful King', *Speculum*, XXXIV (1959).

Richard's reception in York at the end of the royal progress is described by Pamela Tudor-Craig, 'Richard III's Triumphant Entry into York', in Horrox (ed.), *Richard III and the North* and the ecclesiastical welcome discussed by Dobson, 'Richard III and the Church of York'. The account of the October rebellions in Horrox, *Richard III* replaces the reconstruction by A.E. Conway, 'The Maidstone Sector of Buckingham's Rebellion, October 18th, 1483', *Archaeologia Cantiana*, XXXVII (1925) on which all previous discussions were based. Horrox's interpretation is reinforced by I. Arthurson and N. Kingwell, 'The Proclamation of Henry Tudor as King of England, 3 November, 1483', *Historical Research*, LXIII (1990). For the suggestion that Buckingham did indeed aim for the throne see Carole Rawcliffe, *The Staffords, Earls of Stafford and Dukes of Buckingham, 1394–1521* (Cambridge, 1978), pp. 30–5. For participation of Henry Tudor see S.B. Chrimes, *Henry VII* (1972) and R.A. Griffiths and R.S. Thomas, *The Making of the Tudor Dynasty* (Gloucester, 1985).

Chapter 5

The best point of departure now is P.W. Hammond and W.J. White, 'The Sons of Edward IV: A Re-examination of the Evidence on their Deaths and on the Bones in Westminster Abbey', in Hammond (ed.), *Loyalty, Lordship and Law*, pp. 104–47, superseding P.M. Kendall, *Richard III* (1955), Appendix I, 'Who murdered the "Little Princes" ?'. Helen Maurer, 'Whodunit: the suspects in the case', *Ricardian Register*, XVII (1983), offers a good review of all the alternative murderers. Anne Crawford, 'John Howard, Duke of Norfolk: a possible murderer of the Princes', *The Ricardian*, V (1981) effectively disposes of the idea that Howard was the murderer. Charles T. Wood, 'Who killed the Little Princes in the Tower?', *Harvard Magazine*, LXXX (1978) comes up with Jane

Shore as a *jeu d'esprit*. Audrey Williamson, *The Mystery of the Princes: an Investigation into a Supposed Murder* (Gloucester, 1978) sustains the Markham thesis that the children outlived Richard. Lorraine Attreed, 'From *Pearl* Maiden to Tower Princes', *Journal of Medieval History*, IX (1983) revalues medieval attitudes to children.

L.E. Tanner and W. Wright., 'Recent Investigations regarding the Fate of the Princes in the Tower', *Archaeologia*, LXXXIV (1934), as their title reveals, prejudged whose bones they were. Subsequent medical opinion of their report is to be found in Kendall, *Richard III*, pp. 497–8; Ross, *Richard III*, pp. 233–4; Hammond and White, 'The Sons of Edward IV', especially pp. 112–31; and T. Molleson, 'Anne Mowbray and the Princes in the Tower: a Study in Identity', *The London Archaeologist*, V, (1987). A detailed discussion by Helen Maurer of the discovery of the bones in the seventeenth century is to be found in two parts in *The Ricardian*, IX, 111 (Dec 1990) and 112 (Mar 1991).

After careful consideration I have concluded that the Downham Tablet, which purports to be a last message from the Princes in the Tower, is a forgery. See Colin Richmond, *The Penket Papers* (Gloucester, 1986), pp. 61–75.

Chapter 6

The plantation of the south is discussed by W.E. Hampton, 'John Hoton of Hunwick and Tudhoe, County Durham', *The Ricardian*, VII (1985); Horrox, *Richard III*, pp. 178–205, emphasizing the household element; Ross, *Richard III*, pp. 55–9; A.J. Pollard, 'The Tyranny of Richard III', *Journal of Medieval History*, III (1977) and *North-Eastern England*, chapter 14. In the same chapter the political purpose of the Council of the North is emphasized. Earlier discussions of the Council, including R.R. Reid, *The King's Council in the North* (1921) and Ross, *Richard III*, pp. 181–3 emphasize its administrative and judicial role. The case for Richard's good intentions in the administration of justice is put in Anne F. Sutton, 'The Administration of Justice Whereunto We Be Professed', *The Ricardian*, IV (1976). His financial administration is assessed by Horrox, *Richard III*, pp. 299–309 and B.P. Wolffe, *The Royal Demesne in English History* (1974), p. 188 ff.

The most detailed development of the thesis that Richard was an enlightened parliamentary legislator is H.G. Hanbury, 'The Legislation of Richard III', *The American Journal of Legal History*, VI (1962). The context of comparative legislation is to be seen in Ross, *Edward IV* , pp. 341–50, 359–61 and Chrimes, *Henry VII*, pp. 177–84, 220–3. Parliamentary procedure is explained in R.G.

Davies and J.H. Denton, *The English Parliament in the Middle Ages* (Manchester, 1981), pp. 109–84. For the Speaker, William Catesby, see J.S. Roskell, *The Commons and Their Speakers in Parliament* (Manchester, 1965), pp. 293–7.

The degree of support enjoyed by Richard is discussed by Ross, *Richard III*; Pugh, 'Magnates, Knights and Gentry' and Horrox, *Richard III*, who stresses the role of the royal household. It is in Horrox too, in chapter 6, that the most detailed discussion of continuing opposition to Richard is to be found. Margaret Beaufort's role as a conspirator is assessed by Michael K. Jones, 'Richard III and Lady Margaret Beaufort: A Reassessment', in Hammond (ed.), *Loyalty, Lordship and Law*, pp. 25–37. The history of the opposition in exile is to be found in Chrimes, *Henry VII* and Griffiths and Thomas, *Tudor Dynasty*. The support given to them by France is demonstrated by A.V. Antonovics, 'Henry VII, King of England, "By the Grace of Charles VIII of France"', in Griffiths and Sherborne (eds.), *Kings and Nobles*.

The conduct of Richard's foreign policy is discussed in detail and found wanting by Ross, *Richard III*, pp. 191–203. For Scotland, see also Macdougall, *James III*. The particular importance of relationships with the Papacy is brought out by C.S.L. Davies, 'Bishop John Morton, the Holy See, and the Accession of Henry VII', *EHR*, CII (1987).

The high moral tone of Richard's propaganda is stressed by Charles Ross in 'Rumour, Propaganda and Popular Opinion during the Wars of the Roses', in R.A. Griffiths (ed.), *The Crown, Patronage and the Provinces* (Gloucester, 1981). The cult of Henry VI is discussed by B.P. Wolffe, *Henry VI* (1981), pp. 351–8 and Roger Lovatt, 'A Collector of Apocryphal Anecdotes: John Blacman Revisited', in A.J. Pollard (ed.), *Property and Politics: Essays in Later Medieval English History* (Gloucester, 1984).

Bosworth has been much debated in recent years. The site of the field itself has been a matter of fierce controversy since the publication of the essay by Colin Richmond, 'The Battle of Bosworth', *History Today*, XXXV (August 1985). His suggested resiting of the field was rejected by Daniel Williams in *The Ricardian*, VII, No. 90 (Sept. 1985). Further discussion is to be found in *History Today*, XXXV (October 1985) and *The Ricardian*, VII, No. 92 (March 1986), No. 96 (March 1987), VIII, No. 105 (June 1989). A careful assessment of all the evidence, founded on a thorough knowledge of local topography, is to be found in Peter J. Foss, 'The Battle of Bosworth: towards a Reassessment', *Midland History*, XIII (1988). Almost as divisive has been the question of the extent of Richard's support on the field. Ross, *Richard III*, basing his assessment on the 'Ballad of Bosworth Field', concluded that there was a high turn-out of peers and gentry on the king's side. Pugh, 'Magnate, Knights and Gentry', supported by Richmond, '1485 and All That', argues that it was low. In the specific case of the earl of Northumberland, Hicks, 'Dynastic Change', argues that Richard was betrayed; Horrox, *Richard III*, follows him in describing the earl's 'defection'; Ross, *Richard III*, suggests that it was impossible for Northumberland to engage. The behaviour of the Stanleys is more clearcut, although their precise dispositions are obscure. For recent consideration of the role of Sir William Stanley see Michael K. Jones, 'Sir William Stanley of Holt: Politics and Family Allegiance in the Late Fifteenth Century', *Welsh History Review*, XIV (1988).

For the debate over parliamentary sovereignty see W.H. Dunham and Charles T. Wood, 'The Right to Rule in England: Depositions and the Kingdom's Authority, 1327–1485', *American Historical Review*, LXXXI (1976); J.W. McKenna, 'The myth of Parliamentary Sovereignty in late medieval England', *EHR*, XCIV (1979); and Wood, *Joan of Arc and Richard III*, pp. 192–9. The latest discussion of Yorkist and early Tudor Monarchy is Anthony Goodman, *The New Monarchy, 1471–1534* (Oxford, 1988). The significance of Richard III's accession for the future development of royal authority in the north is expounded in Pollard, *North-Eastern England*. For Henry V as hero see G.L. Harriss, *Henry V; the Practice of Kingship* (Oxford, 1985), to which T.B. Pugh offers a welcome corrective in *Henry V and the Southampton Plot*, pp. 137–46.

Chapter 7

Anne F. Sutton, ' "A Curious Searcher for our weal public": Richard III, Piety, Chivalry and the Concept of the Good Prince', in Hammond (ed.), *Loyalty, Lordship and Law* approaches the question of Richard's character from a similar standpoint to mine but comes to a different conclusion. Her footnotes supply a comprehensive bibliography. Ross, *Richard III*, chapter VII is a more conventional, and less friendly, assessment. Hicks, *Richard III as Duke of Gloucester* endeavours to understand Richard's personality before 1483 from a register he kept of his grants of land and offices. The conclusion drawn is that he was proud, ambitious, aggressive, acquisitive and utterly self-absorbed. Not everyone would share Dr Hicks' confidence that the document itself can provide a reliable insight into Richard's mind.

For the fifteenth-century idea of nobility as well as chivalry itself, Maurice Keen, *Chivalry* (Newhaven, 1984) provides an excellent introduction. Richard's books are the subject of detailed analysis in successive editions of *The Ricardian* by Anne Sutton and Livia Visser-Fuchs since 1986. The most recent general discussion of late-medieval spirituality and piety is to be found in R.N. Swanson, *Church and Society in Late Medieval England* (Oxford, 1989), chapter 6. Richard's piety is reviewed in Sutton and Visser-Fuchs, *Hours of Richard III*, 79–85. For Richard's patronage of Coverham and the cult of St Ninian see Pollard, *North-Eastern England*, chapter 7; for the highly plausible suggestion that the foundation in York Minster was intended to provide a mausoleum see Dobson, 'Richard III and the Church of York'. Kendall, *Richard III*, recounts with approval Richard's obsession with sexual morality; Ross, *Richard III*, more cynically questions his sincerity; Colin Richmond, 'Religion and the English Gentleman', in R.B. Dobson (ed.), *The Church Politics and Patronage in the Fifteenth Century* (Gloucester, 1984), p. 201 comments that to describe Richard as a genuinely pious and religious man is like calling Joseph Stalin a genuinely devout Marxist.

For divisions in York see Hanham, *Early Historians*, pp. 60–4 and Palliser, 'Richard III and York', pp. 62–73. For support for Richard's cause after Bosworth see Ian Arthurson, 'A Question of Loyalty', *The Ricardian*, VII (1987) and W.E. Hampton, 'The White Rose under the First Tudors', ibid.; Keith Dockray, 'The Political Legacy of Richard III in Northern England', in Griffiths and Sherborne (eds.), *Kings and Nobles*, pp. 205–227; and Pollard, *North-Eastern England*, chapter 15.

Chapter 8

The revisionist and Ricardian traditions are traced by Potter in the later chapters of *Good King Richard?* Buck's *History* and Walpole's *Doubts* are discussed by their modern editors. Materials for a fuller study of Ricardian novels and other manifestations of Ricardian enthusiasm in the twentieth century exist in the Barton Library, the library of the Richard III Society.

The question of a north-south divide, raised initially in Pollard, 'Tyranny of Richard III', is discussed more fully in *North-Eastern England*, chapter 1. See also Frank Musgrove, *The North of England: a History from Roman Times to the Present* (Oxford, 1990).

Index

Peers are indexed under family names, cross-referenced from titles. Royal dukes are under titles: sovereigns and princes under personal names. Bishops are indexed under surnames. Entries in italic are references to illustrations.

'Deserves special and lasting attention.'
Medieval World

'An excellent review . . . adds a new dimension. It's a gripping read.'
Laura Blanchard, Ricardian Register

'An excellent addition to the many written recently on fifteenth-century topics . . . well worth reading.'
P.W. Hammond, The Ricardian

Richard III has divided opinion for over five hundred years. Traditionally, he has been perceived as a villain, a bloody tyrant and the monstrous murderer of his innocent nephews; to others he was and remains a wronged victim who did his best for kingdom and family, a noble prince and enlightened statesman tragically slain.

This lavishly illustrated and stimulating book explores the story of Richard III and the tales that have been woven around the historic events; discusses his life and reign and the disappearance of the Princes in the Tower; and assesses the original sources upon which much of the 'history' is based. While telling the story as he sees it, Professor Pollard also suggests that 'the truth' may never be known: the controversial nature of the events at the time is partly to blame; but at least as important are the paucity of the surviving evidence and the fact that the received stories are now so deeply ingrained.

The text is illustrated by over 200 manuscript illustrations, engravings, contemporary documents and photographs, in both black and white and colour. In addition, a number of 'picture essays' explore particular aspects of Richard III's life and reign: his birth sign of Scorpio; the portraits of Richard; the symbolism of pigs and boars; Richard's saints; his books; the Princes; historical paintings of Richard III; and cartoons and caricatures. The book is also supported by full source notes and references.

A.J. POLLARD is professor of history at the University of Teesside, where his research specializes in northern England in the fifteenth century. Among his previous books are *The Wars of the Roses* (Macmillan, 1988) and *North-Eastern England during the Wars of the Roses* (OUP, 1990). He also made an appearance in London Weekend Television's *Trial of Richard III* (on the losing side).

Jacket pictures: left, The Princes in the Tower *by Sir John Everett Millais (Royal Holloway & Bedford New College, Surrey; photograph The Bridgeman Art Library); right,* Richard III *(Society of Antiquaries)*

£12.99

ISBN 0-7509-0354-6

9 780750 903547

ALAN SUTTON PUBLISHING
PHOENIX MILL · STROUD · GLOUCESTERSHIRE

ALAN SUTTON PUBLISHING INC.
83 WASHINGTON STREET · DOVER · NH 03820